IMAGES
of America

Along the Battenkill

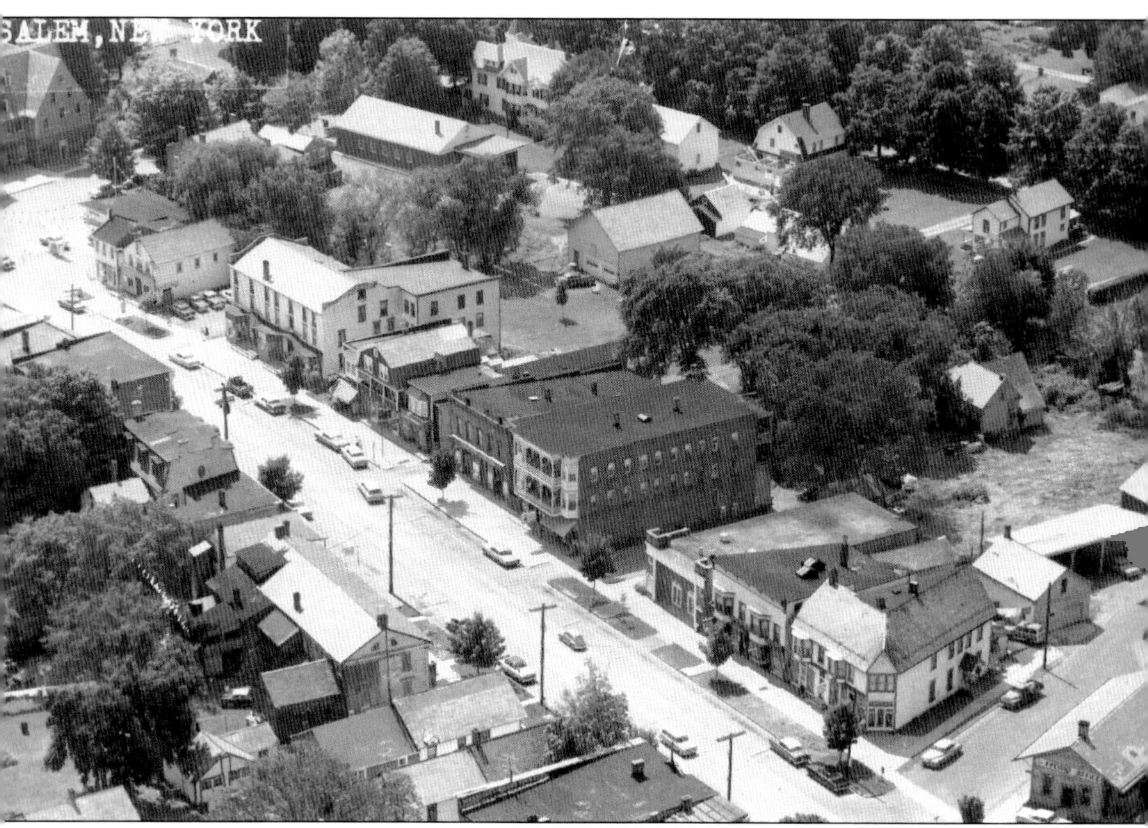

This 1962 aerial view of the village of Salem's Main Street shows a busy street where merchants offered a variety of goods and services. The street, once lined with stately elm trees, is now lined with maple trees. The sign on the Delaware & Hudson Railway passenger depot (lower right) indicates that the depot was being used only as a freight office. (Courtesy of the Salem town and village historical archives.)

On the Cover: This late-1800s photograph shows a smartly dressed foursome with Hedges Lake, Little Pond, and the Battenkill Valley in the distance. (Courtesy of the Salem town and village historical archives.)

IMAGES
of America

ALONG THE BATTENKILL

William A. Cormier

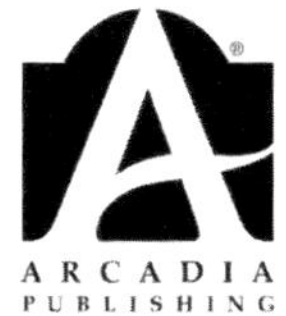

ISBN X978-1-4671-2138-5

Published by Arcadia Publishing
Charleston, South Carolina

Printed in the United States of America

Library of Congress Control Number: 2013948565

For all general information, please contact Arcadia Publishing:
Telephone 843-853-2070
Fax 843-853-0044
E-mail sales@arcadiapublishing.com
For customer service and orders:
Toll-Free 1-888-313-2665

Visit us on the Internet at www.arcadiapublishing.com

To my wife, Sara Jane, whose enthusiasm for history equals mine

Contents

Acknowledgments 6

Introduction 7

1. Fun on the Battenkill 9
2. Shushan on the Battenkill 17
3. Popular Area Lakes 25
4. North by Northwest 33
5. Salem Merchants, Industry, and Agriculture 45
6. Community Life 63
7. Hard Times 83
8. Parades and Patriotism 91
9. Northern Exposure 107

Acknowledgments

Over the years, Salem has been fortunate in having local photographers and historical writers capture life in the area. Town historians, village historians, Bancroft Public librarians, and private history collectors have preserved their efforts, resulting in a large photograph and historical document collection spanning many years, making this book possible. An important contribution was made by Jeffrey and Winston Adler, who discovered the glass negative collection of Robert A. Cruikshank at auction, purchased the collection, and donated it to the village archive in 1993.

I want to thank Peg Culver, librarian, for her encouragement and care in helping to maintain the village historical photograph and material archive in Bancroft Public Library. I also want to thank the following photographers and lenders of their private photographs and historical material: Herbert Eriksson (Shushan's premier photographer), Joan Wulff, Harold "Butch" Gilchrest, Edie Meikle, and William Dean Cormier. Thanks go to Kay Tomasi and Sally Brillon for their research and written works regarding the commercial history of Salem and along the Battenkill. Special thanks go to Gail Bearup, who suggested contacting Herbert Eriksson and Joan Wulff for their historical photographs of the Battenkill. Unless otherwise noted, the Salem town and village historical archives provided all images appearing in this book.

Finally, I want to thank Remy Thurston and Rebekah Collinsworth, of Arcadia Publishing, for their guidance and support in all phases of the book.

INTRODUCTION

"If you step from the Union Depot in Troy into a Delaware and Hudson car attached to the 5 p. m. express on the Fitchburg Railroad, you will find yourself in the prettiest town in Northern New York." A correspondent to the *Troy Daily Press* wrote these words about Salem in 1888.

The Delaware & Hudson Railway, itself an outgrowth of the Delaware & Hudson Canal, was a most scenic route, following the gentle curves of the Battenkill north to Salem and west to the Hudson. The river, like a string of pearls, was the common thread connecting the gem-like communities of Eagleville, Shushan, Salem, Jackson, East Greenwich, Battenville, Greenwich, Middle Falls, and Easton.

For the first indigenous people and early European pioneers, the river was a source of transportation, supplying fertile land, water, and waterpower to the countryside farmers and village merchants who set up shop to serve local inhabitants. Today, the land along the Battenkill remains mostly agricultural, with its small villages nestled in the surrounding valleys. Salem, once the most populated community above Albany, continues to be one of "the prettiest towns" by any measure.

The setting is grand. Salem and its surroundings are framed by the Taconic and Green Mountains on the east, the Hudson River on the west, and, farther north, the Washington County boundaries of Lake George, Lake Champlain, and the Adirondack Mountains. The fertile land in between is nourished by numerous lakes, rivers, and creeks, tying Washington County in a watery web to the North Country.

Life was difficult at times—wars, religious and political differences, natural catastrophes, crop failures, and disease all took their toll. Nevertheless, the early settlers managed to thrive, creating towns and villages with churches, schools, courthouses, factories, retail stores, and opera houses.

Understandably, these things were not done without determined and inventive people, looking for a place in which they could comfortably live, if not prosper. The Presbyterian work ethic, arriving with the pioneering Scottish and Irish in the late 1700s, served them well. They were not alone. Later, other ethnic groups, including French, German, Welsh, Finnish, Norwegian, Swedish, and Italian immigrants, arrived in Salem, also bringing that work ethic with them. Many of these influential people, of all walks of life, are featured in this work.

A walk or drive through these communities today reveals that pride. Battenkill conservancy members will espouse the beauty and magic of the river's quiet babble to heal the weary soul, to offer habitat for fauna and flora, to provide water sport for outdoorsmen and women, to impart water to sustain crops and humans, and to drive mill machinery.

Man-made structures along the Battenkill and in the towns and villages reflect the human element. Water-powered industrial mills, cast of marble and carefully laid bricks, housed the once important flax, wool, paper, and wood industries. Later, electric generators spun by the swirling waters lit up nearby communities. Private homes, on farms and in villages, both modest and extravagant, represent fine examples of a variety of architectural styles dating from the 1700s.

Saltbox, Greek Revival, Georgian, Federal, Victorian, Italianate, and Queen Ann styles are but a few. Main Street commercial districts reflect 19th-century storefronts of brick, iron, and wood, with the common theme of commercial businesses on the first floor and apartments on the second and third floors. Sprinkled throughout the villages and towns were churches, schools, opera houses, firehouses, feed mills, steam and electric power plants, hotels, liveries, and professional offices of lawyers and doctors. Since travel between towns and villages was limited by a lack of good roads, not everyone could appreciate these marvels until the industrial revolution brought mechanization to the rural areas. Eventually, covered bridges crossing rivers and streams, passable roads, and railroads connecting one town to another brought new adventures.

In 1852, a most important method of transportation transformed the towns of Salem, Cambridge, and Greenwich, New York, and Rupert, Vermont, along the line. The door of easy travel was open when the Troy & Rutland Railroad chose to build a line along the eastern side of Washington County bordering Vermont. It was called the Bridge Line. Local lore humorously says that it got its name from all the rivers and creeks it had to cross from one end of the long county to the other.

When the railroad line from Troy reached Shushan, it followed the northerly flow of the Battenkill to Salem. Eventually, the Delaware & Hudson (D&H) Railway took over the Troy & Rutland Railroad, as well as the Johnson & Greenwich Railroad line that ran west along the Battenkill from Salem to Greenwich. The Battenkill, the Hudson River, the Champlain Canal, and the railroads served the public, with natural power or man-made power, traveling north to the Adirondacks. The adventure of cross-country travel to the far West for Washington County residents became a reality with the completion of the Transcontinental Railroad in 1866. Again, the rivers showed the way.

One

Fun on the Battenkill

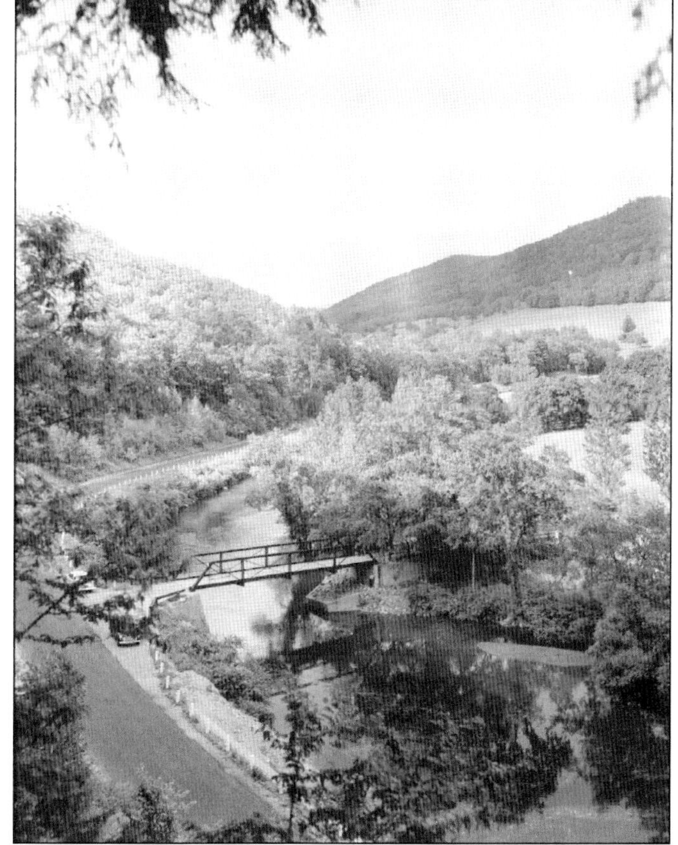

The 53-mile-long Battenkill, emanating from the Green Mountains, contains numerous popular fishing holes. Located just over the border in New York State is Dutchman's Hole, on State Route 313. The river, called Dionondehowa by the early Indians, flows through the New York State communities of Eagleville, Shushan, Rexleigh, and Fitch's Point, forming the southern border of the town of Salem. (Photograph by Herbert Eriksson.)

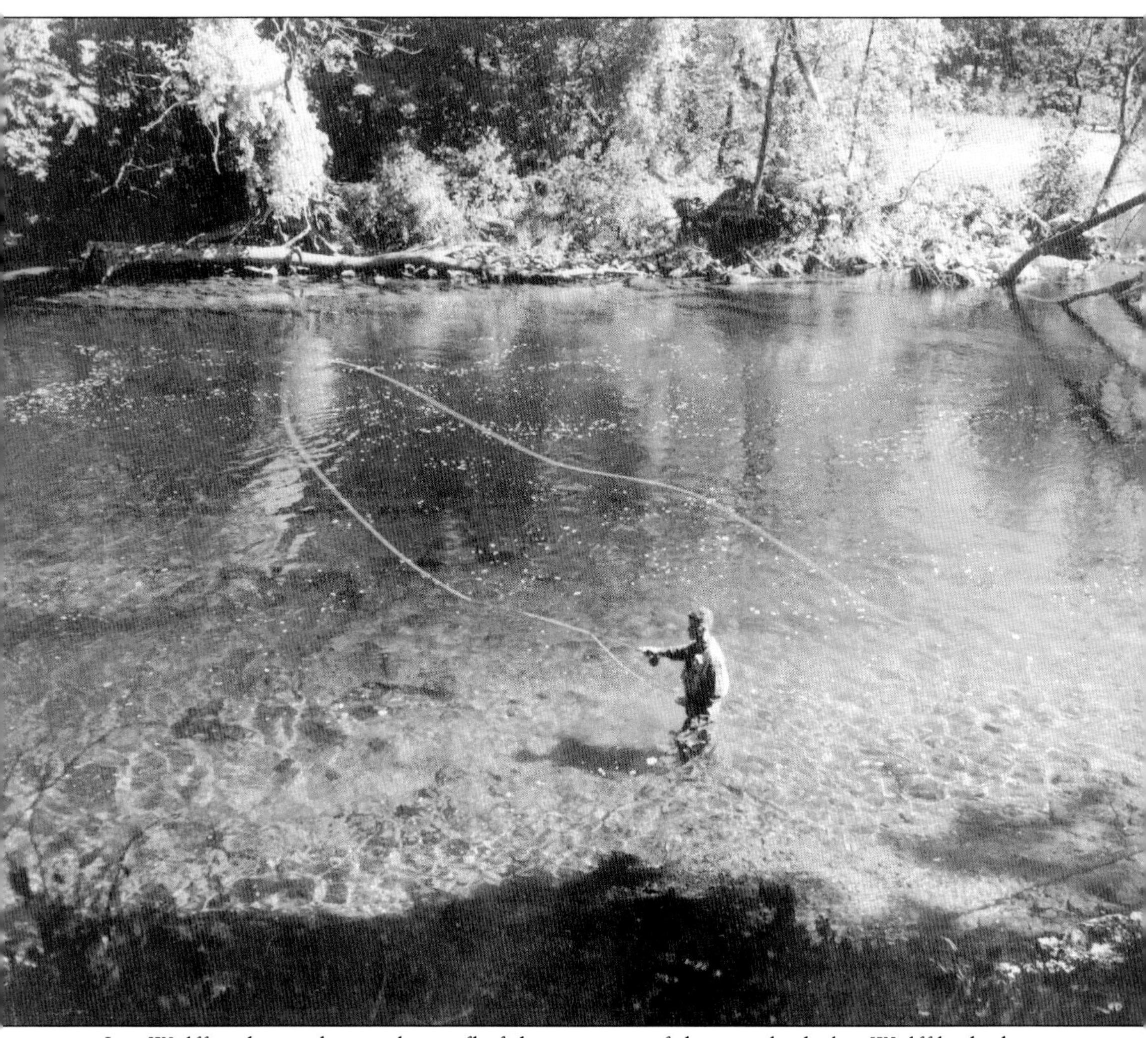

Lee Wulff, in his waders, is shown fly-fishing in one of the popular holes. Wulff had a home on the Battenkill in Eagleville between 1940 and 1960 and was a proponent of the catch-and-release philosophy, as outlined in his 1939 book *Handbook of Fly-fishing*. His early Grey, White, and Royal Wulff flies, among others, became very popular with fly-fishermen. (Courtesy of Joan Wulff.)

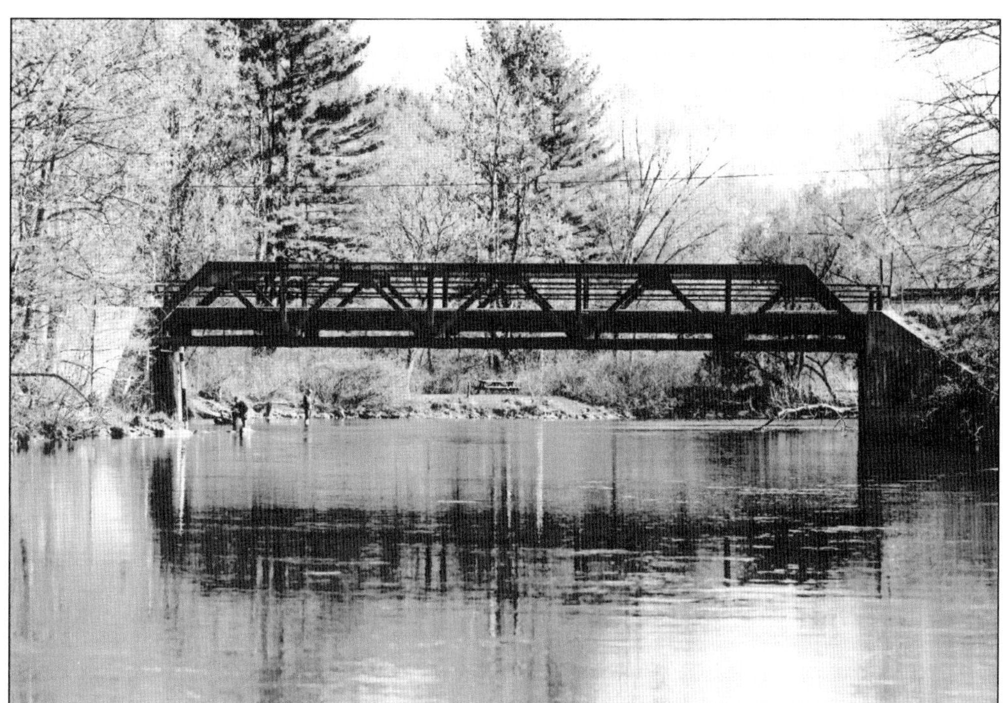

This photograph shows the Tackle Box fishing hole at Buffum's Bridge. Note that two fishermen can be seen near the left riverbank. This is a full shot of the Buffum Bridge, which Lee Wulff, wearing waders, dove from to prove that waders were safe. Today, the use of fishing waders is widespread. (Photograph by Herbert Eriksson.)

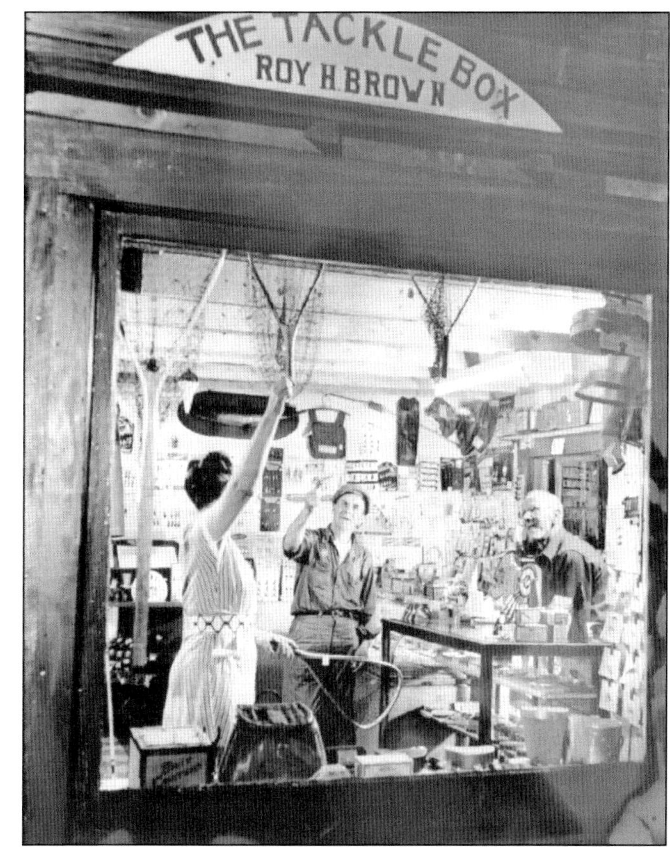

Seen through the large Tackle Box window are Ann Brown (left) and Roy Brown (right); they are helping a fisherman decide which fishing net to use on the river. Fishing advice, gear, food, and other supplies kept visiting fishermen well stocked. The Tackle Box continues to be popular with fishermen today. (Photograph by Herbert Eriksson.)

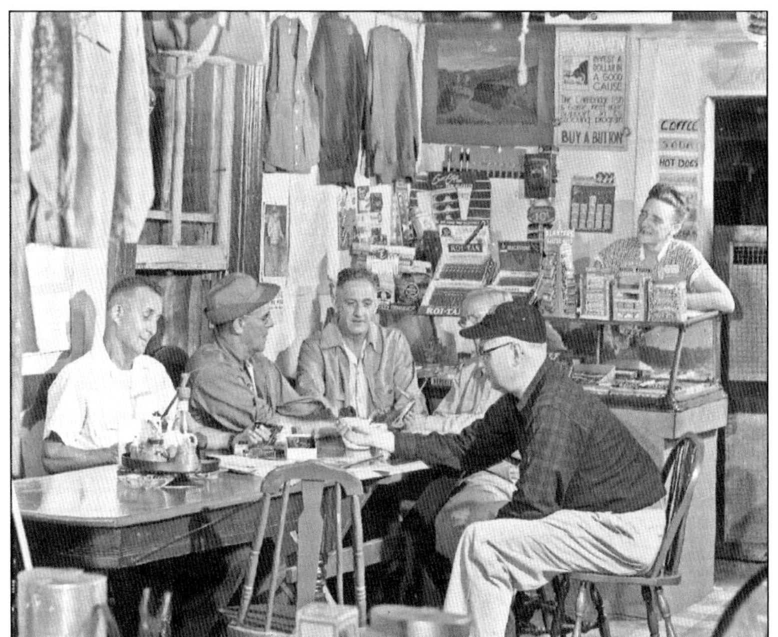

When fishing was not good or bad weather intervened, Roy and Ann Brown discussed recent catches, fishing tackle, and fly-tying with regulars. Pictured are, from left to right, Harry Harlow, John Eriksson, unidentified, Roy Brown (partially hidden), Homer Peters, and Ann Brown (counter) at the Tackle Box. (Photograph by Herbert Eriksson.)

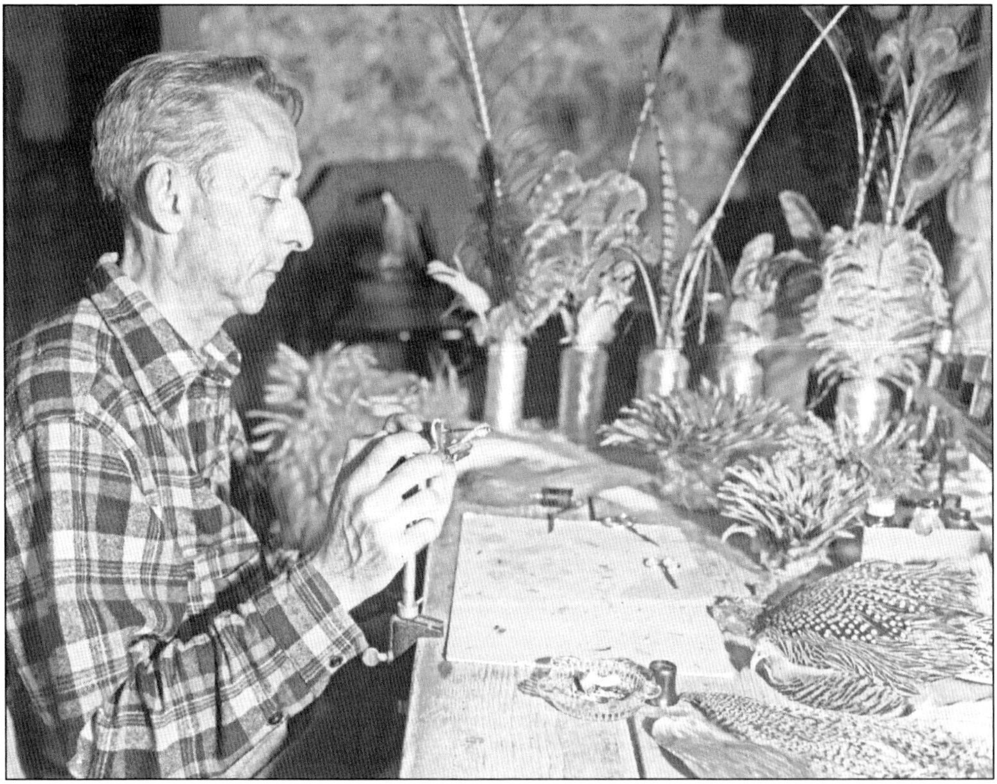

Lou Oatman, a nationally known expert on fly-fishing and fly-tying known for his "exact imitations," is shown at his fly-tying table. As one can see, many different types of feathers were used in fly-tying, to mimic the natural flies on the Battenkill. Of his many flies, he developed 17 popular streamer patterns, closely resembling native forage fish. (Photograph by Herbert Eriksson.)

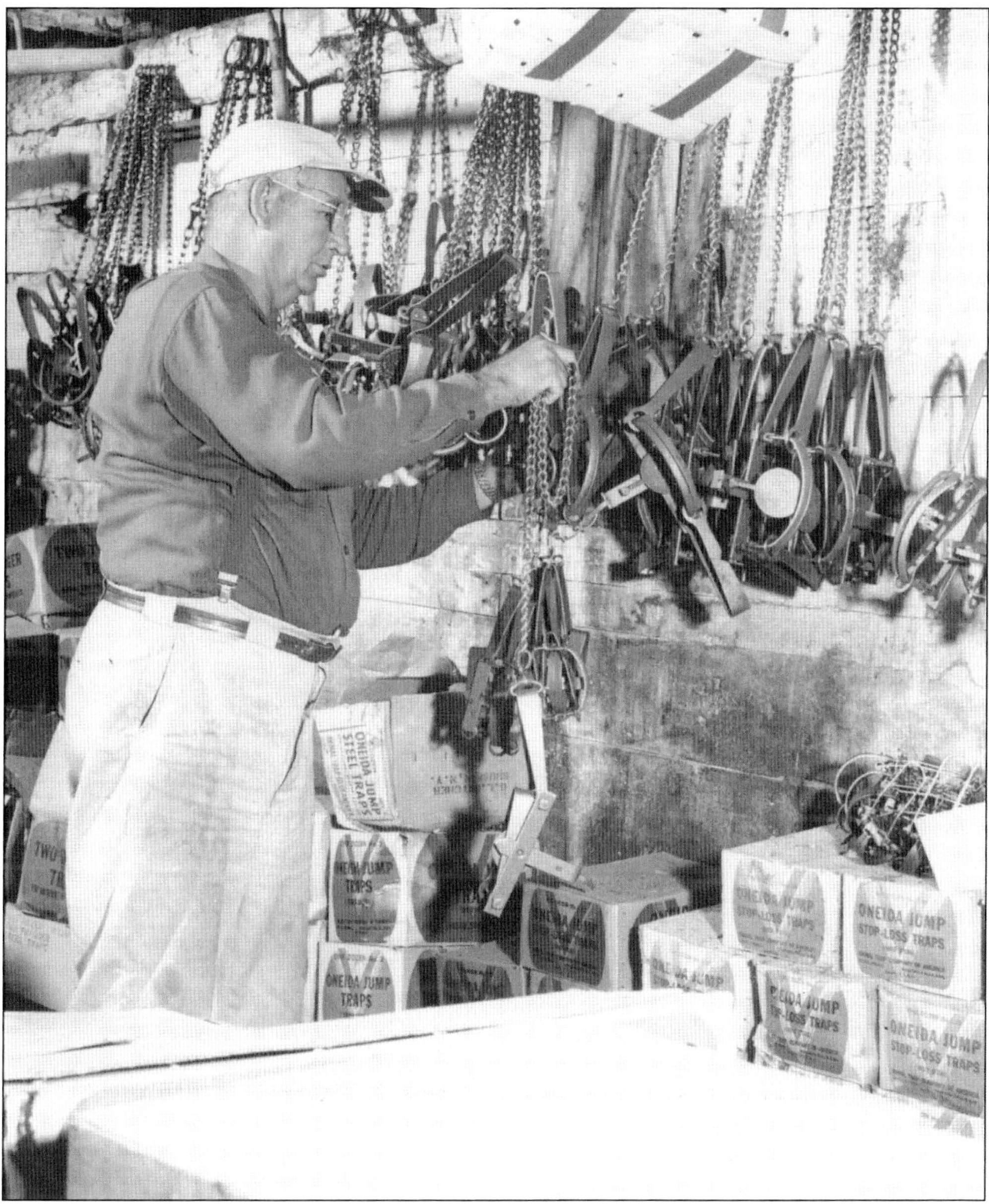

As popular as fishing was on the Battenkill, so was trapping for small animals such as muskrat, beaver, and mink in the neighboring forests and streams. O.L. Butcher operated a well-known trapping shop in Camden Valley, where he sold all kinds of traps and gave free advice. (Photograph by Herbert Eriksson.)

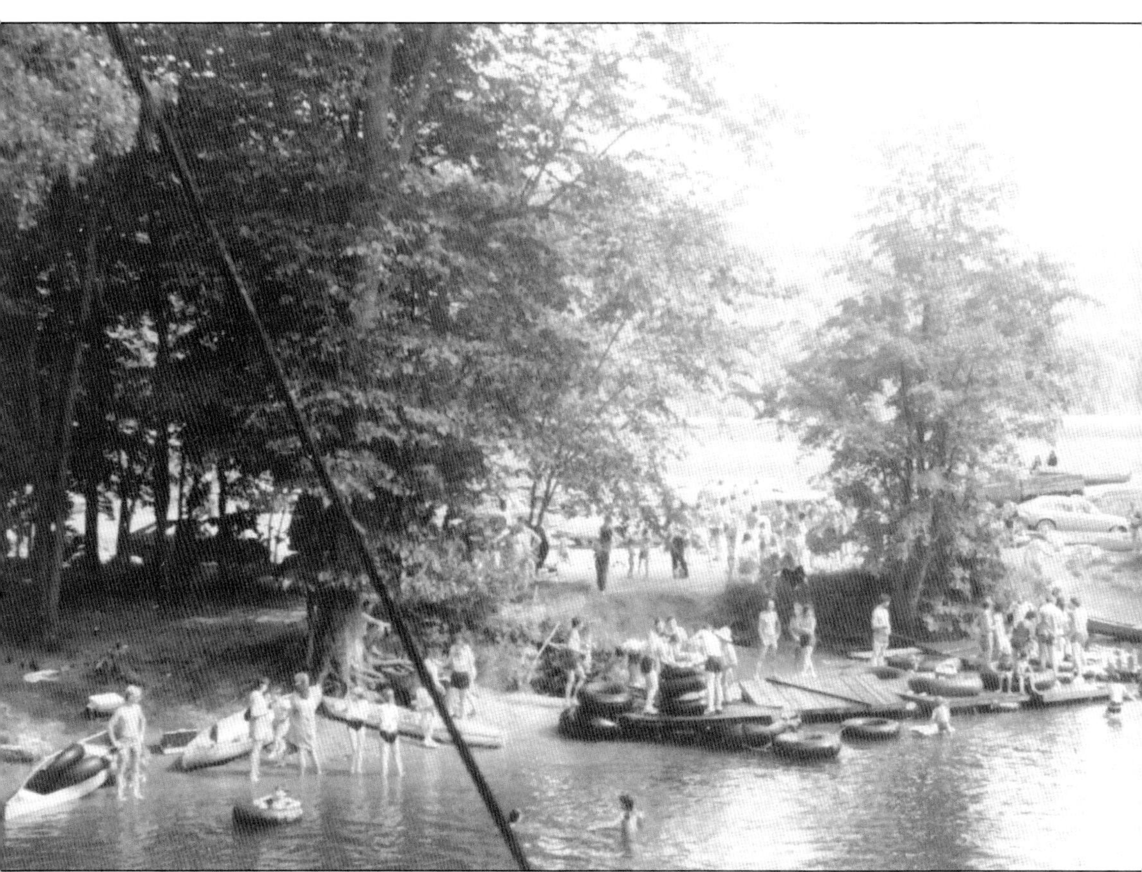

In the summer, the Battenkill was a popular playground for locals and visitors. This 1970s photograph shows that, in addition to swimming in the river, adventurers also launched tubes, canoes, and kayaks from the site of the Eagleville Covered Bridge. Popular stops on the river were in Shushan and Rexleigh. (Photograph by Harold "Butch" Gilchrest.)

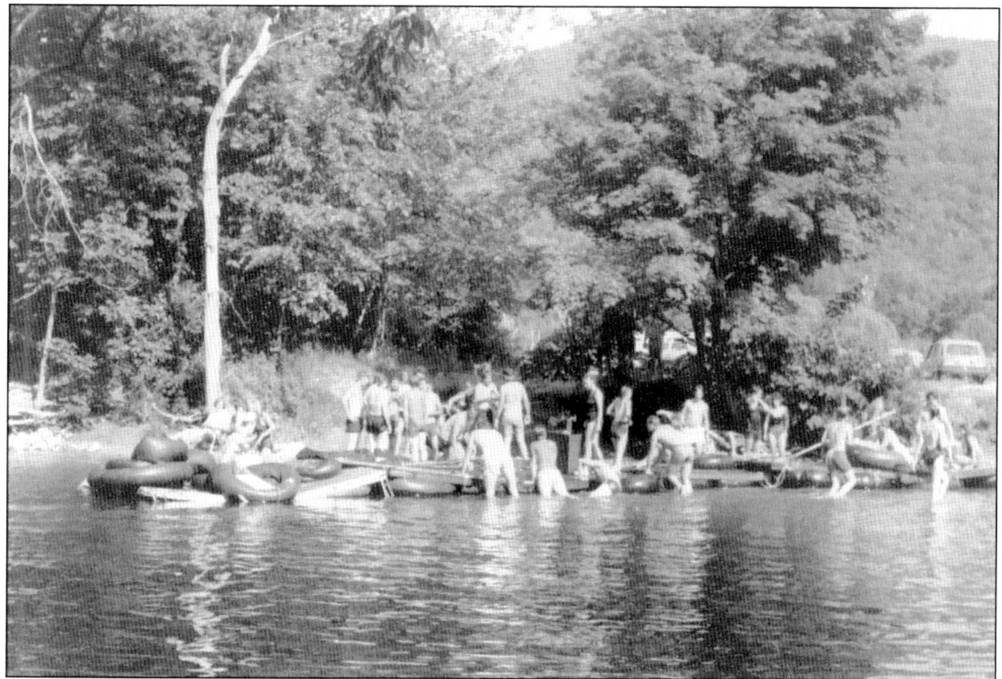

This photograph, taken in the late 1970s, shows another group getting ready to launch their tube rafts. The tubers and fly fishermen did not always get along, with the fishermen claiming that the tubers disturbed the fishing sites. Fortunately, most tubers and canoe riders respected the fishermen's space. (Photograph by Harold "Butch" Gilchrest.)

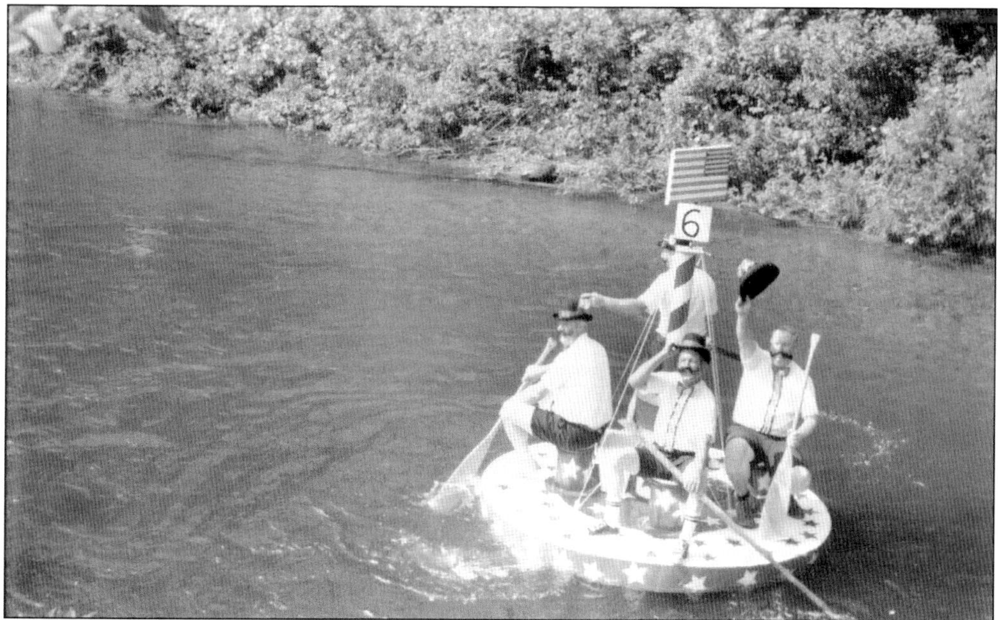

Beginning on July 4, 1962, boaters and spectators participated in the annual Cambridge Invitational predicted log race on the Battenkill. On July 4, 1976, costumed revelers decorated their rafts in celebration of the bicentennial of the signing of the Declaration of Independence. This float appears to have a barbershop quartet theme. (Photograph by Harold "Butch" Gilchrest.)

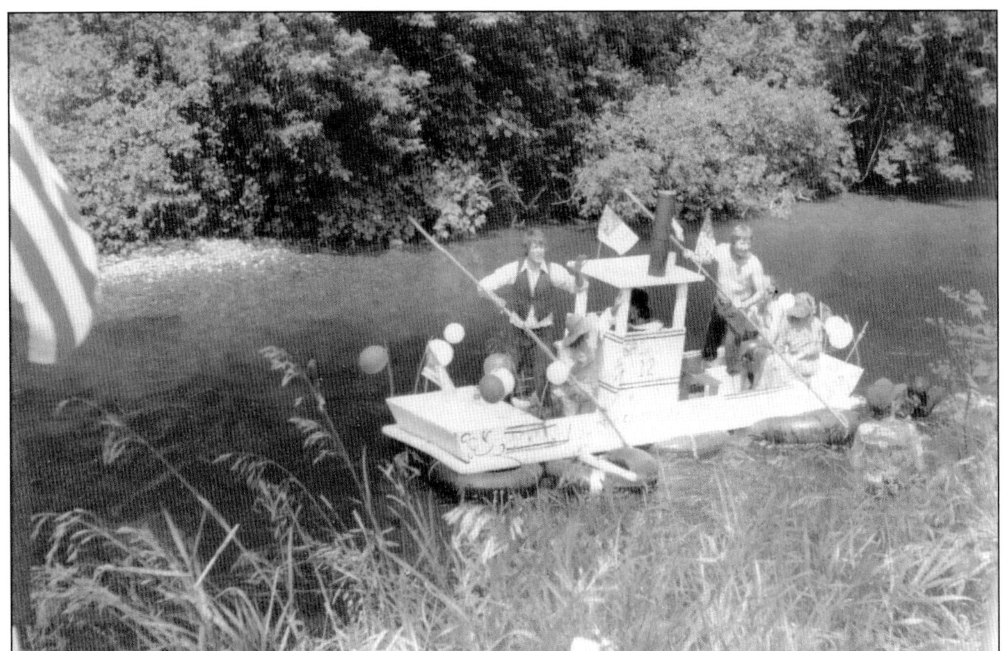

Another July 4, 1976, decorated float, named *Showboat*, was reminiscent of a Mississippi River steamboat. Large tire inner tubes kept the boat afloat, while the men with poles supplied the power. The float parade was held early enough in the day so that people could also view the street parade in Salem Village. (Photograph by Harold "Butch" Gilchrest.)

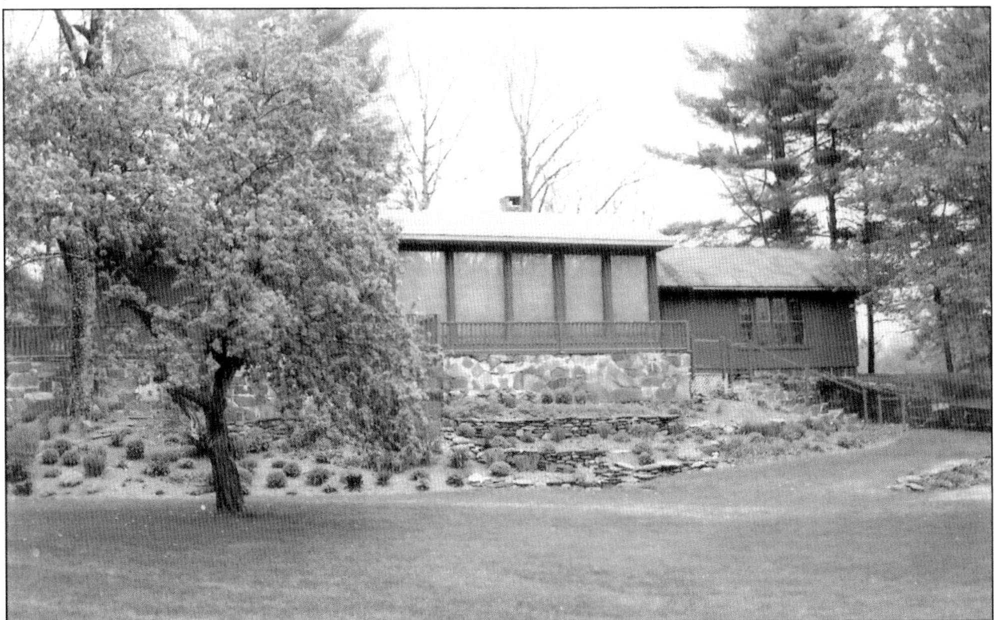

In 1952, John Eriksson built a house on the Battenkill for Maria and William Georgi, but their daughter Jesse Georgi was the only family member to live in the Shushan house. When she died in 1988, she bequeathed the property to the Shushan people, with the town of Salem as the legal owner. Today, the town operates the house and its landscaped grounds as the Georgi on the Battenkill Museum and Park. (Courtesy of the Georgi on the Battenkill Museum and Park.)

Two

Shushan on the Battenkill

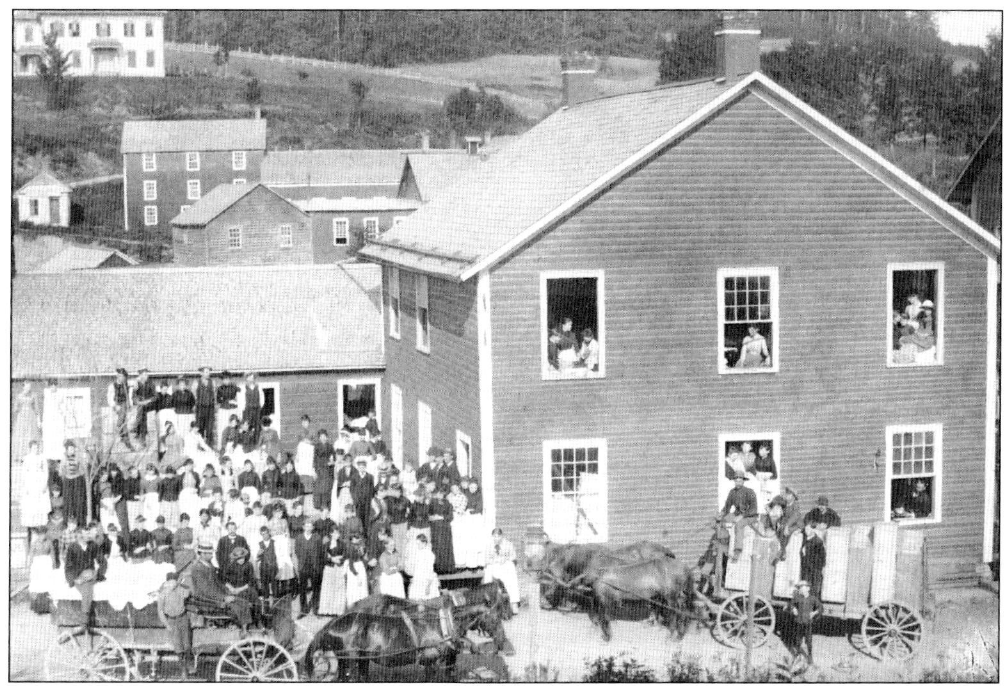

In 1876, Shushan businessman L.C. Piser built the Shushan Shirt Factory on the banks of the Battenkill. At one time, the business employed 175 people, mostly women, who lived in boardinghouses that charged $2.50 a week. In 1891, the Hercules Manufacturing Company placed electric generators in the shirt factory, making Shushan one of the earliest communities to have lights in the area.

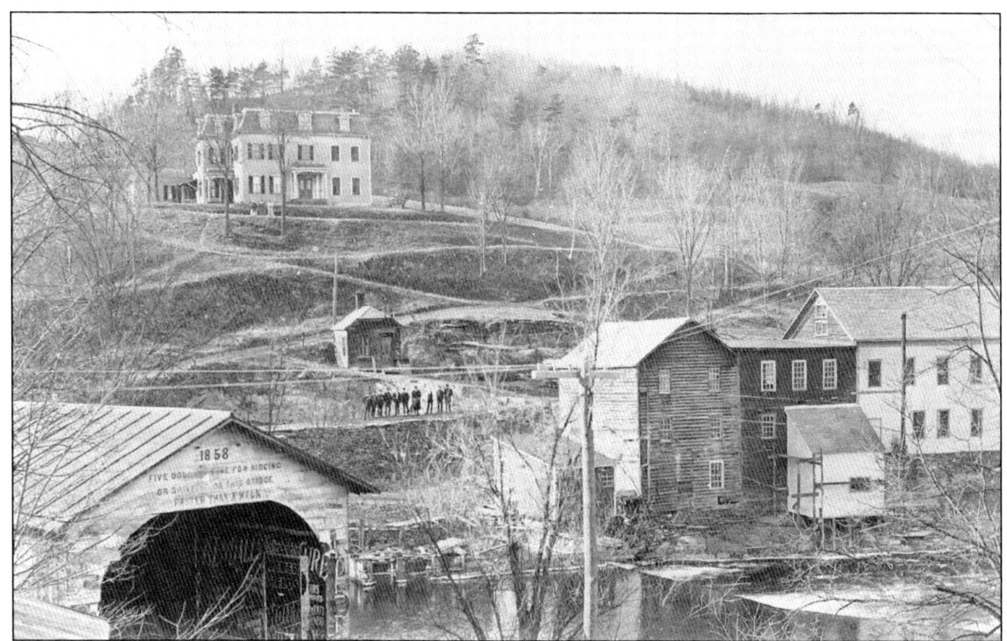

These Battenkill mills are shown on the town of Jackson side. In 1858, Milton and John Stevens built the Shushan Covered Bridge over the Battenkill, using Town's lattice truss. The covered bridge sign says, "Five Dollars Fine for Rideing or Driving on this Bridge Faster Than a Walk." The house on the hill in the photograph was the home of L.C. Piser.

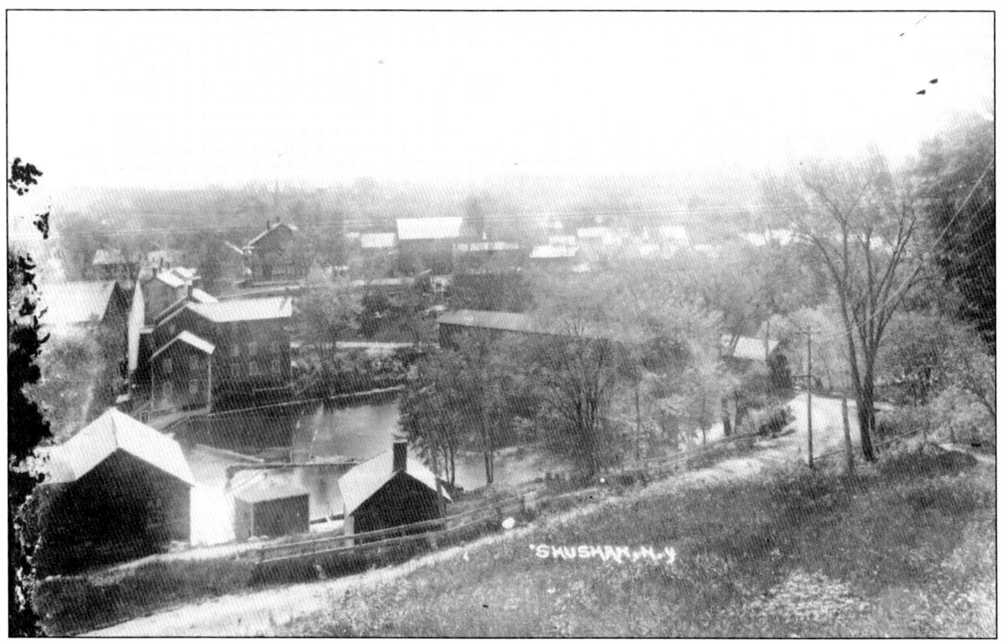

This late-1800s photograph shows the Shushan Covered Bridge and milldam and the Piser Shirt Shop, located to the left of the bridge. The milldam directed the water to the waterwheels in the mills on both sides of the Battenkill. The now-gone Baptist church can be seen in the center of the photograph.

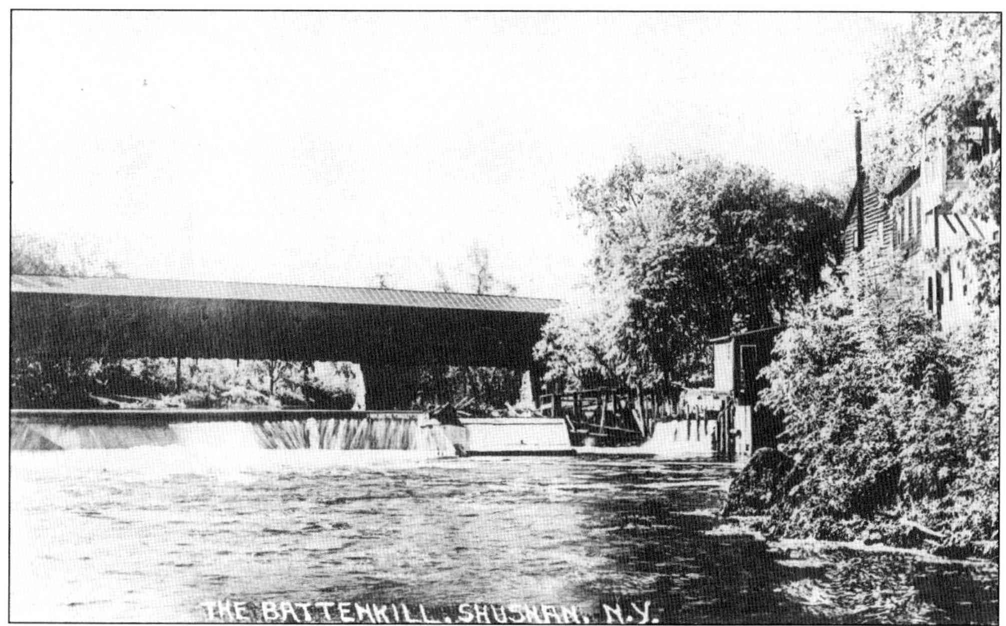

This photograph, looking east, shows the Shushan Covered Bridge, the dam, and Lovejoy's Tin Mill (right). The mill flume gates can be seen at the left of the mill. By 1876, Shushan had situated two woolen factories, a gristmill, a sawmill, a tin mill, a woolen mill, a flax mill, and a shirt mill on the river. (Courtesy of Edie Meikle.)

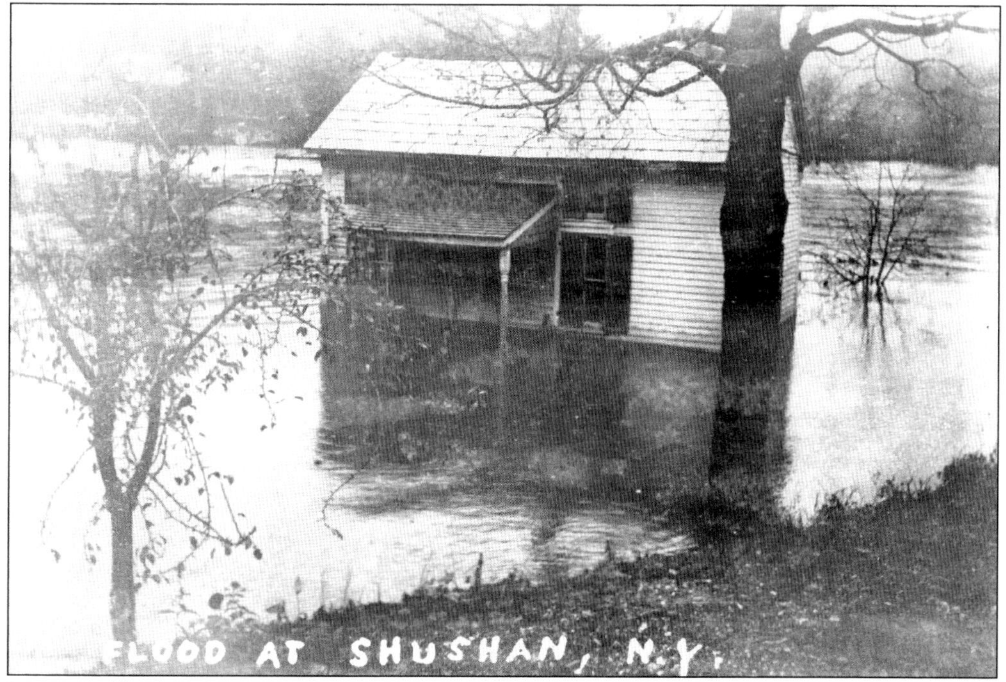

In 1936, a flood took out the Shushan dam, never to be rebuilt. The water-powered mill era was at an end. Shown here is the home of Fred Marco surrounded by water; the surging Battenkill can be seen in the background. At one time, 14 dams on the Battenkill supplied power to 73 mills, from Eagleville to Clarks Mills in Greenwich. (Courtesy of Edie Meikle.)

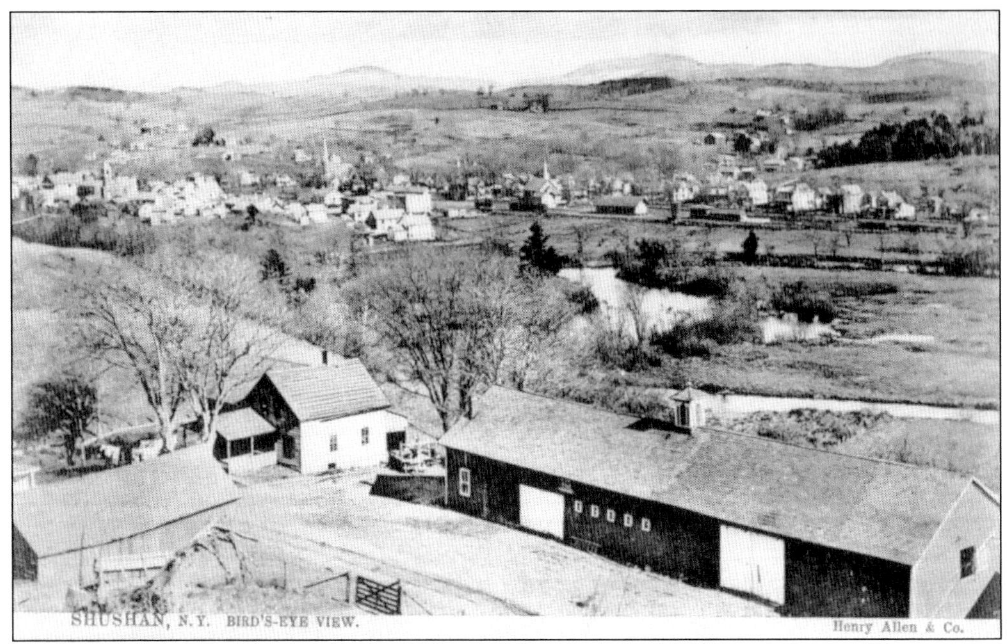

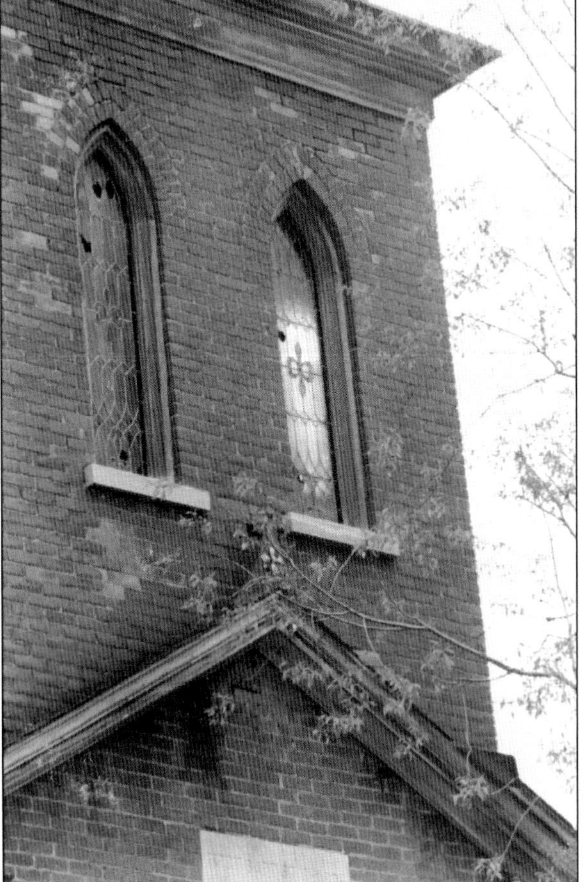

Looking east over Shushan, this bird's-eye view shows the Delaware & Hudson tracks, town buildings, and the Battenkill. The Baptist church (far left) was built in 1800, the large Presbyterian church in the left center was built in 1878, and the Methodist church (center) was built in 1847. The Baptist church no longer stands.

This abandoned Baptist church close-up shows two Gothic windows with stained-glass windows. The church, organized in 1790, was one of the earliest in the area, but the church building itself was not built until 1800. The church closed in the early 1900s and was torn down in the early 1970s. (Photograph by Edie Meikle.)

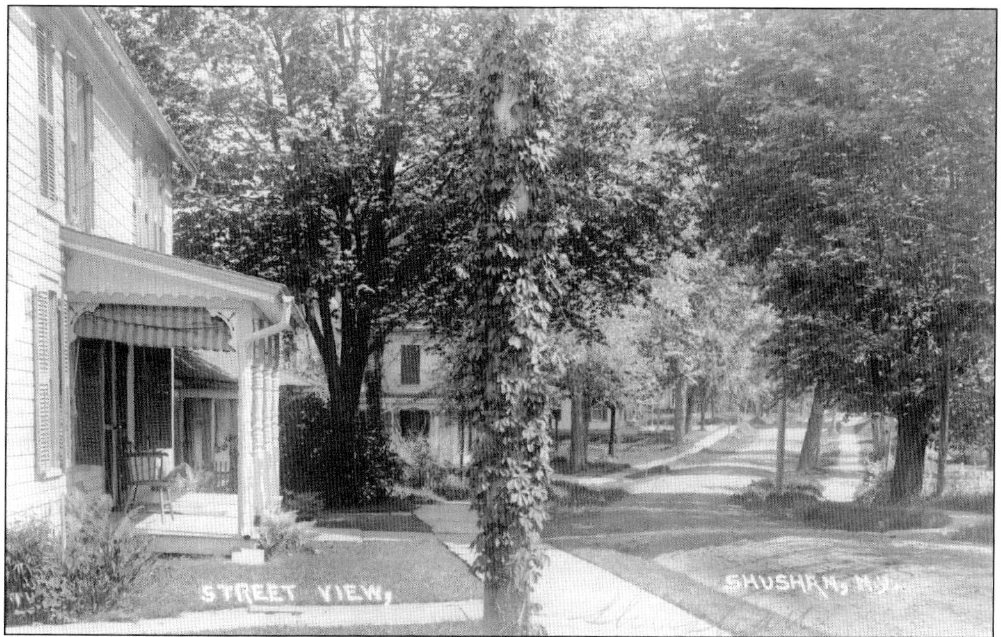

This 1910 photograph shows the dirt road north (today's County Route 64) from Shushan to Salem Village. Mica flagging, obtained from a nearby quarry, made for smooth, dry sidewalks in the village during mud season, when the dirt roads turned to ruts and mud holes. The slate sidewalks continue to serve the hamlet.

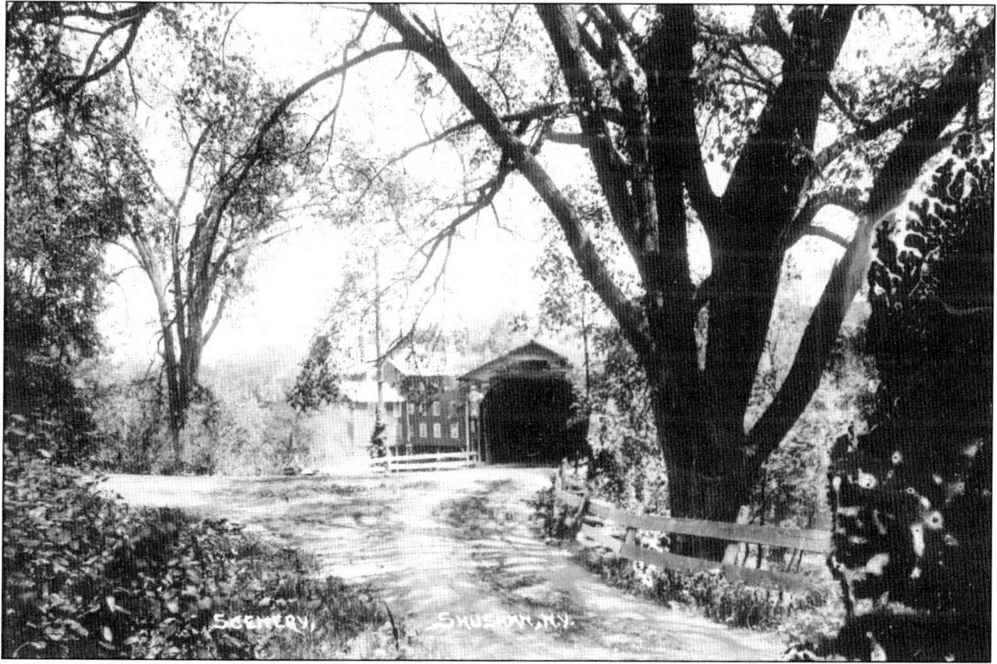

This photograph shows the west road (left) from the town of Jackson entering the Shushan Covered Bridge. The Piser Shirt Factory is seen to the left. The road today is County Route 61, leading to the Jackson glacier lakes, Lauderdale and Hedges. Both lakes continue to be popular summer retreats for vacationers.

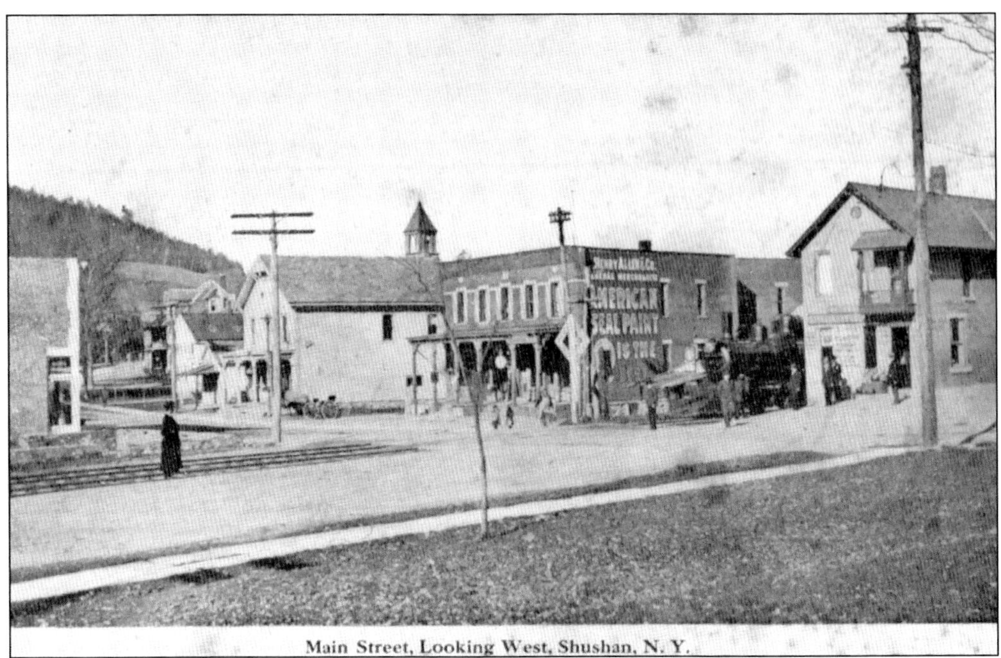

Stevens' Corner on the Shushan Main Street was named for Gilbert H. and Martin Stevens, prominent businessmen in Shushan. They owned the sawmills together, but Martin, alone, owned the potato storage building on the right, next to the Delaware & Hudson tracks. Note the steam engine and the large advertising sign pictured. The Baptist church steeple can be seen in the center of the image.

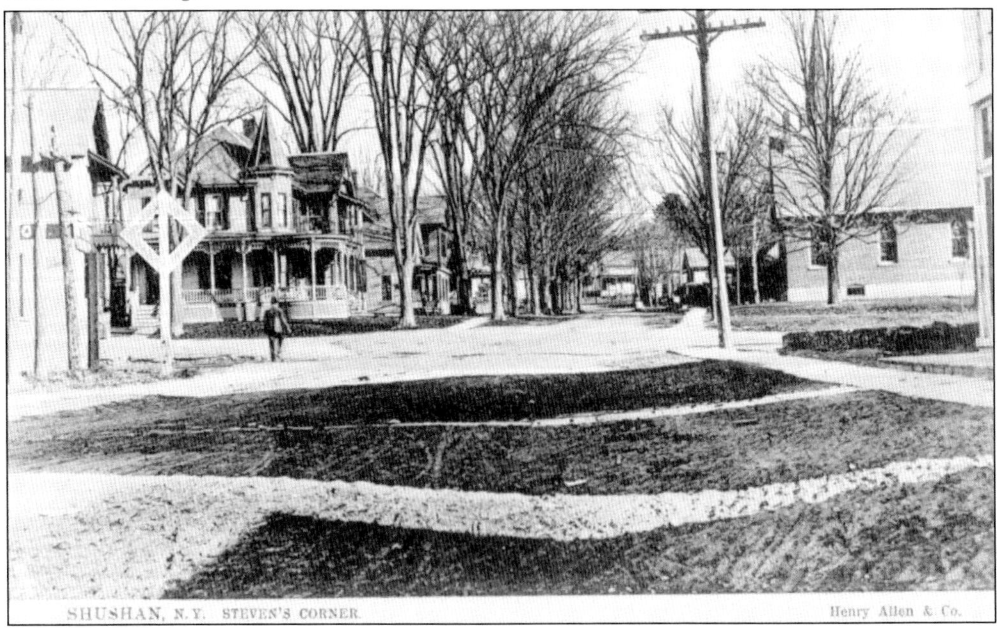

This photograph shows today's County Route 61 headed east from Stevens' Corner to Buffum's Bridge and New York State Route 313, which followed the Battenkill to Arlington, Vermont. Seen on the right is the Methodist church. On the left is a large Queen Ann–style house, owned by Martin Stevens, typical of the architecture of the fancier homes in the village.

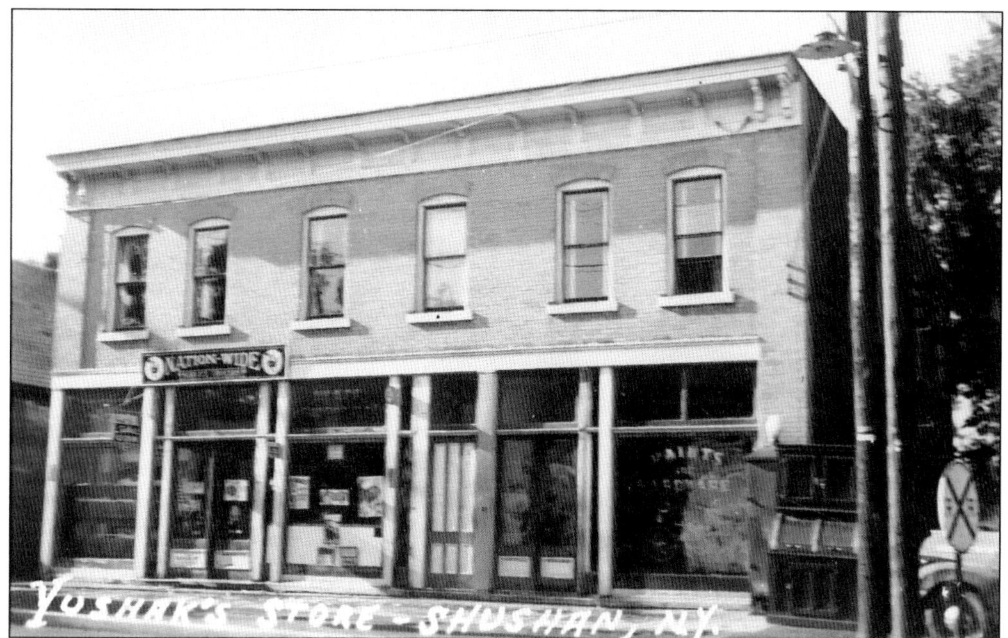

Yushak's Store on Main Street, purchased in 1941 by the Michael Yushak family, is shown in this 1948 photograph. It still provides the people of Shushan and summer vacationers with fine meats, wet and dry goods, and a cup of coffee if needed. The store is now run by second-generation owner Dennis Yushak and his wife, Debbie.

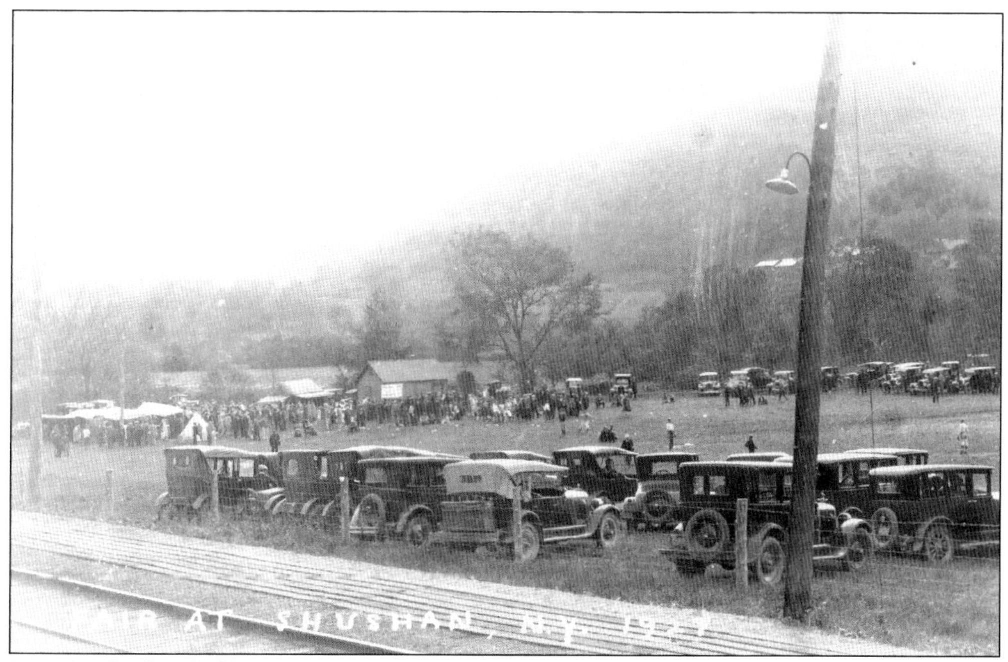

In 1927, Shushan held its own fair in a field south of the railroad depot on County Route 64. The number of cars indicates that people came from far and wide to attend the fair. A baseball game appears to be in progress on the right side of the fairgrounds.

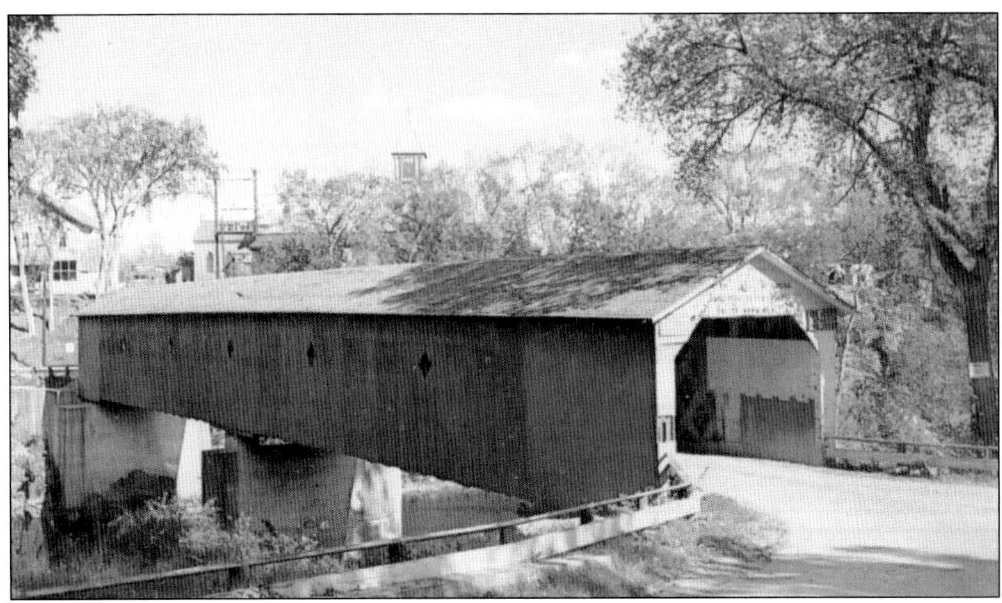

This photograph shows the Shushan Covered Bridge just before it was closed to traffic, when a modern steel bridge replaced it in 1962. In 1974, the Washington County Board of Supervisors deeded the wooden structure to the Shushan Covered Bridge Association, organized by John Robert Rich. Today, the Shushan Covered Bridge serves as a museum.

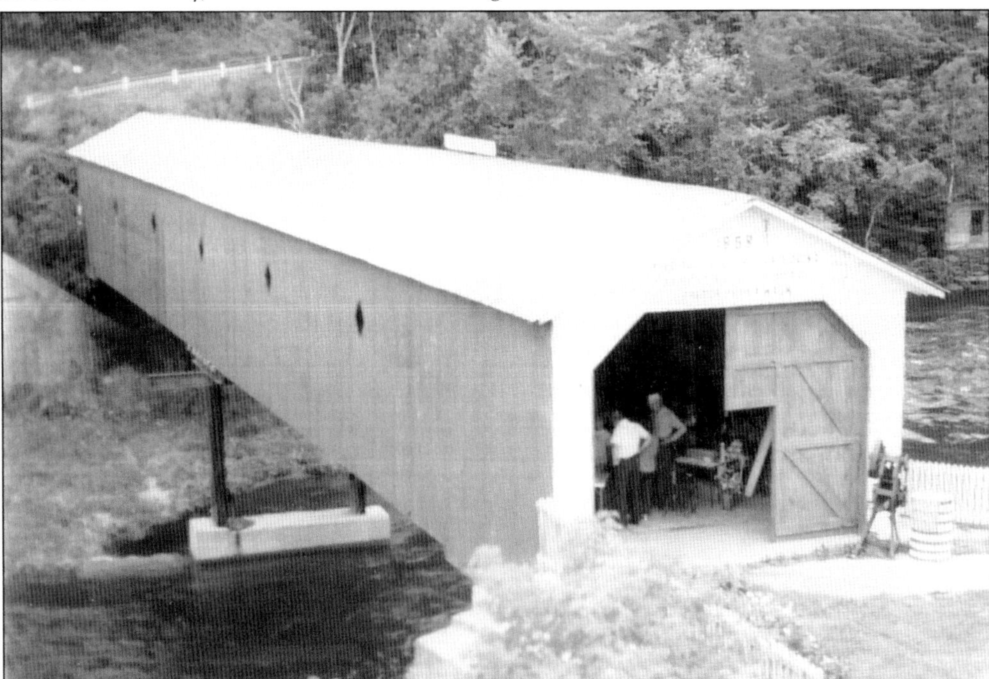

This 1976 photograph shows the Shushan Covered Bridge as a farm implement museum. The Shushan Covered Bridge Association opened the museum on June 28, 1975. Officers in 1975 were president Carlton A. Foster; vice president Everett Stromberg; secretary Mary Buffum Hamlin; and treasurer Frederick Fortmuller. Directors were Nancy Clark Sheldon, Gunnar Johnson, and Robert W. Raymond.

Three

POPULAR AREA LAKES

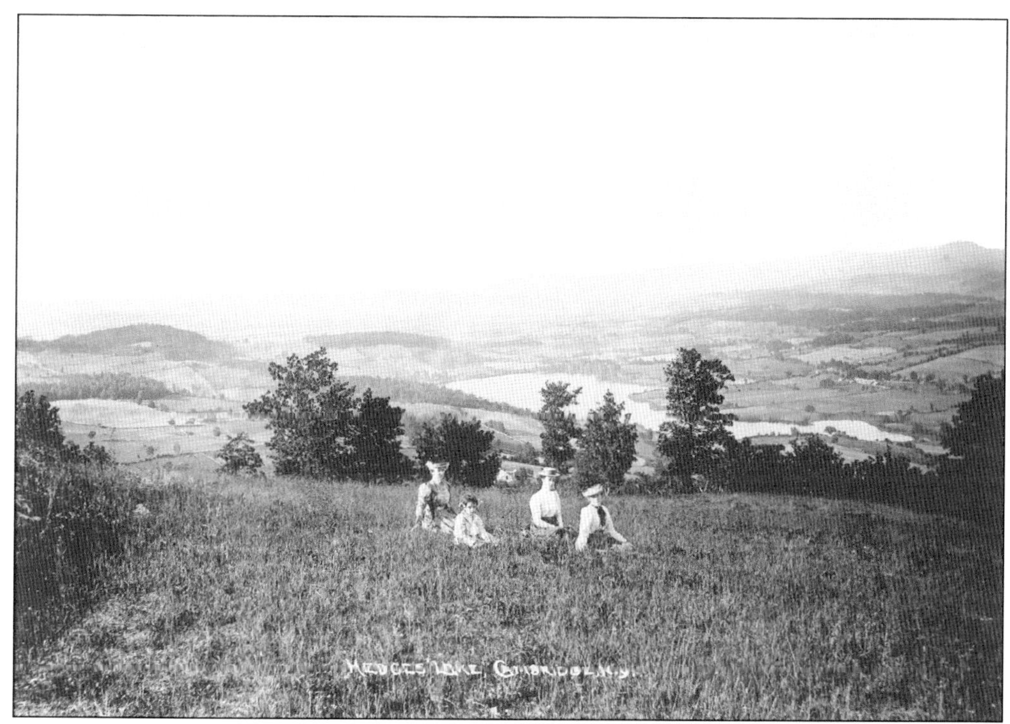

This scenic view from O'Donnell Hill in the town of Jackson shows Hedges Lake. In the distance are the Battenkill Valley, the Taconic Range, and the Green Mountains. In Shushan, the Battenkill and the two nearby glacier-formed lakes of Hedges and Lauderdale were popular vacation spots easily reached by taking the train from New York City or Boston to the Shushan depot.

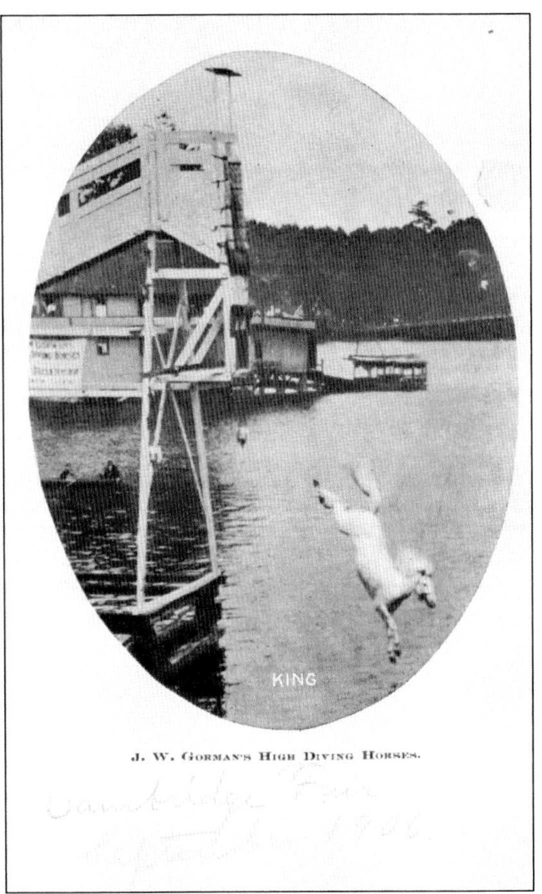

From 1890 to 1943, the village of Cambridge held an agricultural fair adjacent to the Troy & Rutland Railroad tracks. The Delaware & Hudson Railway would put on extra passenger cars to accommodate the crowds. One of the features of the fair was J.W. Gorman's High Diving Horses, which would dive into a large tank of water at the fair.

Automobiles and buses appear to be the modes of transportation taken to this special outing on Hedges Lake around 1910. The pavilion on the left is teeming with people, while others crowd the dock. A Texaco gas pump in the center of the photograph is ready to serve automobile customers and their Ford Model Ts.

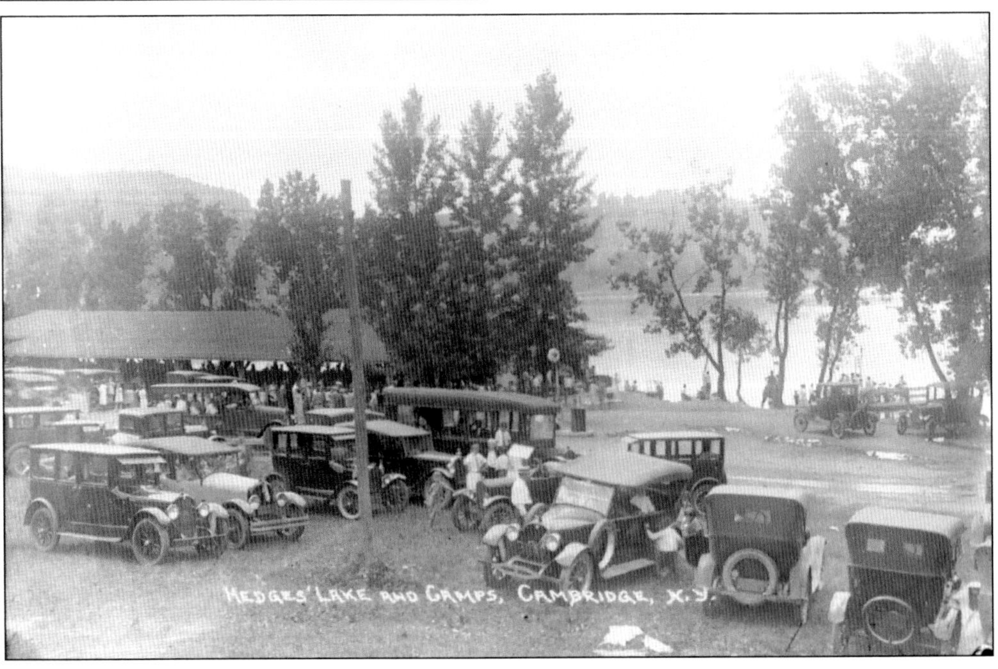

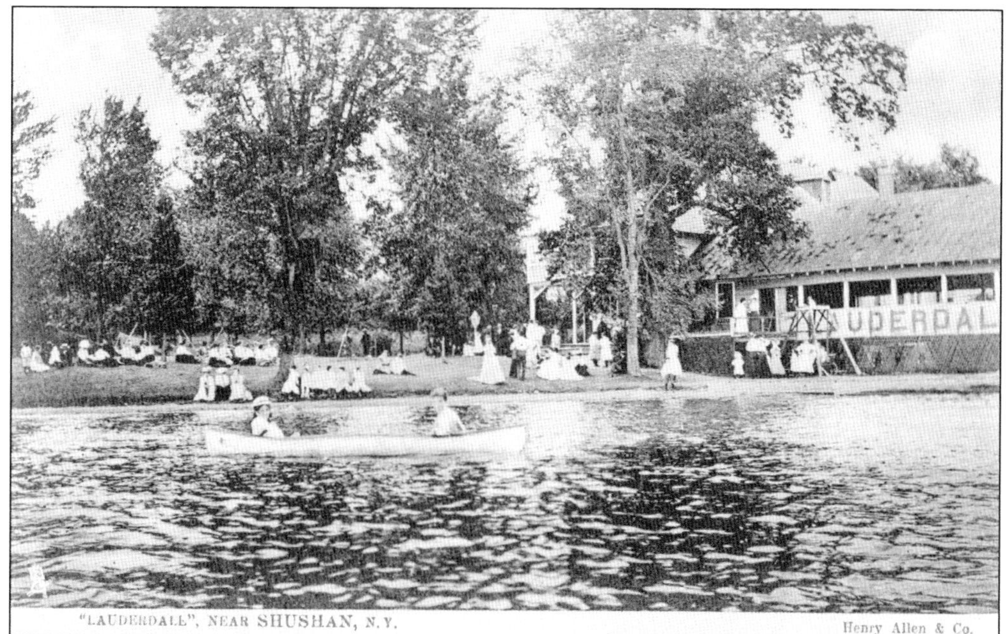

In this 1909 photograph, Lake Lauderdale, once known as Long Lake, according to the 1866 Atlas of Washington County, the pavilion, and the beach are crowded with visitors. The formal dress suggests that the photograph was taken on a Sunday. Hats were fashionable for men and women.

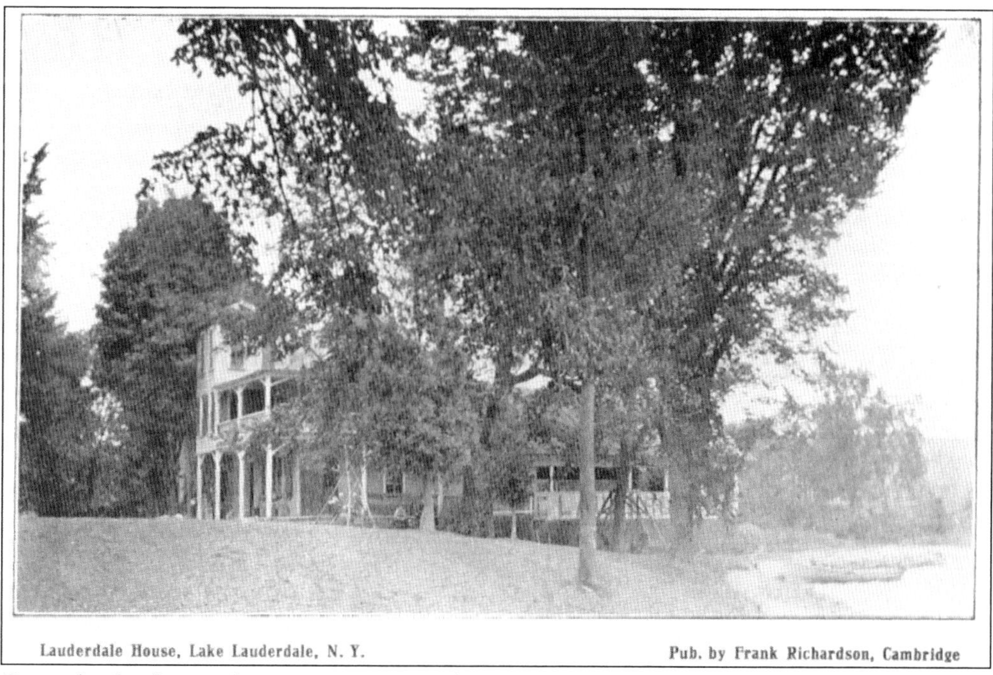

Guests by the day, week, or summer were welcome to stay at the Lake Lauderdale House, with its connected pavilion. Early on, the hotel was a regular stagecoach stop for the Whitehall-to-Albany stagecoach line. The hotel burned in 1926, leaving only the pavilion intact. Two of the Northern Turnpike milestones can be found in the "ponds" area today.

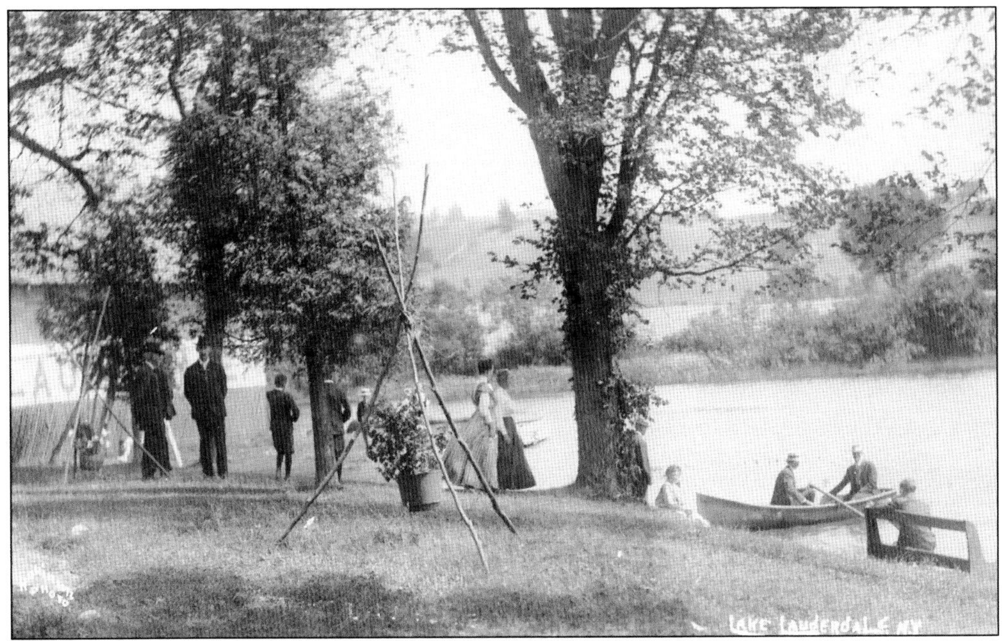

Here is another 1909 Lake Lauderdale Pavilion scene, perhaps taken on the same day, with people watching the two men going for a rowboat ride on the lake. In addition to Lake Lauderdale and Hedges Lake, Clark's Pond, Dead Pond, and Schoolhouse Pond are nearby.

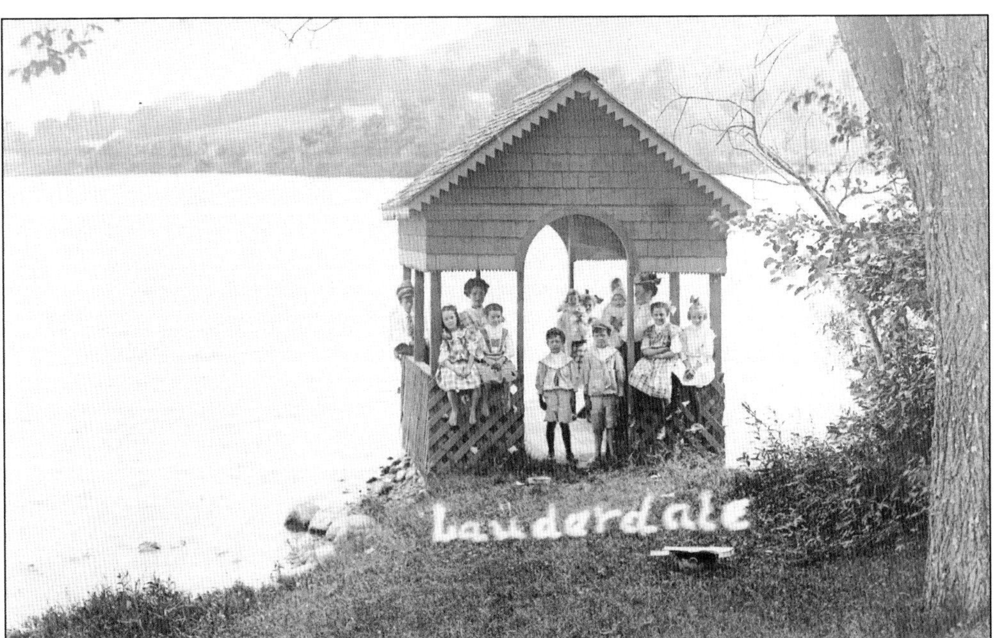

This 1903 photograph shows two women with numerous children in the Lake Lauderdale boathouse. The children are dressed in the fashions of the day for an outing at the lake, with the young boys in knickers, blouses, and caps and most of the girls in plaid dresses.

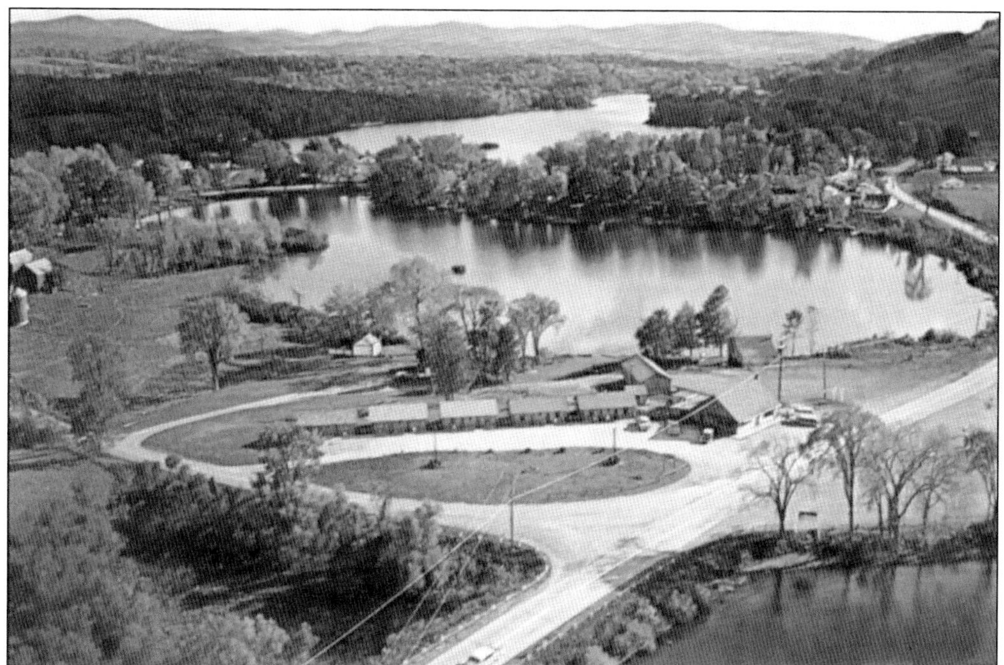

This 1950s aerial view shows part of Dead Pond (right), the Log Cabin Motel and Restaurant (center), and Lake Lauderdale in the fall of the year. The lined highway, State Route 22 in the photograph, follows much of the original 1799 Northern Turnpike from Lansingburg to Granville. Dead Pond is stocked with rainbow trout each spring and is a popular fishing spot.

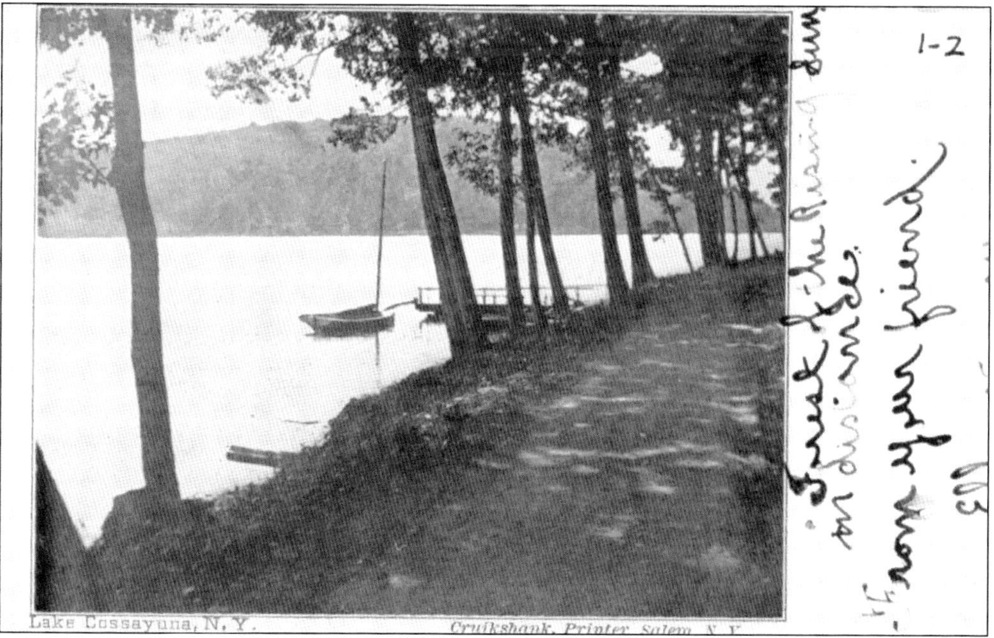

The Salem depot was used by vacationers going to the Indian-named Lake Cossayuna. Horse-drawn wagons and, later, automobiles waited at the depot to transport baggage and people. This 1910 photograph by Salem's Robert A. Cruikshank shows a small sailboat and dock on the east shore of the lake. The hill in the background was known locally as "the forest of the rising sun."

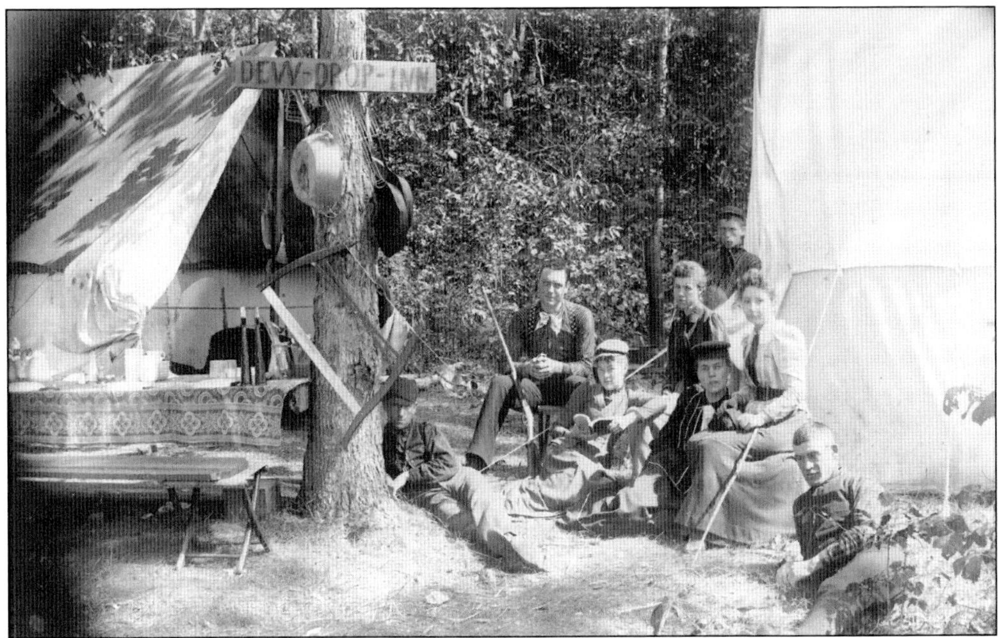

As the railroads expanded, vacationers could travel miles away from home. The Delaware & Hudson Railway was fast transportation from Troy to Shushan, Salem, and the Adirondack towns on the railway, making North Country camps, hotels, and boardinghouses popular destinations. Here, in an 1888 photograph, adventurous campers roughed it at the "Dew-Drop-In" at Lake Cossayuna, northwest of Salem.

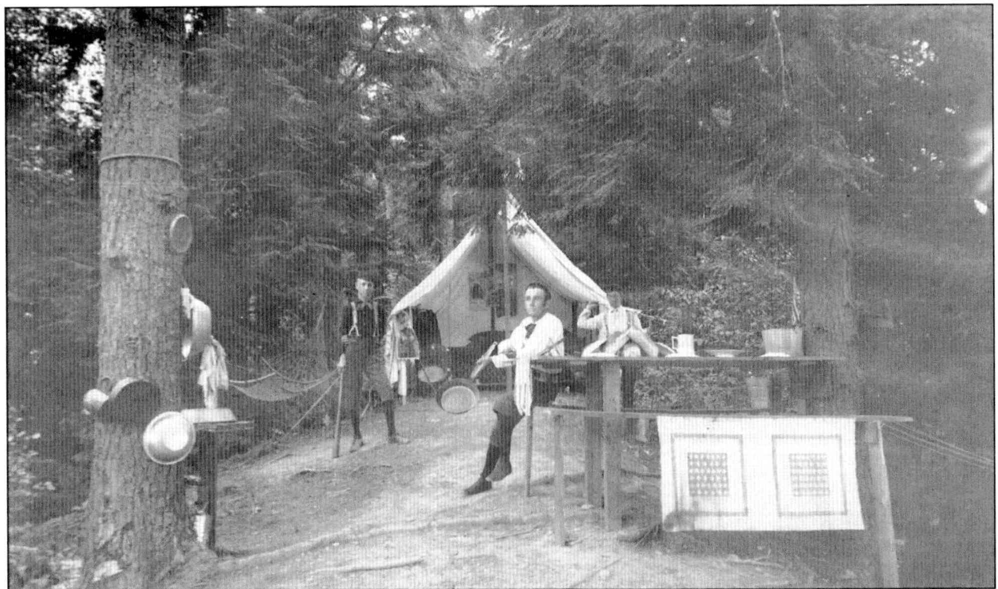

Gentile camping was the preferred method for many adventurers, including Salem people. Posing in this 1888 photograph at Star Camp are cook James Kerslake (left), boss W. Hill (center), and porter W.H. Reid (right). The props—a baseball bat, frying pan, and rifle, individually held by each man—appear to be symbols of their positions in the camp.

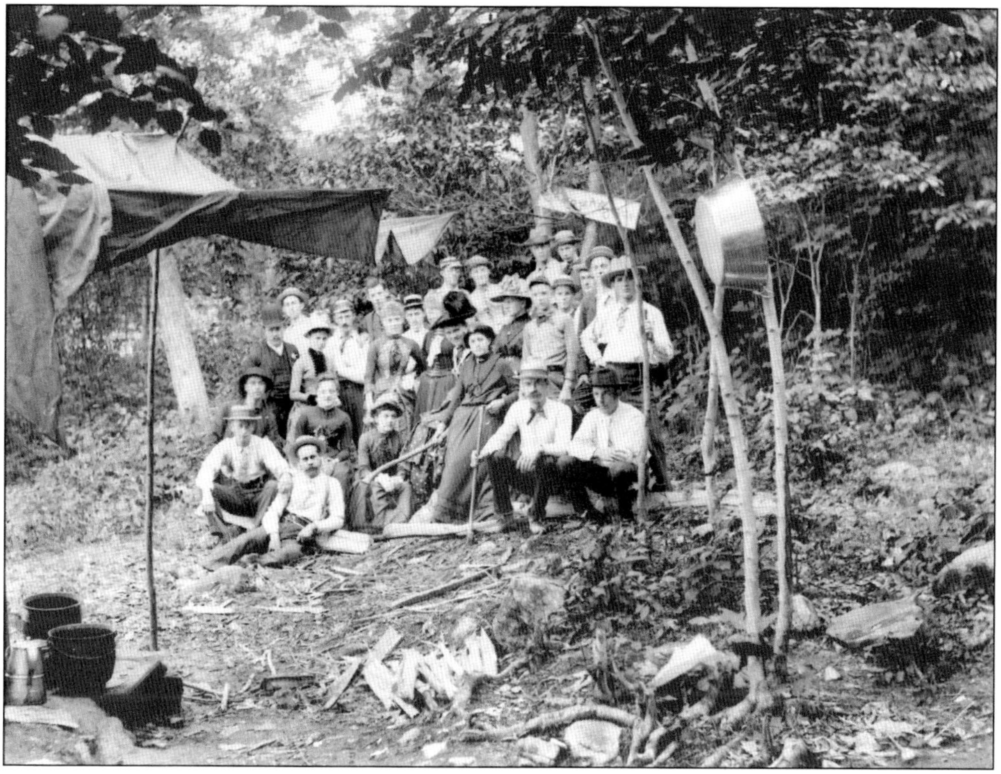

Posing at Camp Hard Luck is a large gathering of young men and women, contrary to social norms of the day. In this 1888 photograph, the large kettles, coffee pot, and split wood (perhaps split by the man and woman holding the axes) indicate that preparing a meal was imminent.

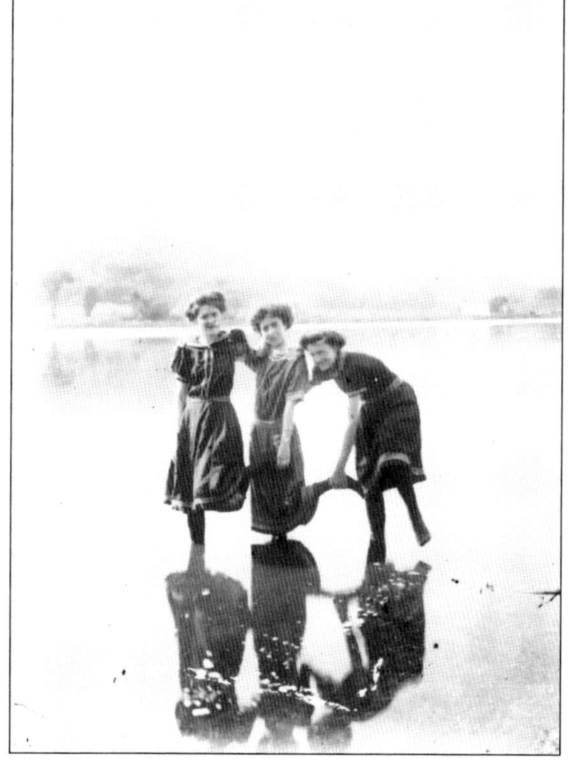

In this 1888 photograph on Lake Cossayuna, the three young girls have ventured out for a humorous photograph, their reflections making six of them. Swimming apparel for men included shorts and shirts, and apparel for women consisted of full-length bathing suits and stockings, which were dictated by the social norms of the day.

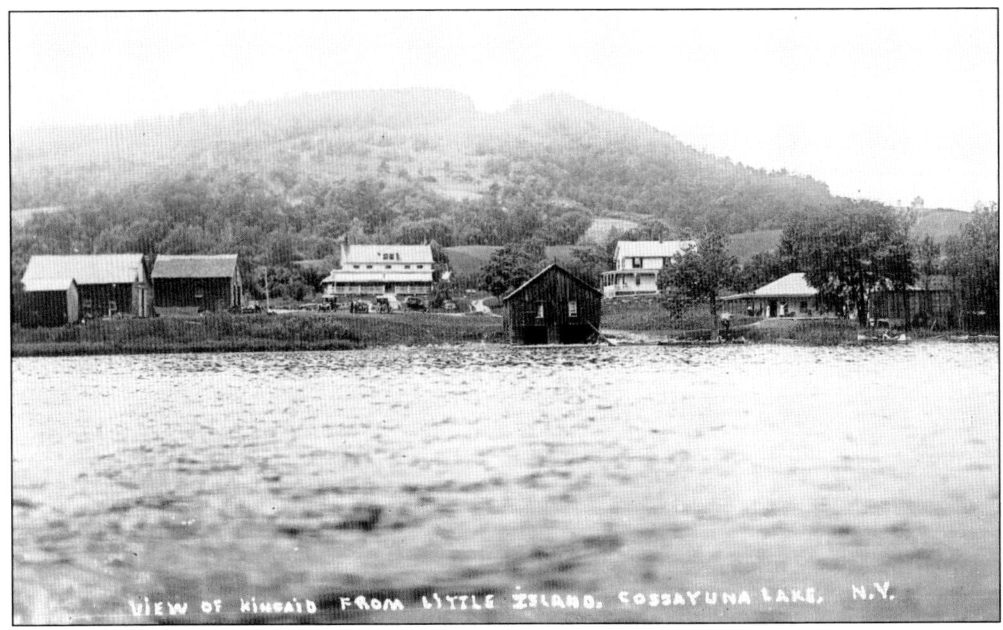

By 1939, the Delaware & Hudson Railway traveler guide, *A Summer in Paradise*, advertised numerous boardinghouses for vacationers in the Jackson and Salem area. Here, Kincaid's Resort, called the "most popular resort on the lake," is seen from Little Island in Lake Cossayuna. Note the woman on the right waving at the photographer.

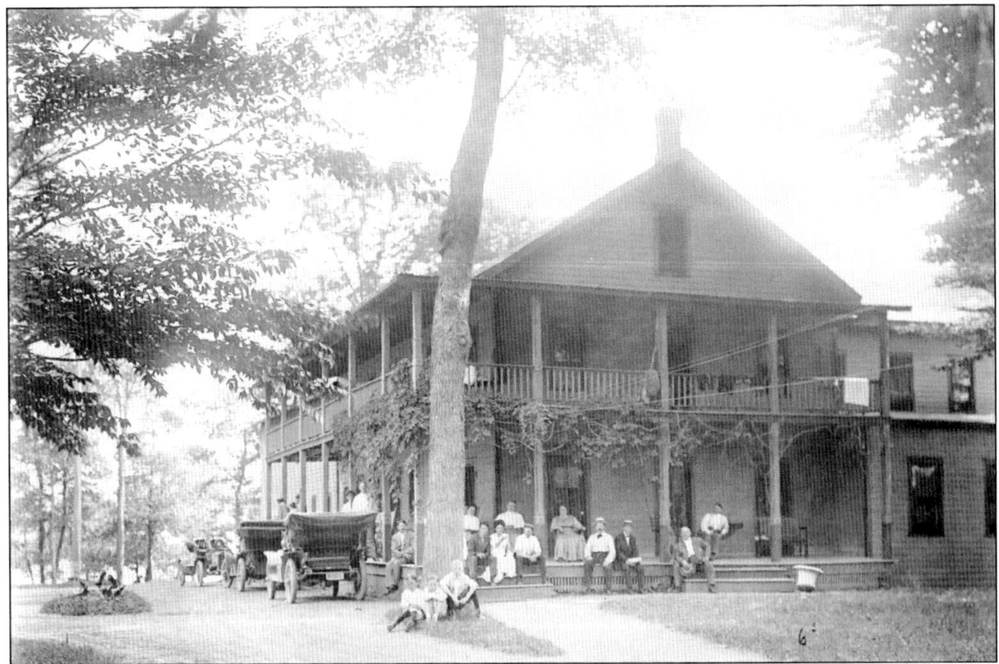

Another popular boarding resort was the Oaks, on Lake Cossayuna. This 1915 photograph shows the patrons posing for the photographer. The two-story porch gave the visitors a good view of the lake, as well as a cool, breezy place to be in the evenings. The woman sitting on the stairs (center) is clearly proud of her fishing catch.

Four

North by Northwest

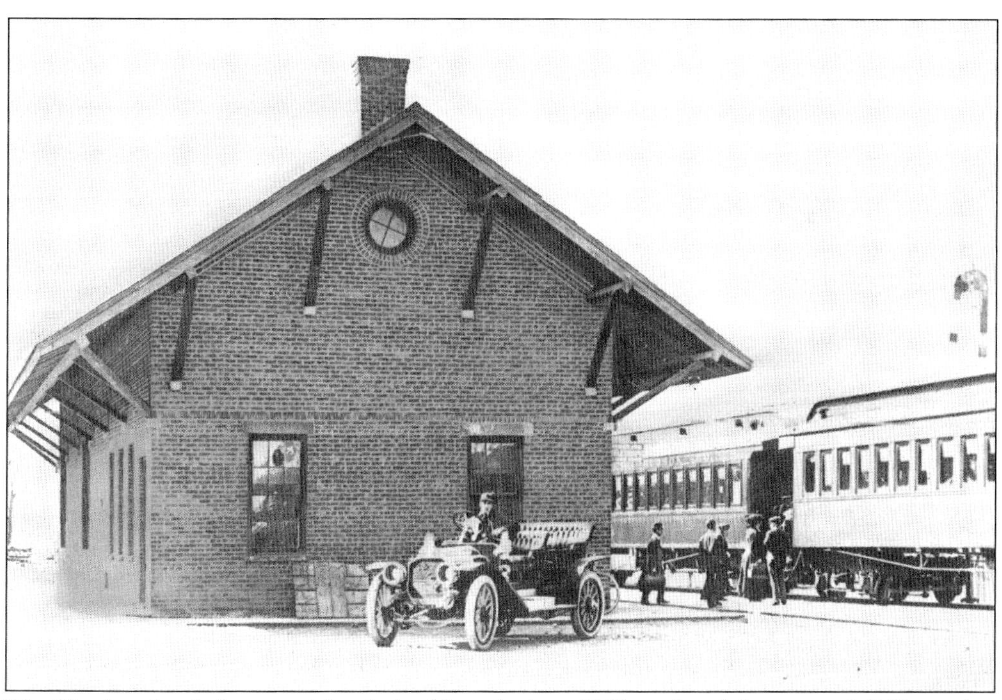

The Shushan brick depot and freight building, built in 1860, replaced the original 1852 wooden depot after it burned. This 1915 photograph shows passengers boarding the coaches. High school students took the train to Salem Washington Academy until June 22, 1934, when, due to a lack of patronage, the Delaware & Hudson Railway shut down the passenger business the next day. The automobile had become king.

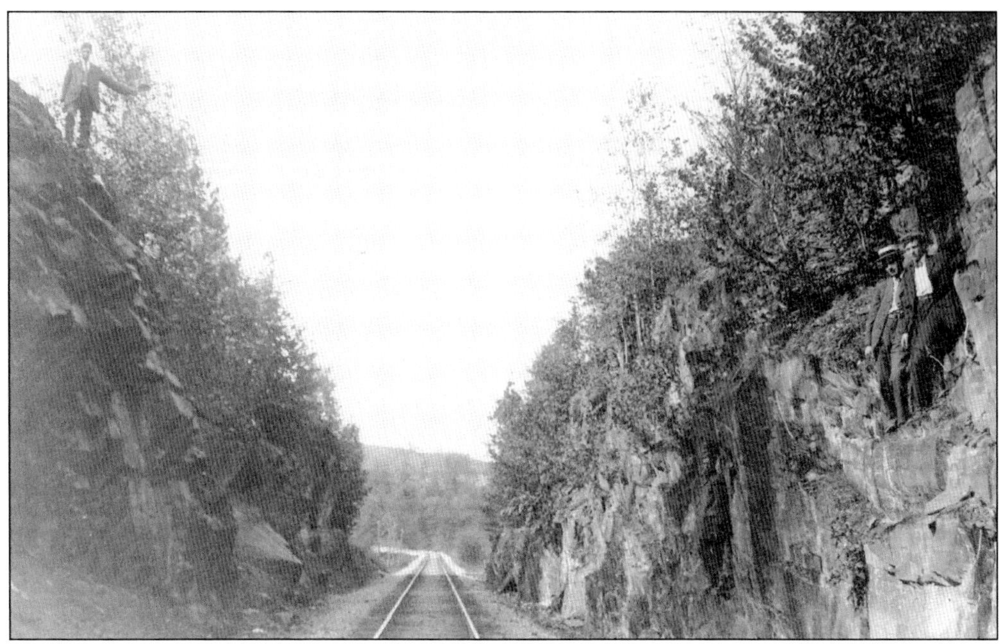

A short distance north of the Shushan depot is a railroad cut through a stone ridge. A traditional story is that when the railroad men blasted the cut in 1850, the people of Shushan were told to stay inside on that day to avoid flying rocks. The cut was a popular spot for locals, as shown by the men on the right.

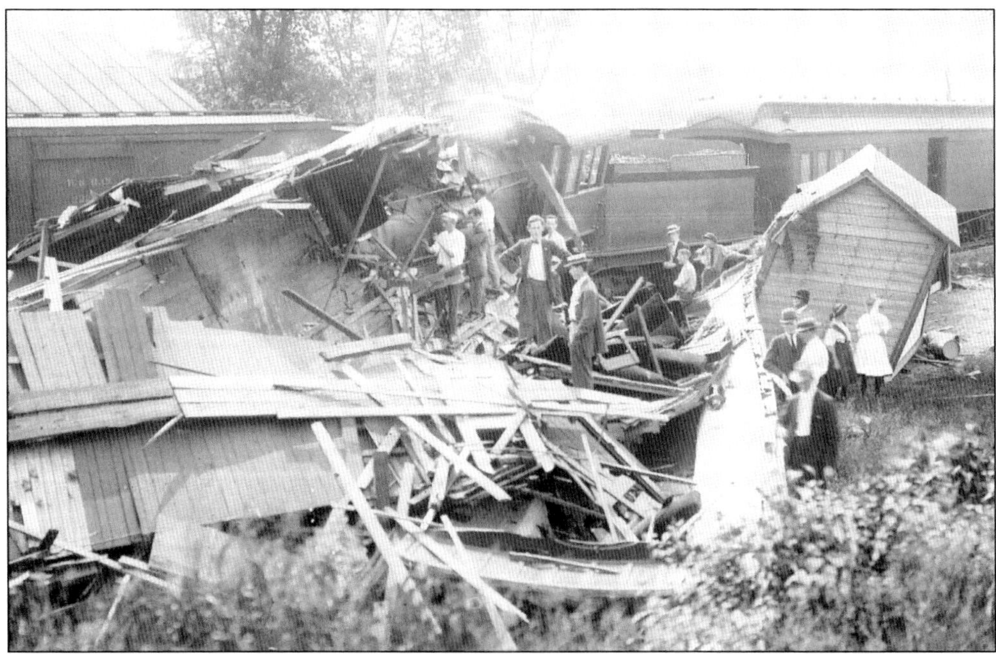

Wrecks were common on the rails. On June 12, 1909, one such wreck took place at Rexleigh (formerly called Baxterville). Here, a freight train loaded with marbleized slate ran into the rear of the milk train. Made of wood, the boxcars easily shattered, leaving only the trucks (wheels) intact.

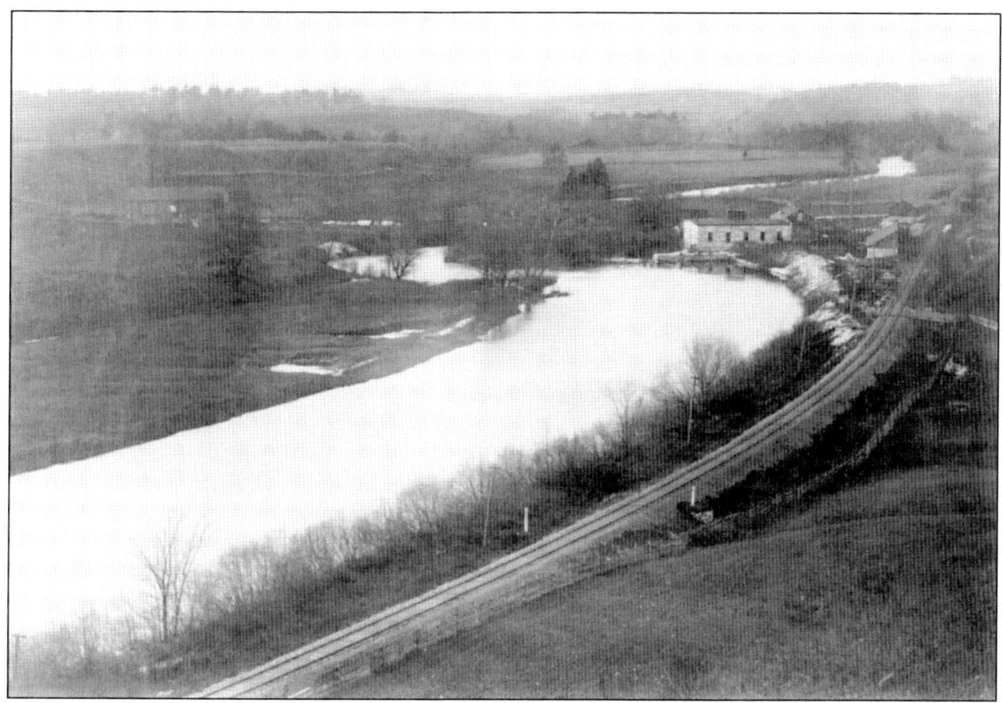

Pictured running side by side are the Battenkill and the Delaware & Hudson tracks at the Baxterville Mill. The dam and flume are to the left of the marble mill. From Shushan, the tracks and the river ran north alongside each other for five miles before both turning west to the Hudson River.

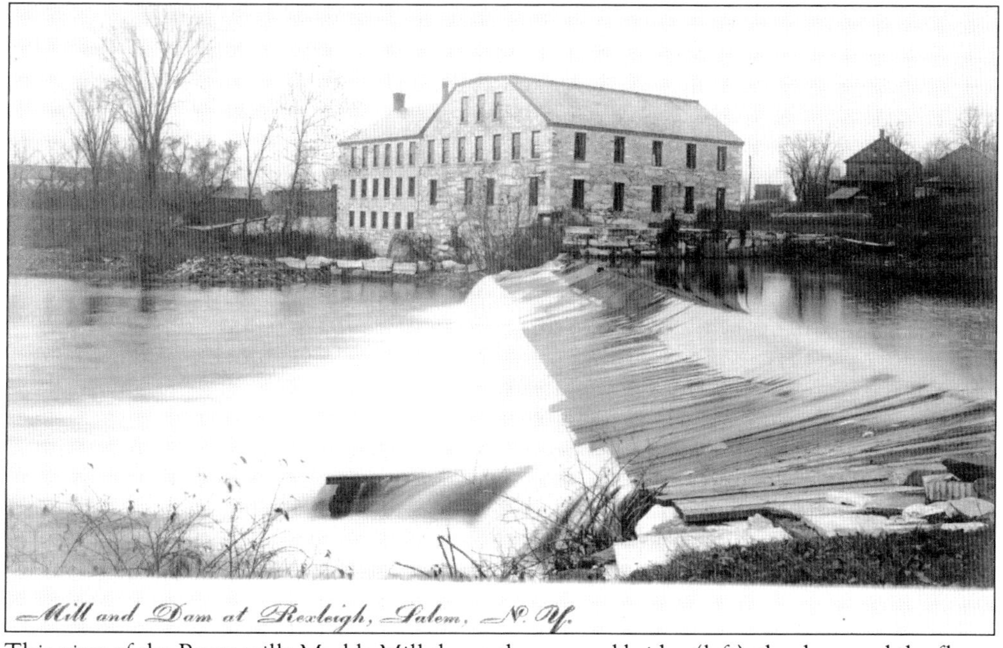

This view of the Baxterville Marble Mill shows the covered bridge (left), the dam, and the flume gates, which controlled water to two power wheels. To the right of the mill are private homes and boardinghouses for upwards of 200 millworkers. The mill was built in 1865 by A.S. Baxter of New York as a sawmill for marble shipped by rail from the Rutland Marble Company.

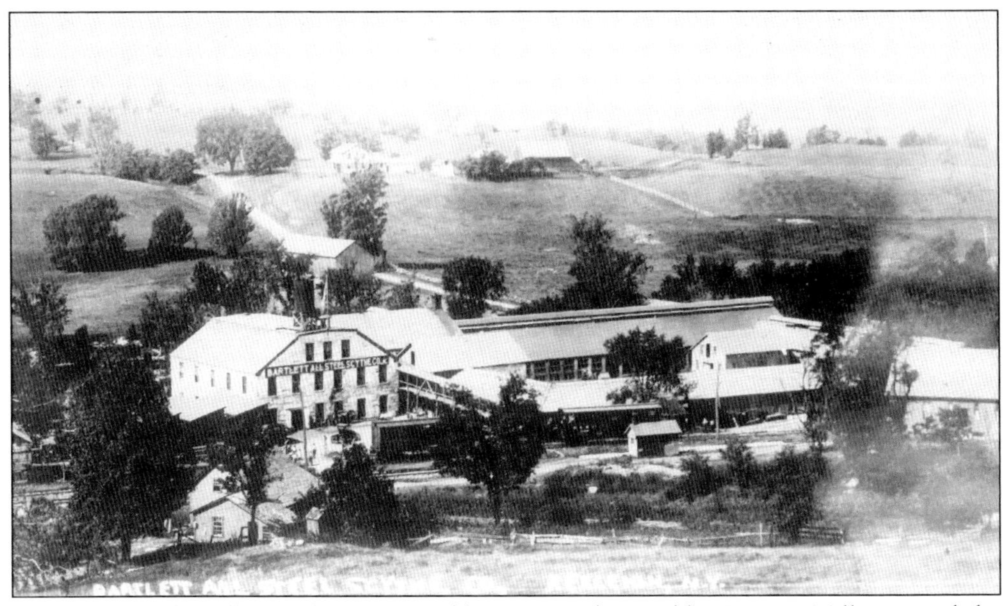

After the marble mill ceased cutting marble in 1896, the Marble Knitting Mill occupied the building until 1910. Then, the Bartlett All Steel Scythe Company moved in, making scythes, grass hooks, and machetes from steel shipped in by rail. Business boomed during World War I, but when the war ended, slow business caused the company to sell out.

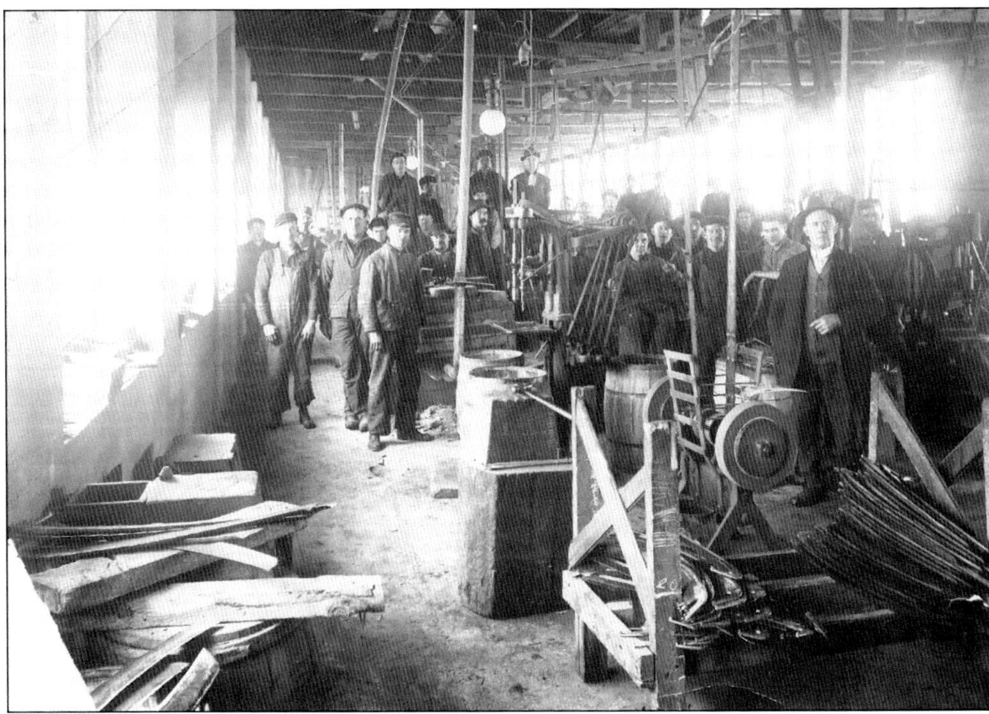

This photograph shows the workforce of the Bartlett All Steel Scythe Company during World War I. By this time, the building was lighted and powered by an electric generator. This group of men is manufacturing scythes. The company had a large war contract with the tsar of Russia for scythes, sickles, and machetes.

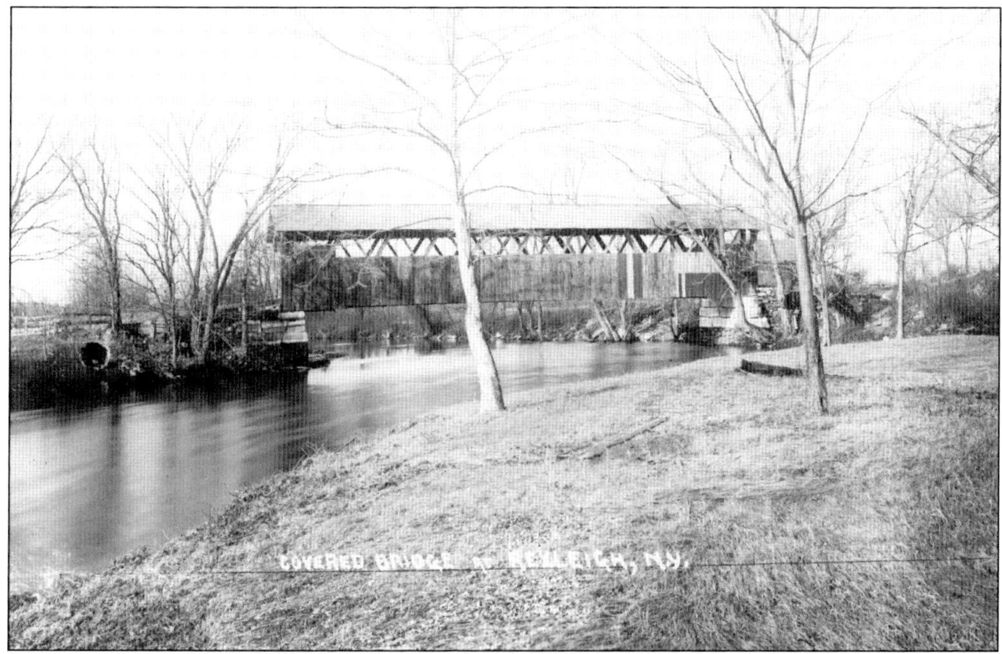

Today in Salem, three covered bridges, one of which is a museum, span the Battenkill. In 1890, the community called Baxterville had a name change when St. Paul's Episcopal Church bought property across the river and named it Rexleigh (King's Meadow), with the idea of building a private school. The school was never built, but the name Rexleigh stuck. The Howe-truss Rexleigh Covered Bridge was built in 1874 and is 107 feet long.

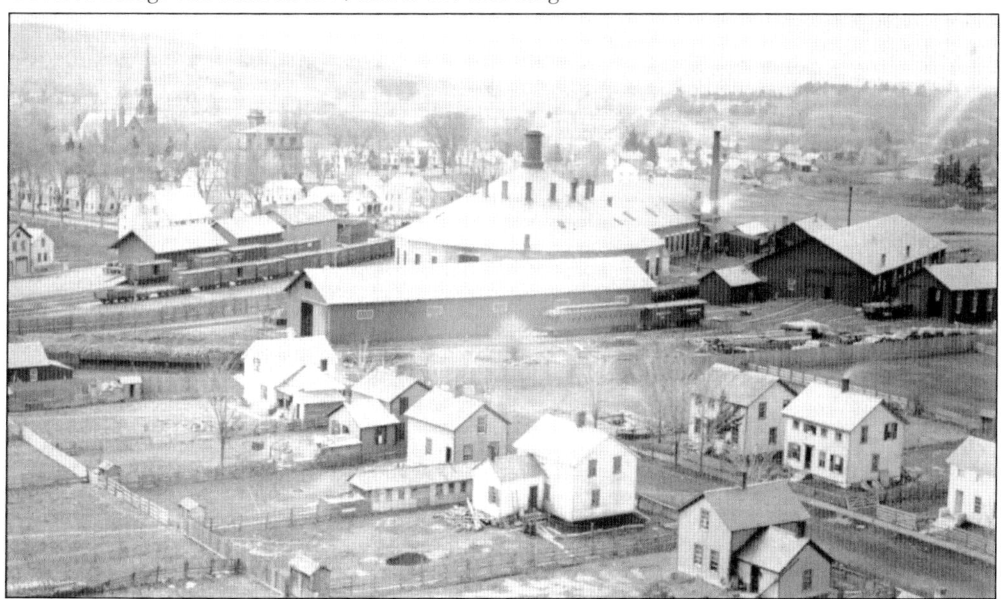

In 1852, the Troy & Rutland Railroad built a large railroad yard in the center of the Salem Village. In 1871, the Delaware & Hudson Canal Company purchased the railroad. Shown in this 1888 photograph are the large engine roundhouse, the repair shop, construction shops, paint shops, and freight buildings. In the foreground is Irish Town, named for its railroad-worker occupants. Some 300 people worked for the railroad.

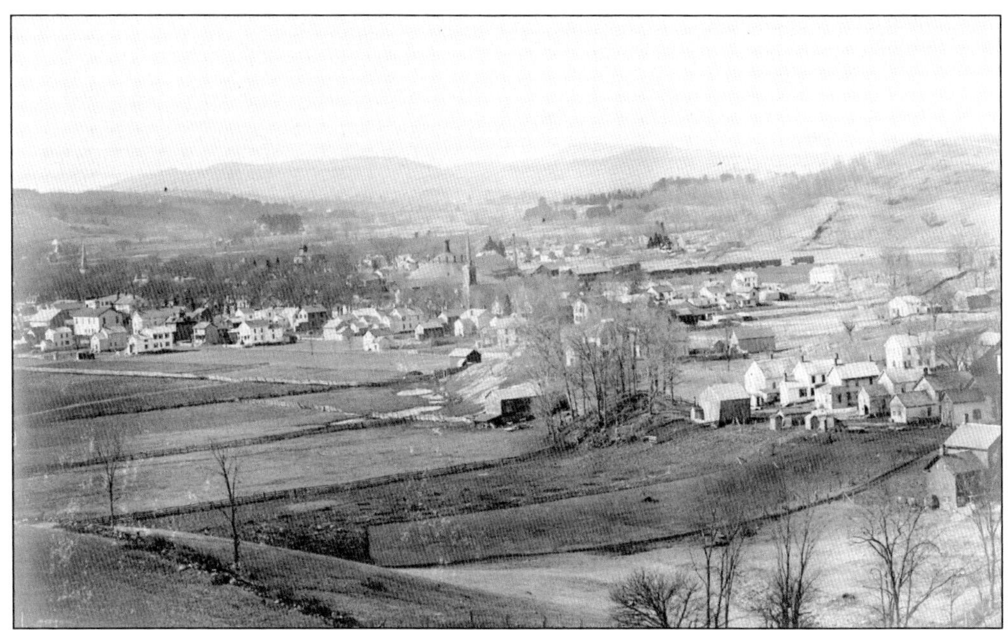

Taken looking southwest from East High Street in Salem Village, this c. 1900 photograph shows the railroad roundhouse and a long line of boxcars. The Holy Cross Church steeple (center), Salem Washington Academy, with its cupola (left), and the steeple of the United Presbyterian Church (far left) can be seen.

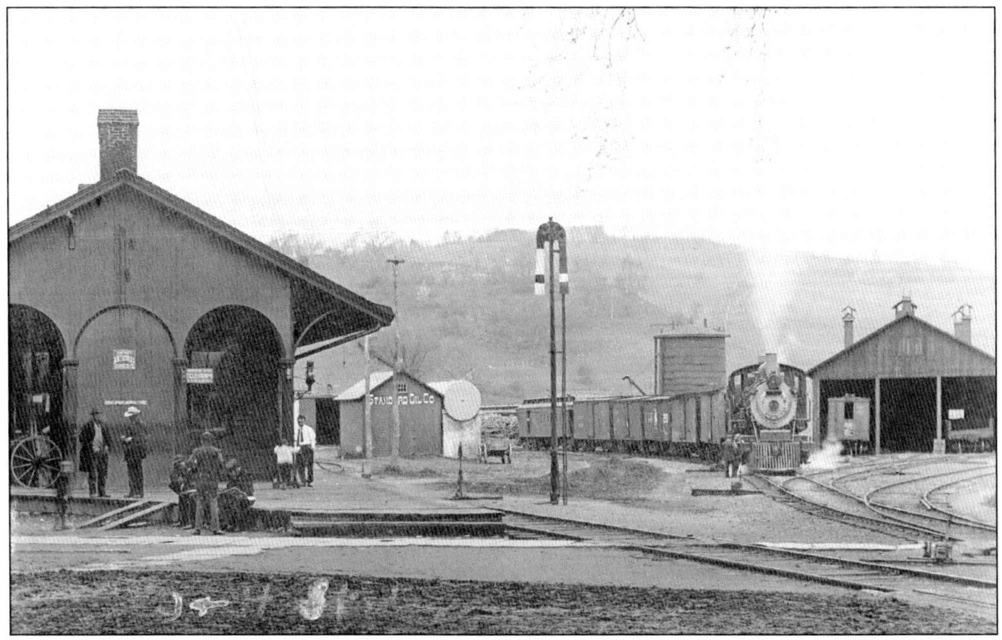

This c. 1905 photograph shows the original Salem depot, with a coal-burning freight train idling in the yard. The Standard Oil Co. storage building and tank, a sign of the new automobile transportation, are to the right of the depot, and the water tower can be seen beyond the train. The roundhouse closed in 1891 and was razed in 1904.

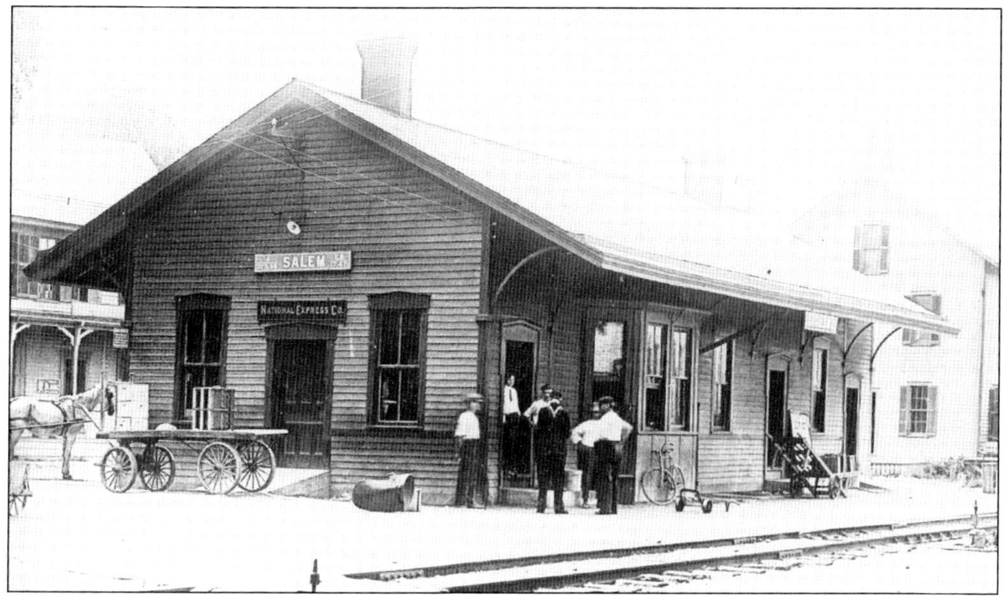

With the advent of passenger service, a new and larger Salem depot was erected in 1909. The following year, electric lights, including the one over the main door of the depot, lit the streets and homes of Salem. The National Express Company name on the sign was the forerunner to the Railway Express Company. A typical hand-pulled express cart awaits its cargo.

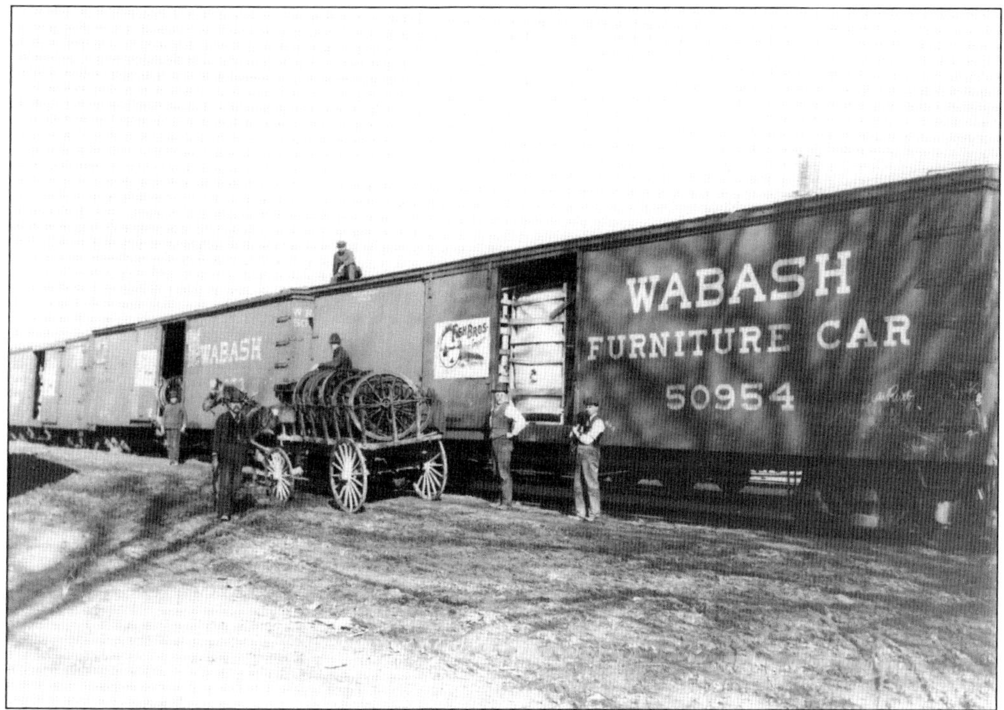

Shipped by rail, Studebaker wagon parts arrived by freight car at the Delaware & Hudson Railway yards. Frank Wright ran the Studebaker Wagon Emporium, selling wagons, buggies, carts, and sleighs that he fabricated in his building on West Broadway. He is standing next to the horse in this 1880s photograph.

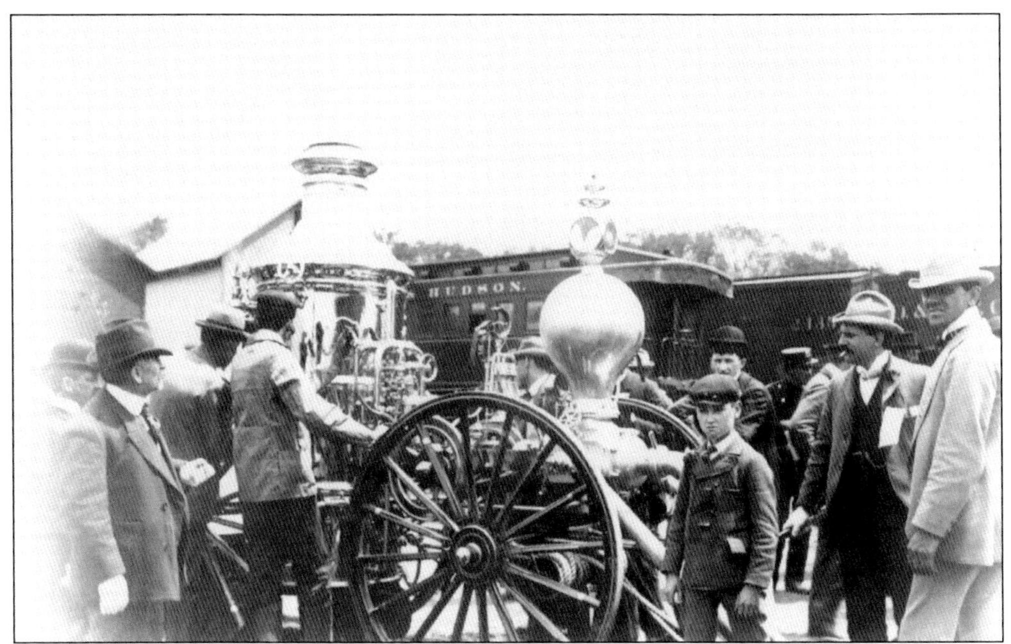

One of the exciting moments in the village was when the firefighting Osoma Steamer arrived by rail freight in 1875. Because a fire had to be kept burning in the steamer firebox at all times, the steamer was kept at the railroad roundhouse, where railroad workers were on duty around the clock. Today, the steamer is on display in the New York State Museum in Albany.

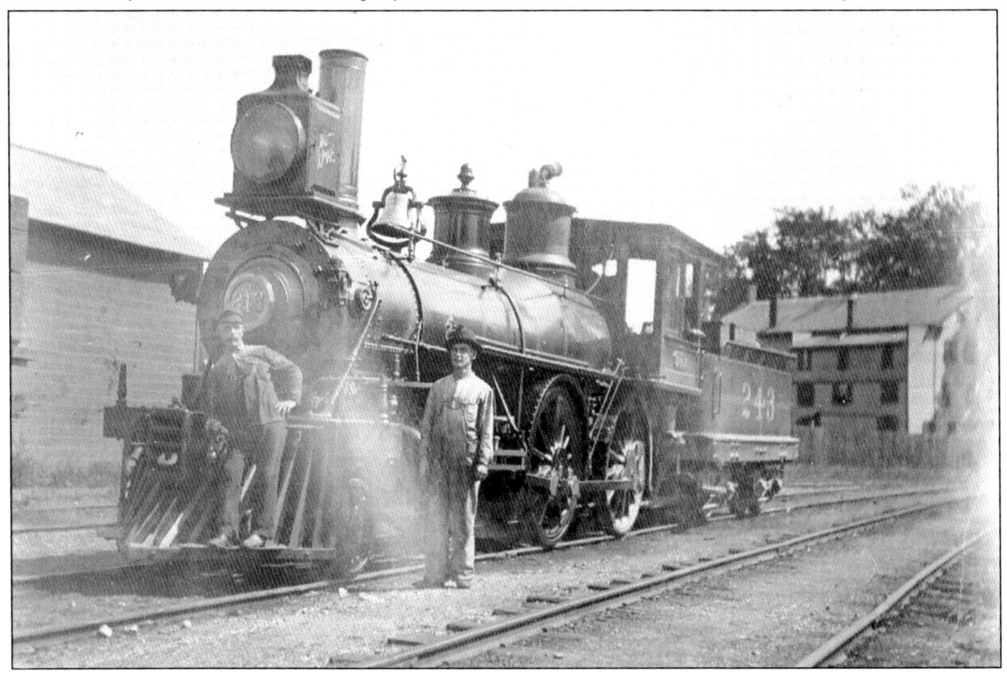

One of Salem's Delaware & Hudson Railway career engineers, Albert Broughton, is standing on the cowcatcher of Engine No. 243 in the Salem yards in 1920. The man next to him was most likely his fireman, who stoked the engine's coal-burning furnace. Broughton came from a family of railroaders, following in the footsteps of his father, Ira.

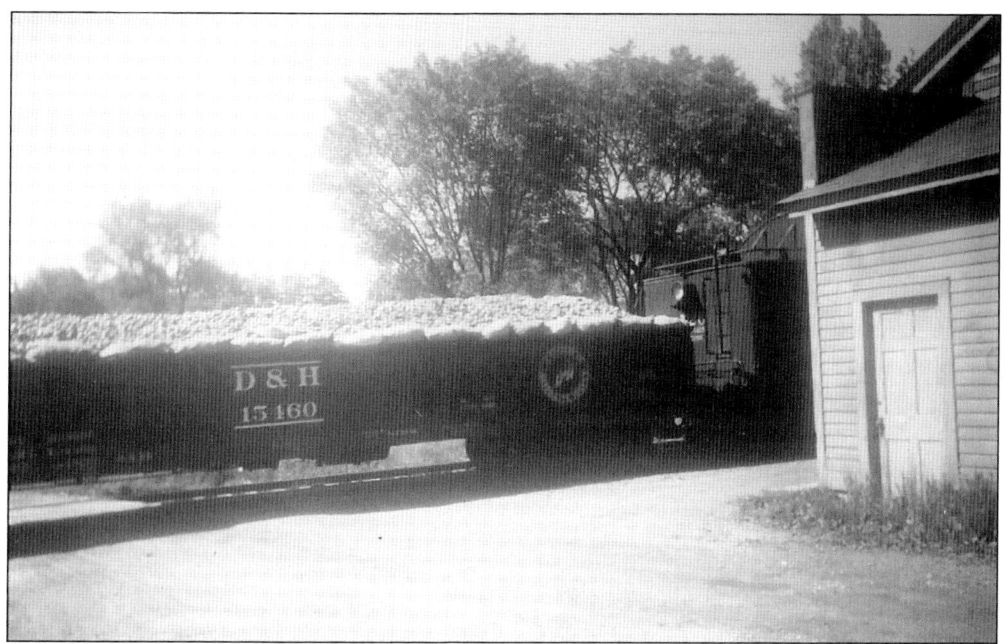

Potato farming was popular in the Salem area, and the best way to get the potatoes to market was by railroad gondola cars. Potatoes were once the leading agricultural crop in the county, and the Irish farmers of Salem and Hebron grew large fields of them. These potatoes, leaving the Salem depot in 1942, are headed east to Rutland, Vermont.

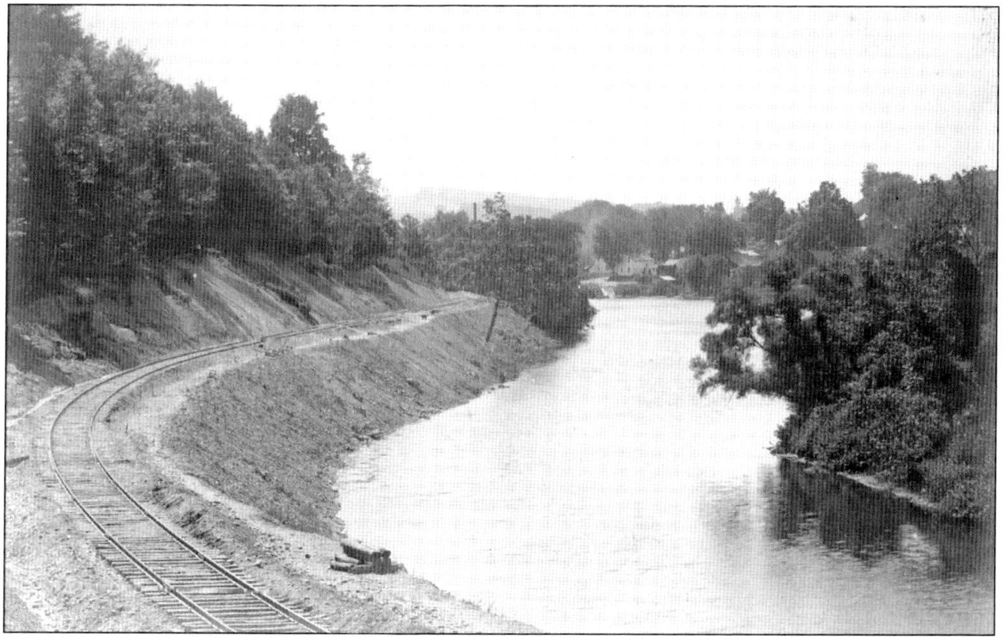

The Battenkill, in its westerly flow to the Hudson River, saw the Greenwich & Johnsonville Railroad build a Salem branch along its southern banks in 1906. By 1907, the Delaware & Hudson had assumed ownership of the Greenwich-to-Salem line, but it still operated under the Greenwich & Johnsonville Railroad name. Around 200 Italian immigrants, with picks, shovels, carts, and wheelbarrows, built this line.

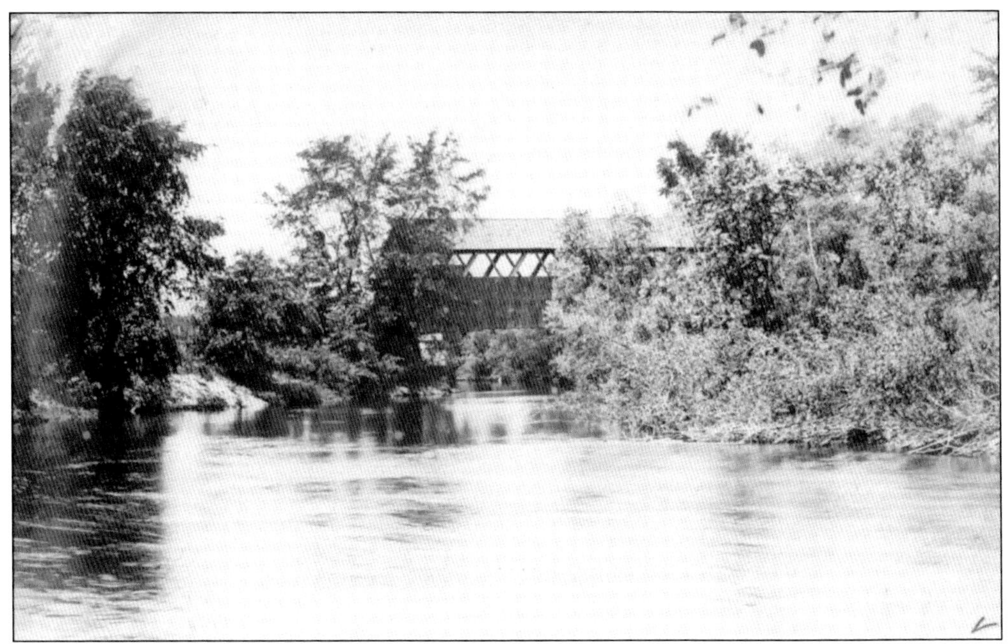

Before the railroad came to Salem, a covered bridge spanned Black Creek at Fitch's Point, enabling farmers to wagon their goods to markets as far as Schuylerville, where canal transportation was available south to Albany and north to Whitehall. In 1906, an iron railroad bridge was built across the Battenkill at Fitch's Point, and, in 1915, an iron highway bridge replaced the covered bridge across Black Creek.

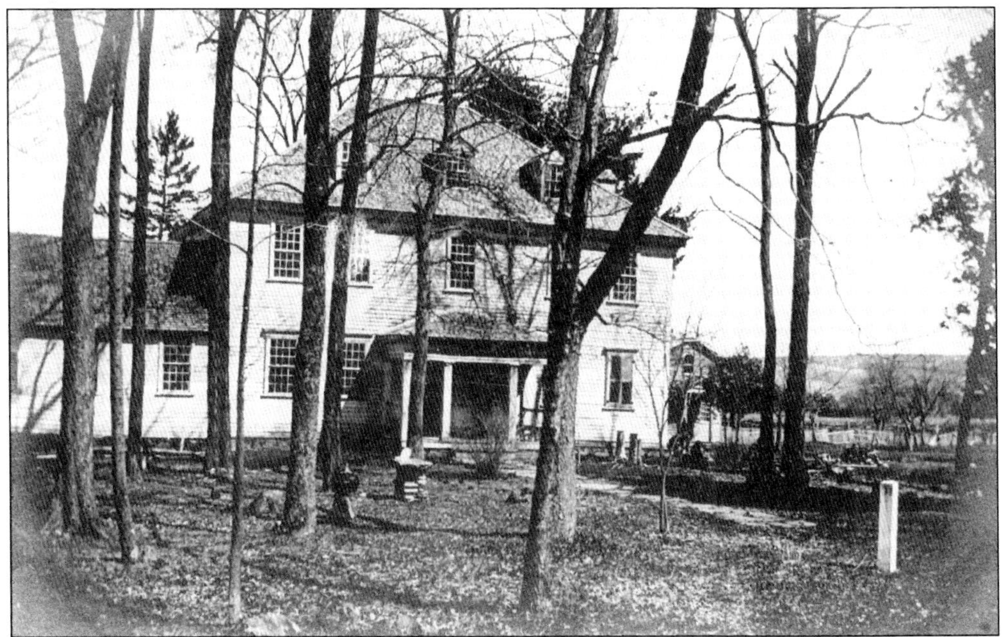

At Fitch's Point, on State Route 29, is the house and laboratory of Dr. Asa Fitch Jr., who became New York State's first appointed entomologist in 1854. The "bug house," as it was known locally, is seen to the right of the main house. Fitch's Point was named for the Fitch family. Hon. Asa Fitch Sr. was a Revolutionary War soldier and a prominent figure in politics.

Dr. Asa Fitch Jr. was a prominent citizen in Salem and New York State. He left his medical practice to become a pioneer in scientific farming, studying noxious insects. As state entomologist, Dr. Fitch was known as the "Bug-Catcher of Salem." Among his scholarly writings is the book *The Noxious and Beneficial Insects of New York State*.

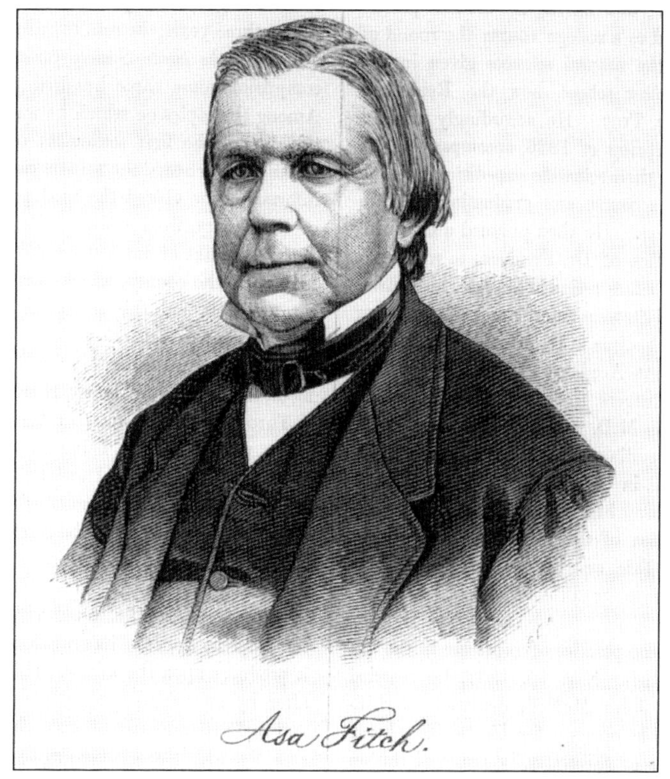

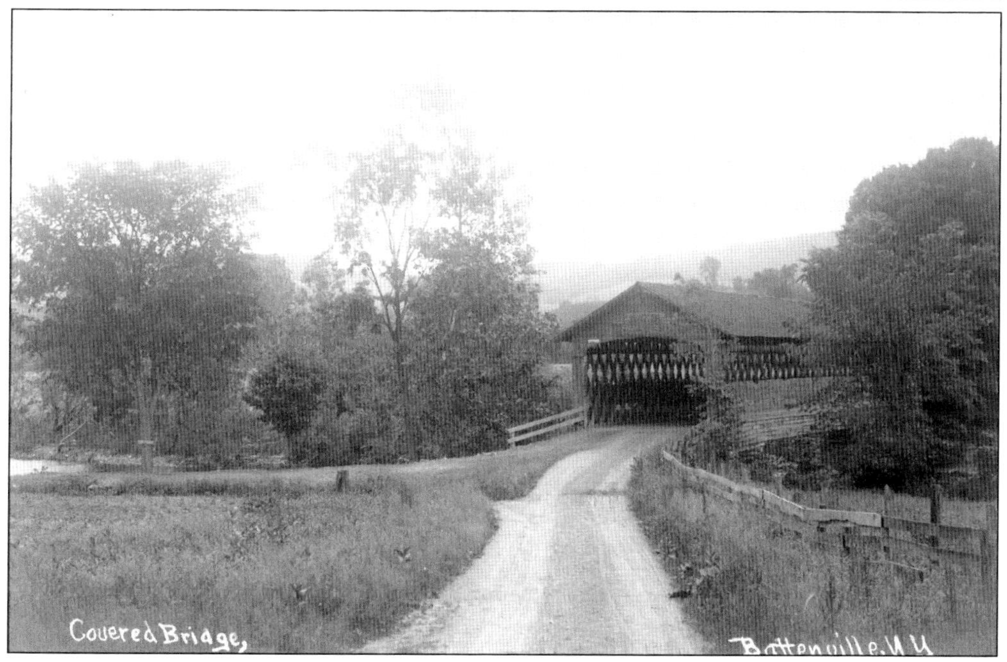

At one time, 10 covered bridges spanned the Battenkill between the Vermont border and the Hudson River. The last four of them were at Fitch's Point, Battenville, Greenwich, and Middle Falls. The Battenville Bridge, shown here, was built of Town's lattice construction in 1840. The bridge was replaced with an iron truss bridge built by the Union Bridge Company in 1916.

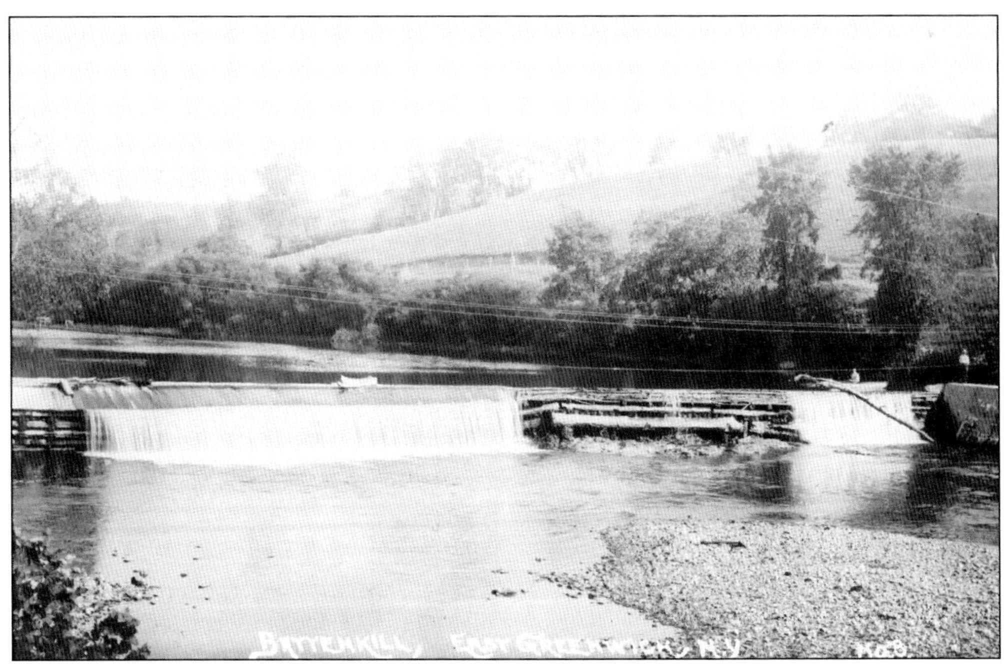

The Battenkill was always a great source of waterpower, which was used by mills at Shushan, Eagleville, Rexleigh, Battenville, East Greenwich, Greenwich Village, and Middle Falls. The dam at East Greenwich, over the years, supplied power to a sawmill, a gristmill, and, eventually, an electric company. It was a popular fishing spot for the two fishermen on the right, as it is to today's fishermen.

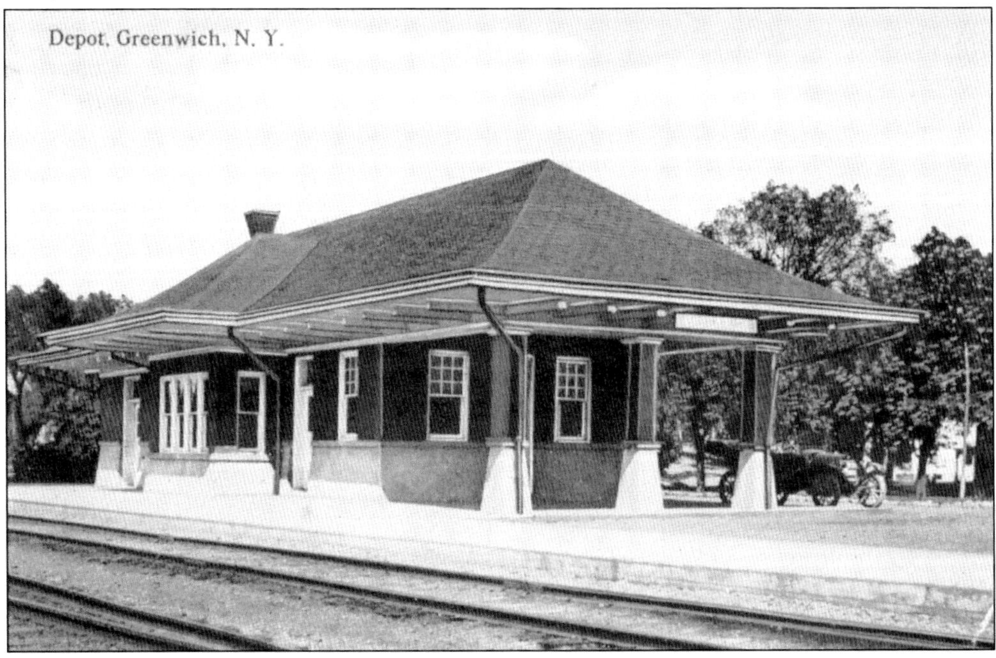

Serving the passengers on the Greenwich & Johnsonville line was the Greenwich depot, built in 1912 at the foot of John Street. From here, passengers could board trains for Johnsonville, Greenwich Junction, Salem, Troy, and Rutland, Vermont.

Five

Salem Merchants, Industry, and Agriculture

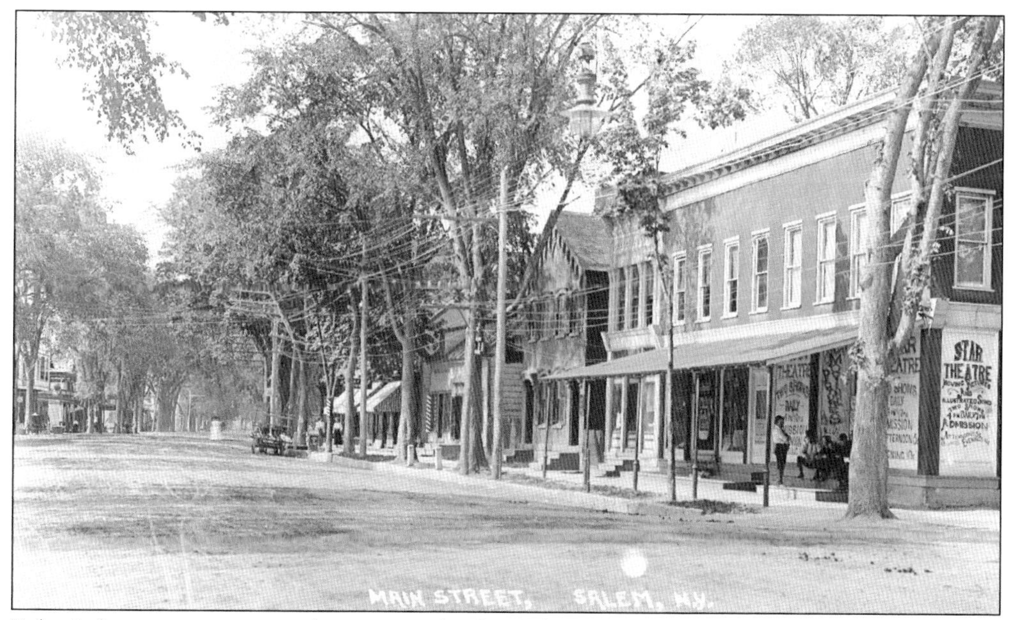

Salem's first motion picture theater was the Star Theatre. It was located in what was known as the Tomasi Building in later years. Here, local folks in 1913 could go to watch Salem's silent film star Jane Gail in her first major film, *Traffic in Souls.*

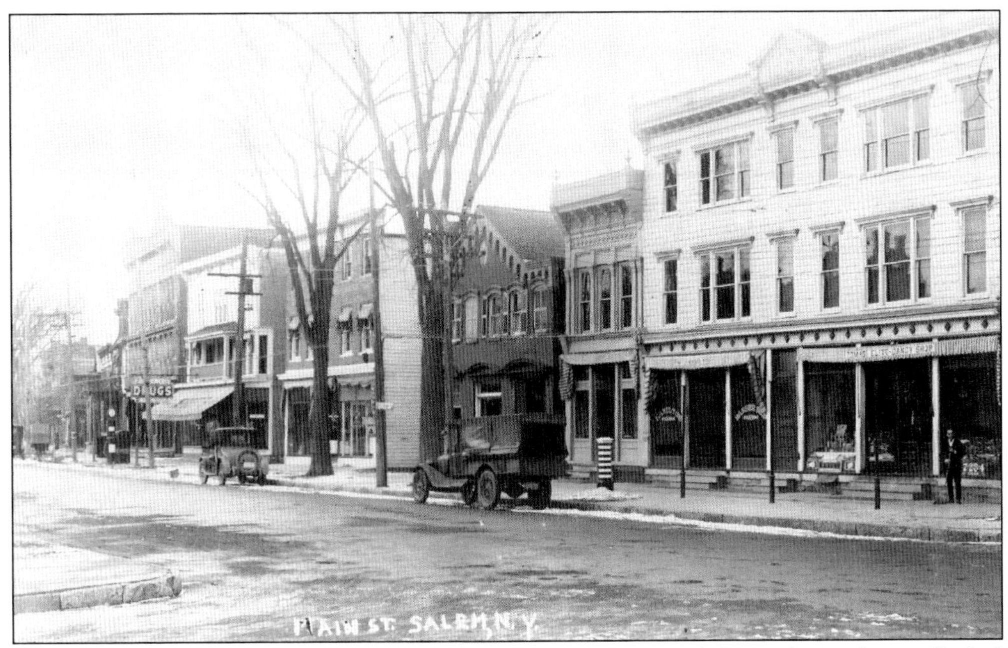

By 1921, the Star Theatre had moved to another location on North Main Street. James "Jacko" Tomasi rented that end of the Odd Fellows Building in 1921 and opened the Tomasi Elite Candy Shop (right). He is standing with a broom in front of his shop. He purchased the building in 1943.

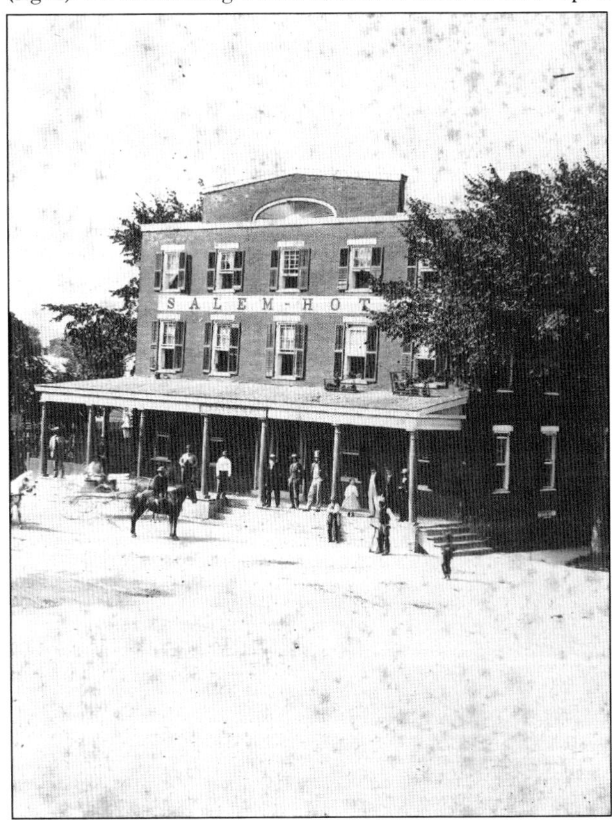

The Salem Hotel, on the corner of West Broadway and South Main Street, was a popular place in 1869. The hotel was the regular stagecoach stop from Fairhaven, Vermont, to Albany. In 1877, the hotel burned down. The Fairchild House, built on the vacant site, would suffer the same fate.

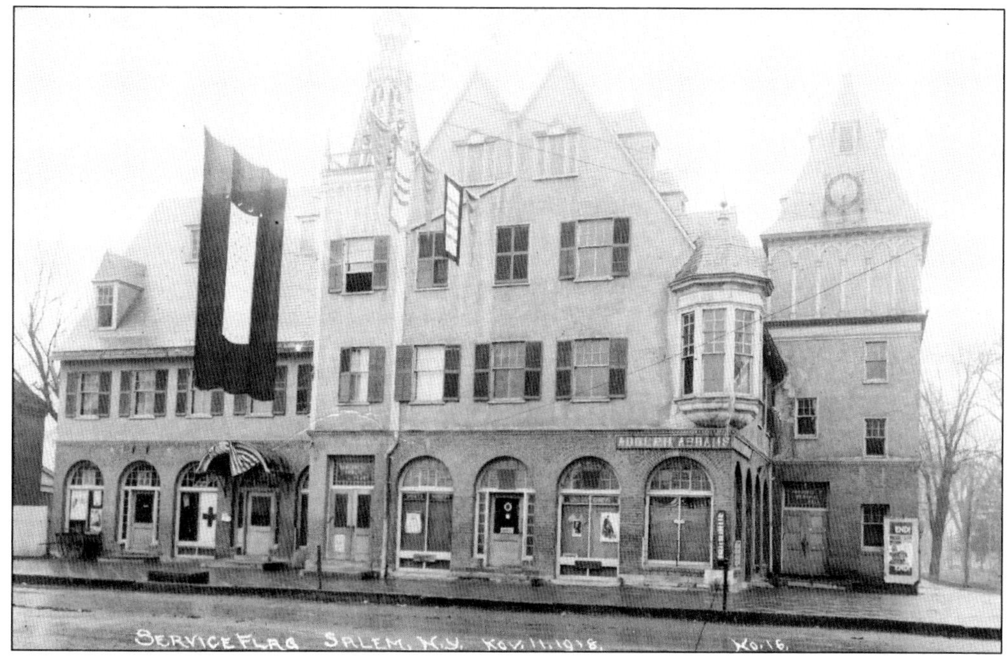

After the Fairchild House burned in 1889, the Proudfit Building was built in 1890. When this photograph was taken, on Armistice Day, November 11, 1918, the building contained commercial shops and a room for the volunteer fire department on the first floor. The Bancroft Public Library, Proudfit Memorial Hall, and the village offices were on the second floor. The Irving Memorial Family Clock Tower is on the right.

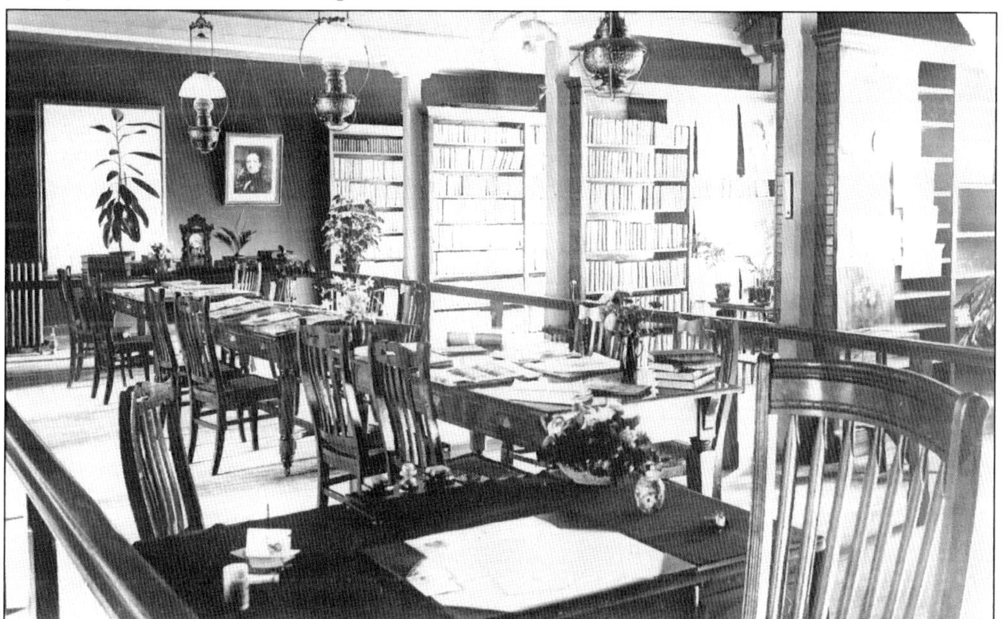

The Bancroft Public Library, on the second floor of the Proudfit Building, was made possible by a bequest of banker Benjamin Bancroft. In addition, Alexander Williams Proudfit gave money in his father's name for a memorial hall. Seen hanging on the back wall is a portrait of former Salem merchant Alexander Moncrief Proudfit, for whom Proudfit Memorial Hall was named.

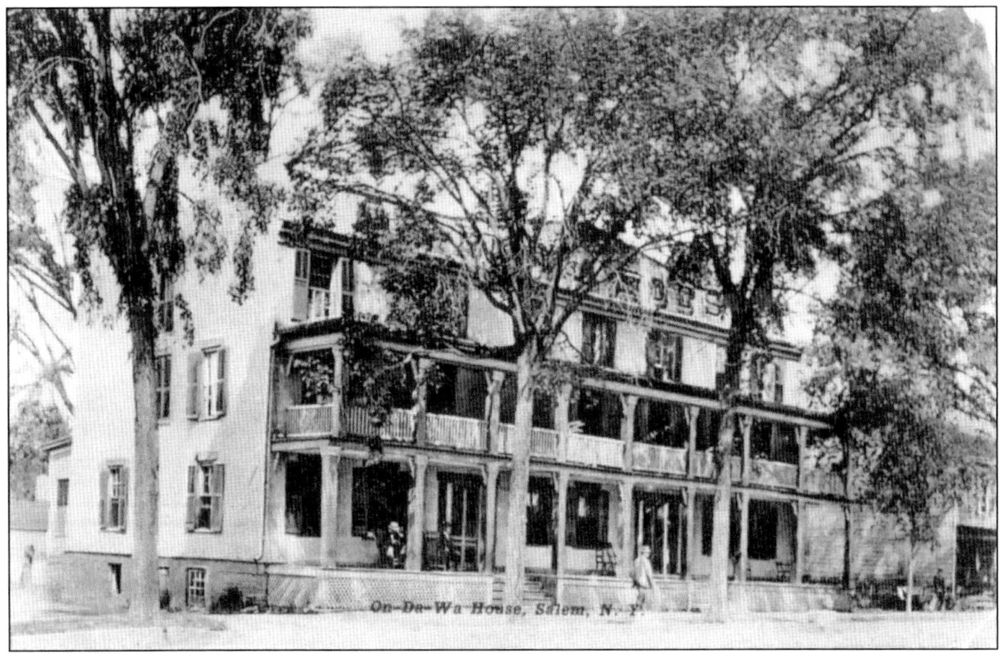

Travelers needed places to stay, and two Main Street hotels were located a short walking distance from the Salem depot. Towering elm trees fronted the Ondawa Hotel in 1913; the trees created a cool spot on the two-story porch for guests to watch Main Street activities. The hotel featured a large dining room open to the public.

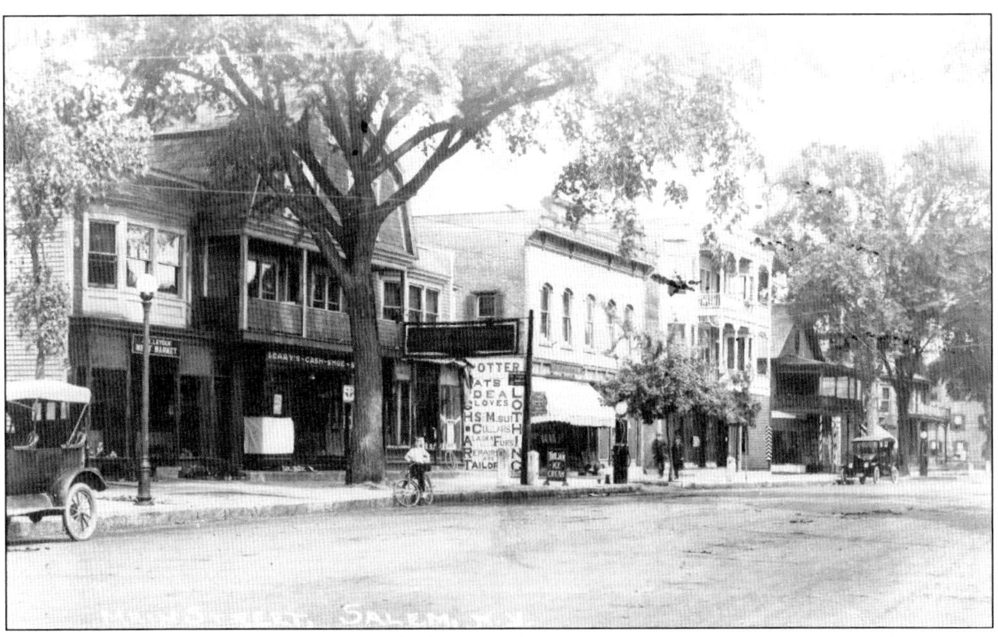

The gambrel-roofed Layden Building (left) housed the James Layden Meat Market, John Leary's Cash Shoe Store, and the Carrolan & Darmody Drug Store in 1920. The Layden family lived on the second floor. This building was destroyed by fire in 1970. J.H. Potter advertised his goods on the side of the next building.

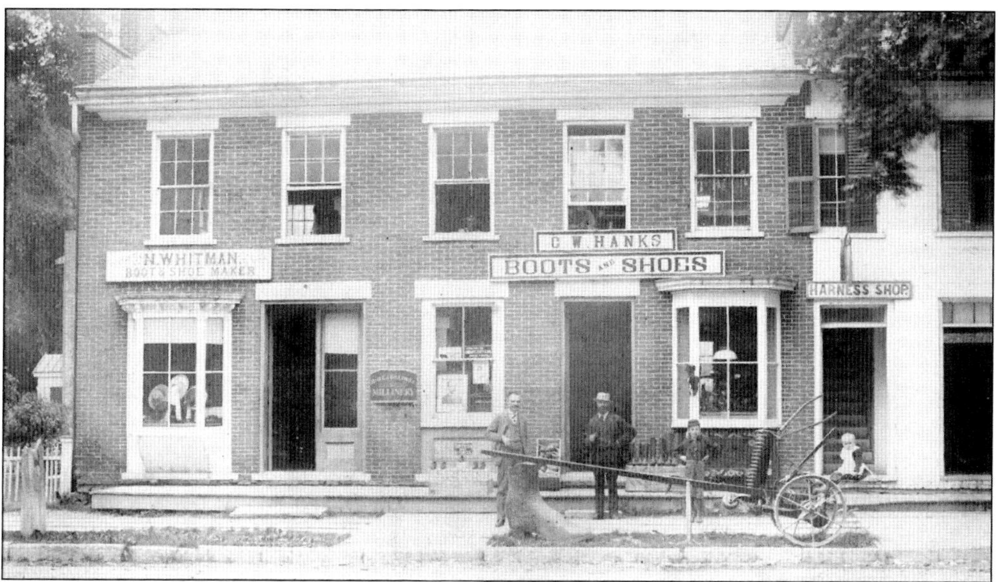

The redbrick Gibson Block stood on the corner of West Broadway and North Main Street. The building was most likely built after the great fire in the center of the village in 1840. In this 1886 photograph, N. Whitman and C.W. Hanks pose in front of their stores. Baby Clifford Hanks is sitting in the hay mower.

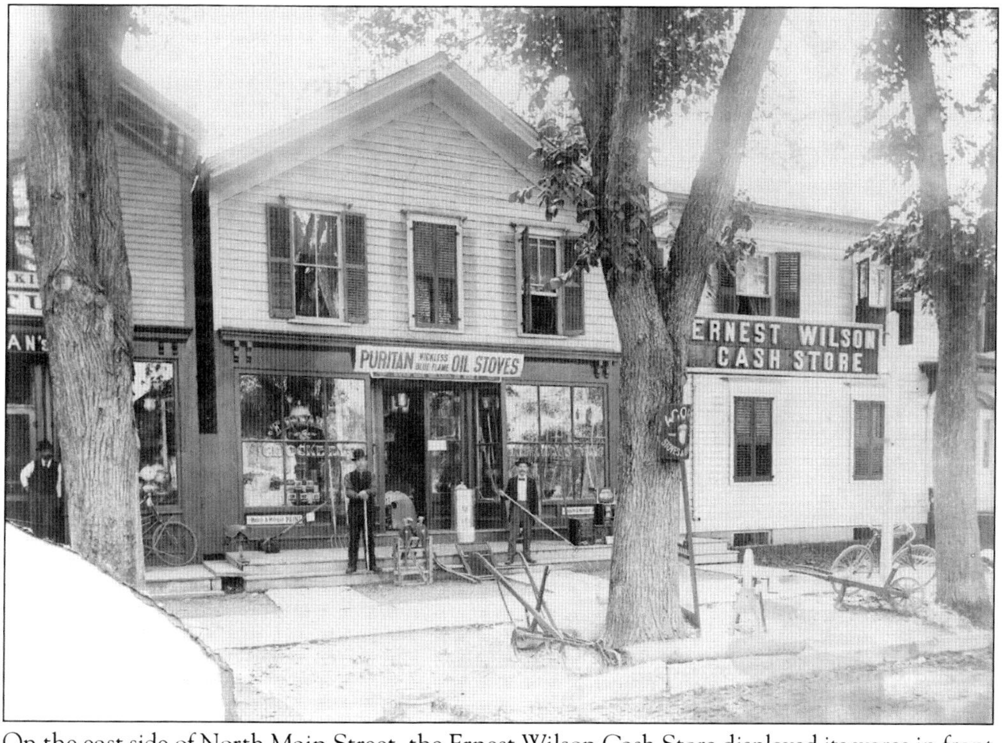

On the east side of North Main Street, the Ernest Wilson Cash Store displayed its wares in front of the building, including lawn mowers, pitch forks, a washboard, a cultivator, a sharpening wheel, stoves, a screen door, and a wheelbarrow. The display of a store's goods on the sidewalk was a common practice and was great for advertising.

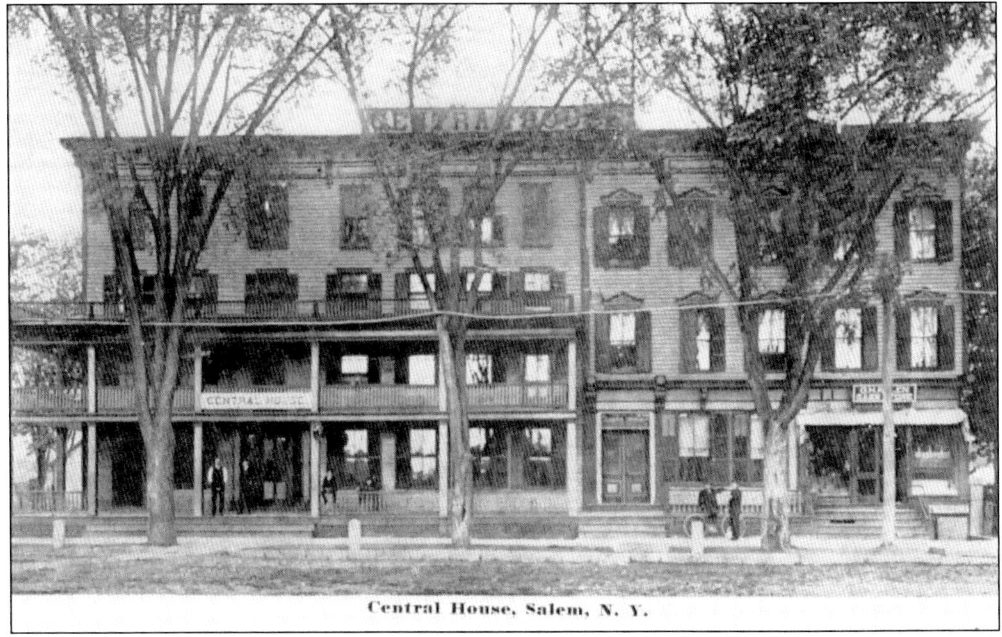

Directly across the street from the Delaware & Hudson depot was the expansive Central House. Like the Ondawa Hotel, it had an airy two-story front porch, giving customers a good view of the railroad cars and passengers as they arrived and departed in 1884. A fire in 1906 destroyed the left side of the hotel, next to the tracks. A spark from a passing train was suspected as the culprit.

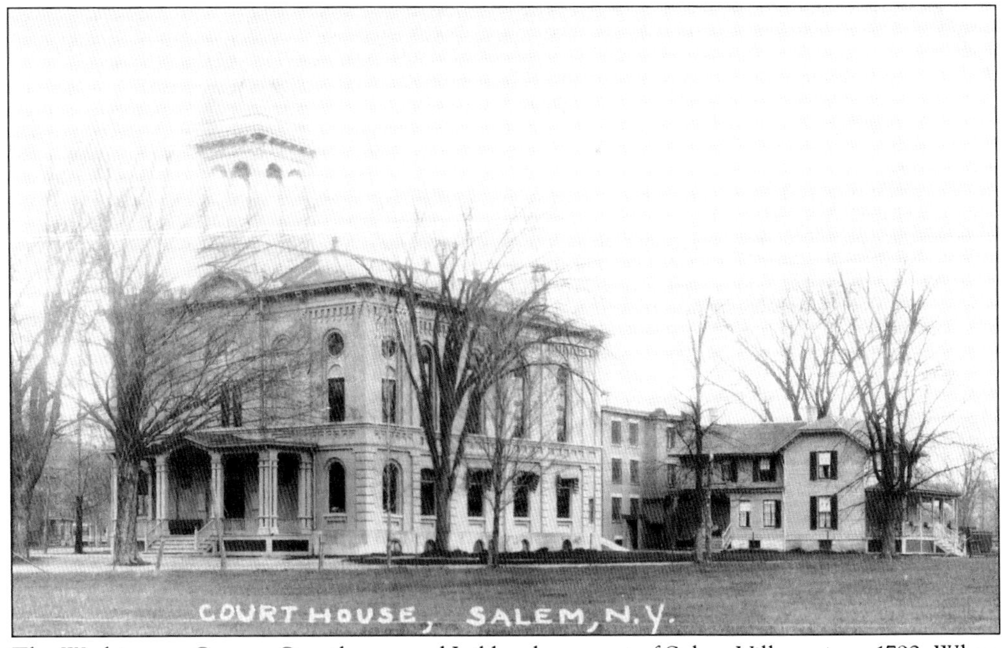

The Washington County Courthouse and Jail has been part of Salem Village since 1792. When the wooden courthouse on North Main Street fell into disrepair, this new courthouse was built on East Broadway in 1869. The original wooden jail behind the new structure was replaced with a brick jail in 1906. The building on the right housed the jail warden and his family.

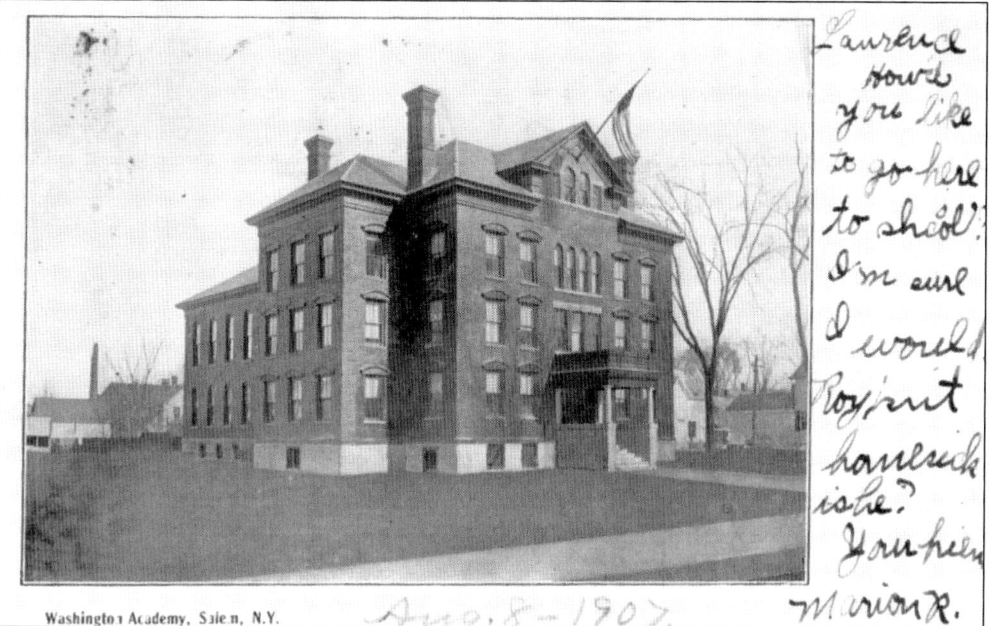

Salem Washington Academy was chartered in 1780 in a wooden schoolhouse on East Broadway. A series of fires convinced the academy trustees to build a large brick school on West Broadway. This photograph shows the academy in 1905. The building served the youth of Salem until 1938, when a new, modern school on East Broadway was constructed during the Great Depression, with the aid of Works Progress Administration (WPA) funds.

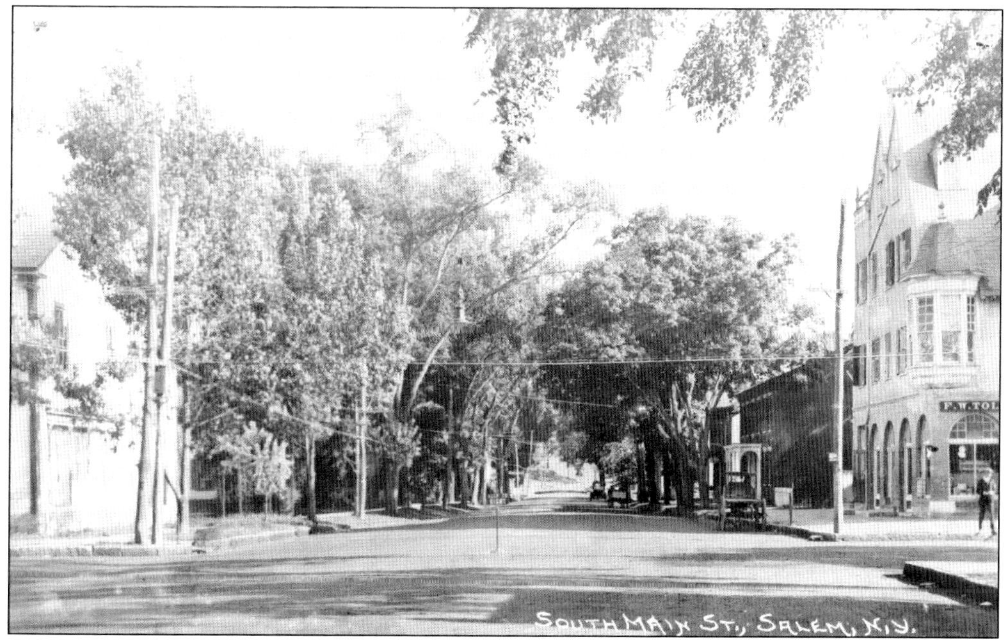

Taken around 1919, this photograph of South Main Street shows the Proudfit Building, in the right corner, and the stately elm trees. Signs of progress are seen in the multitude of electric wires serving private homes and commercial buildings. A light hanging over the intersection illuminates the "Keep to Right" post for automobile traffic.

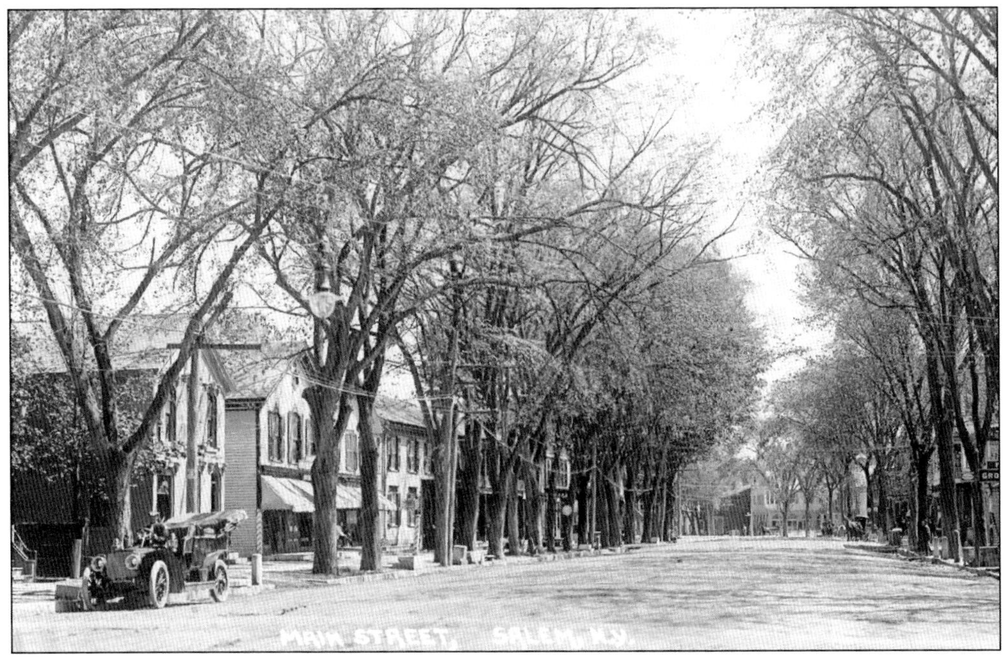

This photograph looking south from North Main Street shows the extent of the dominating elm trees, hanging over the old Northern Turnpike, now State Route 22. Another electric streetlight hangs in front of the Central House railroad crossing. The open touring car on the left is a harbinger of new transportation. Nevertheless, horse-and-buggy transportation continued to use the hitching posts and stepping-stones found along the street.

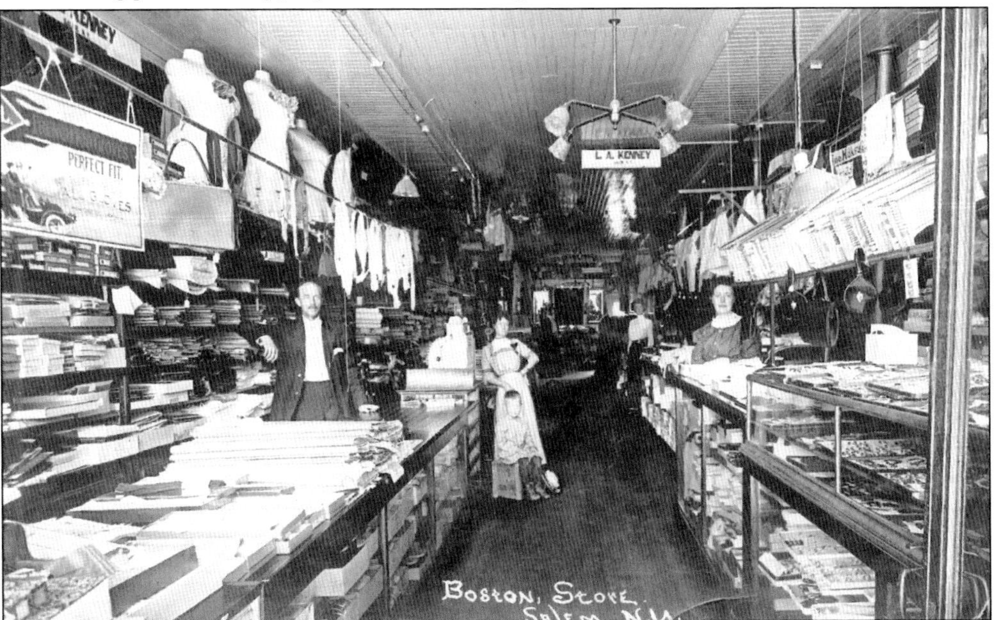

Laurence A. Kenney (left) opened the Boston Store in 1900 on the first floor in the Edgar Philo Building on North Main Street. This 1911 photograph shows Kenney, members of his family, and store clerks. Under different ownership over the years, the Boston Store operated in this site until 1947. The Boston Store advertised, "Eggs and butter as good as cash here."

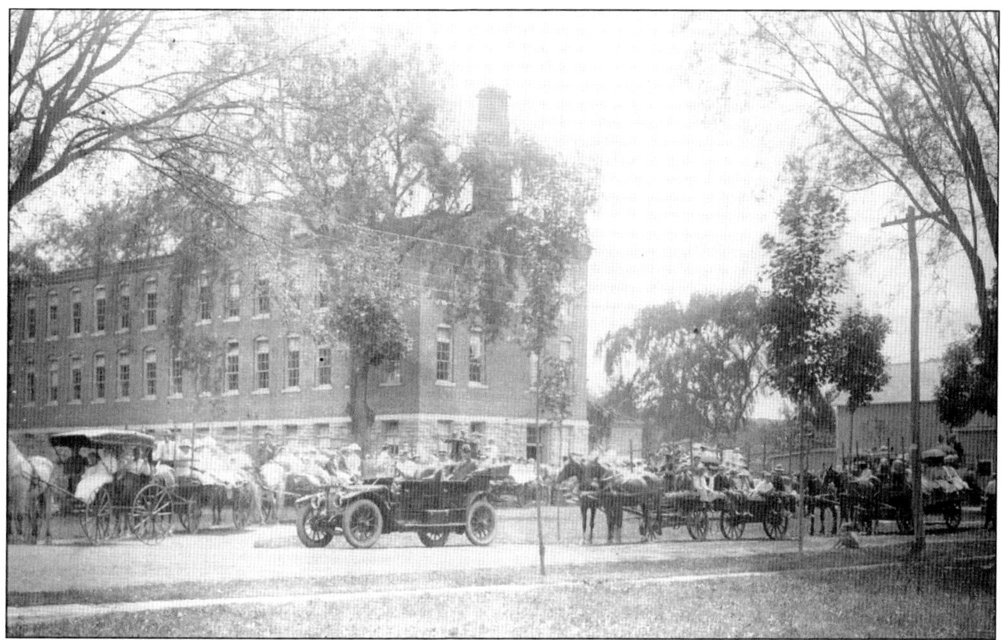

Management treated the employees of the Manhattan Shirt Shop well, with picnics and holiday parties. This 1920 photograph shows the employees going on a summer outing. Manager Henry Spallholz, wearing a fedora, is in the back seat of his open touring car.

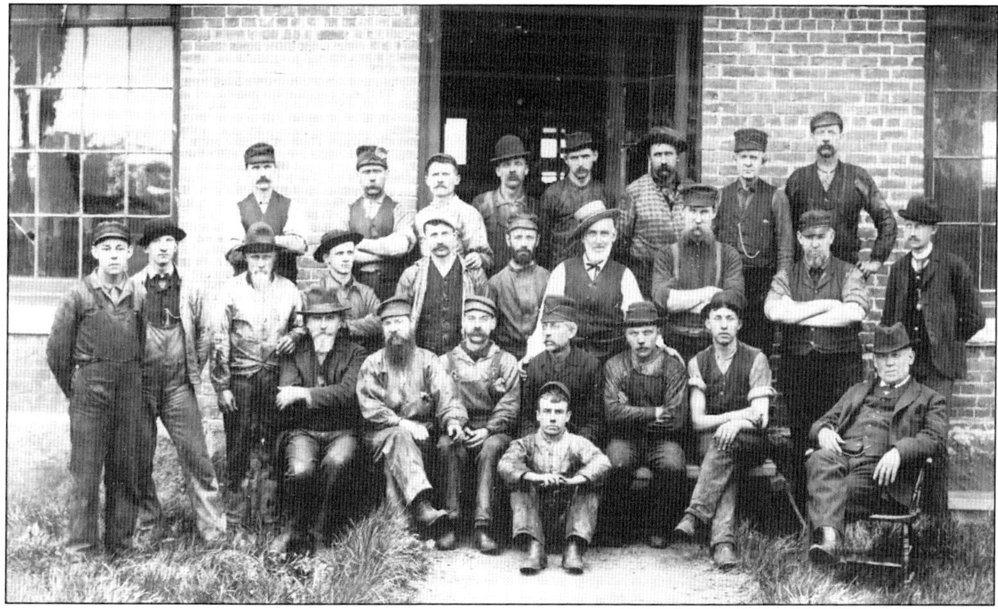

The workmen of the Delaware & Hudson Railway roundhouse and back shop in Salem posed for this photograph on May 9, 1891, the day the back shop closed in Salem. Fred Kegler, master mechanic, is seated at the right. For economic reasons, most of these men were sent to work in the Whitehall Delaware & Hudson shops. Kegler stayed in Salem.

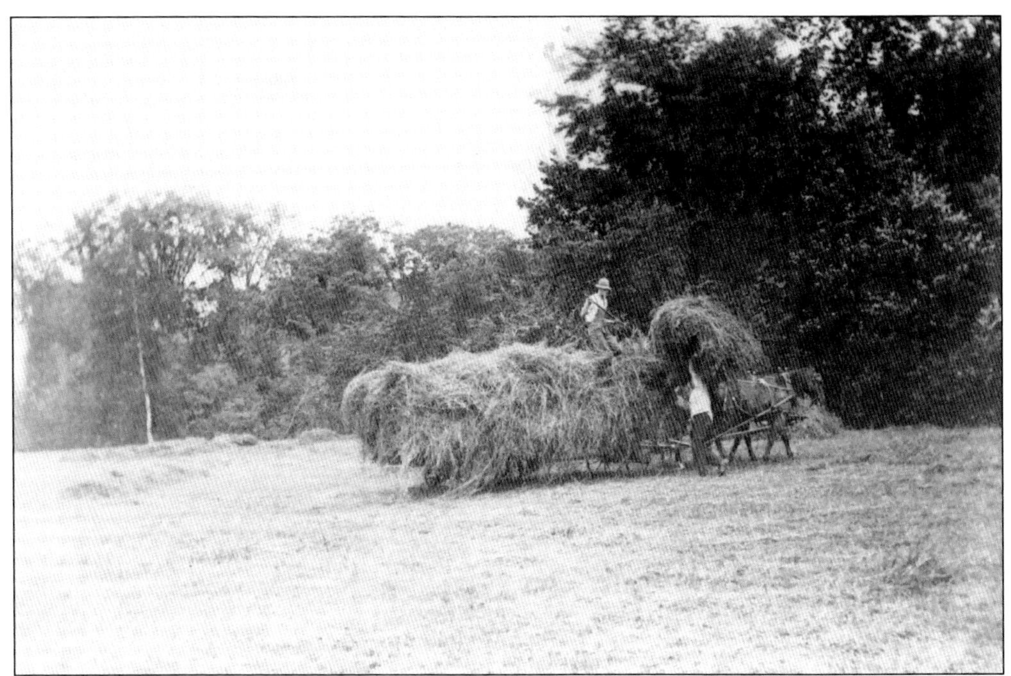

The rich soil in the Battenkill, Slate, and White Creek Valleys invited farmers. Among the popular crops raised were flax, hay, rye, wheat, potatoes, and other vegetables. Common farm animals were sheep, dairy cows, and poultry. Early farming was labor-intensive, and families relied on all family members, as well as hired hands, to harvest their crops. These men are shown harvesting the hay crop in 1880.

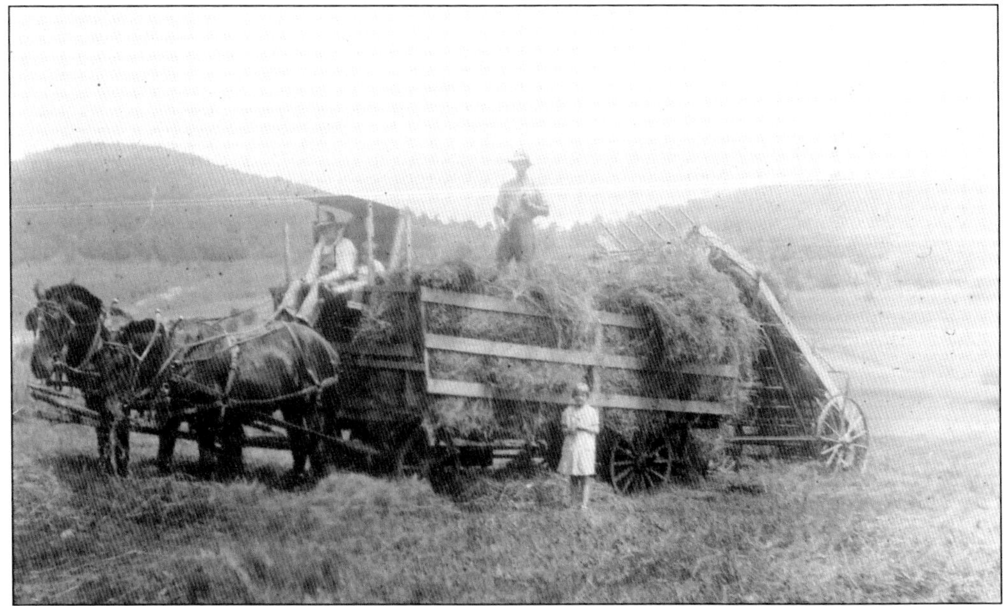

The industrial revolution brought with it farm machines that made life on the farm somewhat easier. Here, in 1929, a mechanized cylinder rake hay loader assists a Camden Valley family. Other mechanical equipment could be rented, if not owned outright. Sometimes, farmers would join forces to rent a piece of equipment to be used among them.

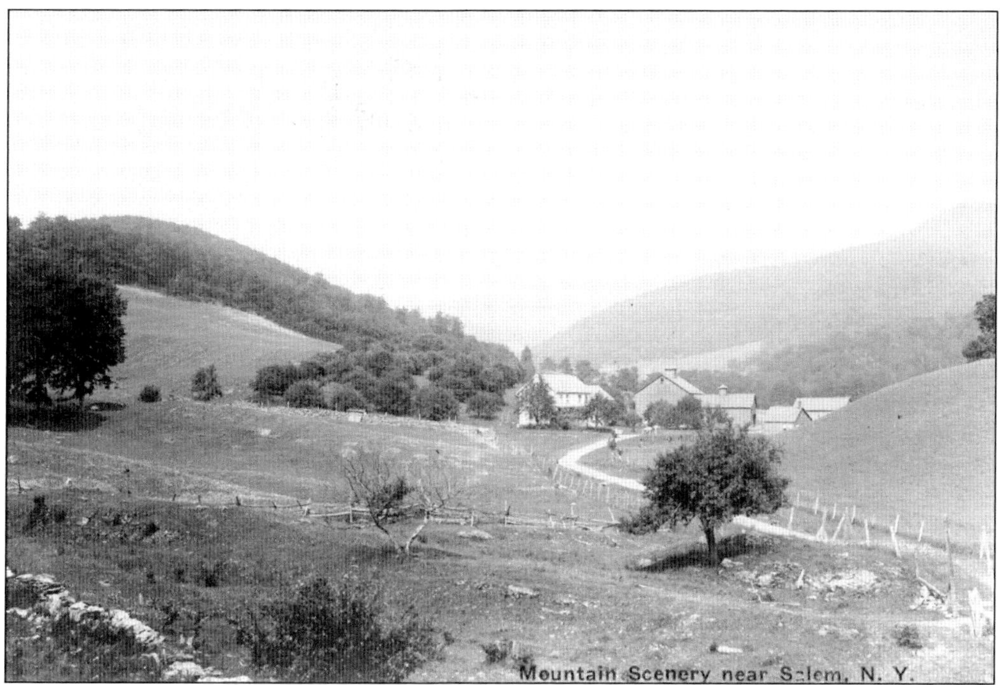

Farms were often isolated on narrow valley dirt roads, which were sometimes made impassable by spring mud and winter snow. The William J. Beaty farm, known as Golden Valley Farm, in Beattie Hollow, was pioneered by the Thomas Beaty family in 1769. The main residence was a log cabin until 1879, when William Beaty built a new house, seen here in 1910.

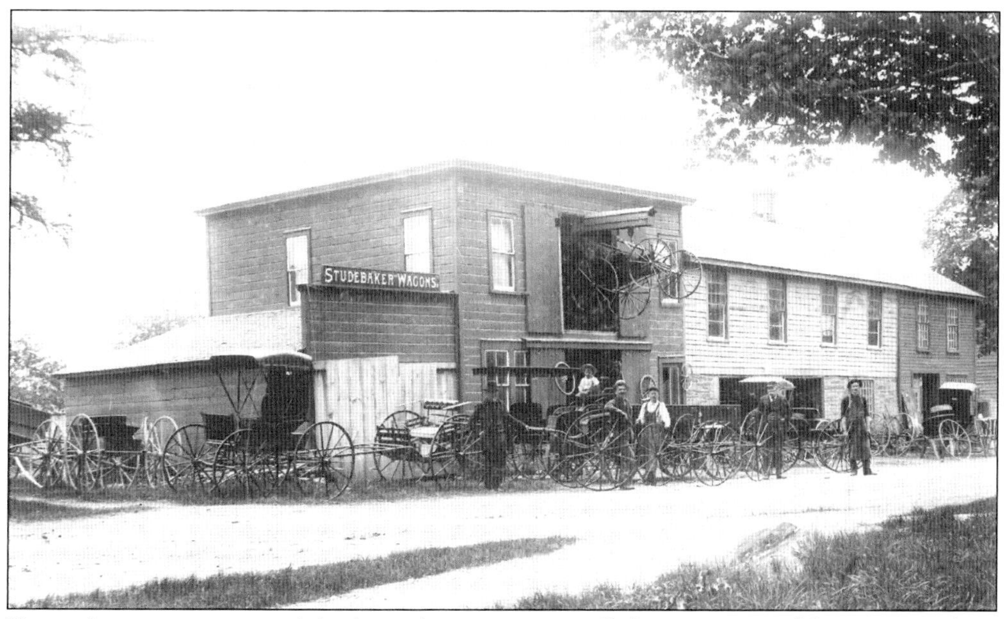

Horses, buggies, wagons, and sleighs in the winter were still the ways to travel for many people in 1912. Frank Wright (center), with his arm on the wheel, stands in front of his business on West Broadway. Seen here are a variety of wagons and carriages. The far end of the building housed the blacksmith shop.

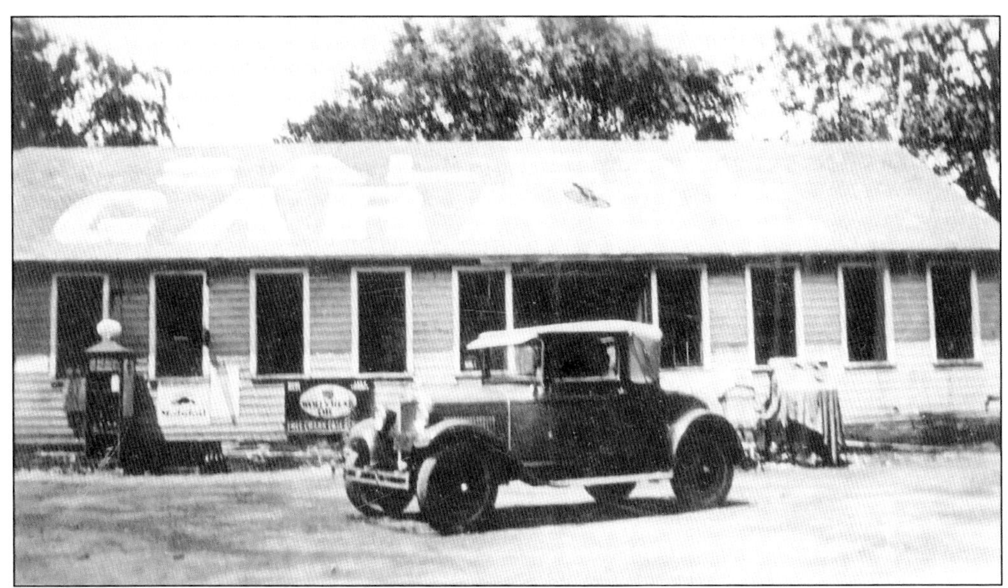

By 1929, the automobile had become the mode of travel, and repair shops and gas stations on the village's Main Street welcomed local customers and travelers. On South Main Street across from the Manhattan Shirt Shop, the Salem Auto Garage, with a 1929 Chevrolet coupe awaiting service, was one such business.

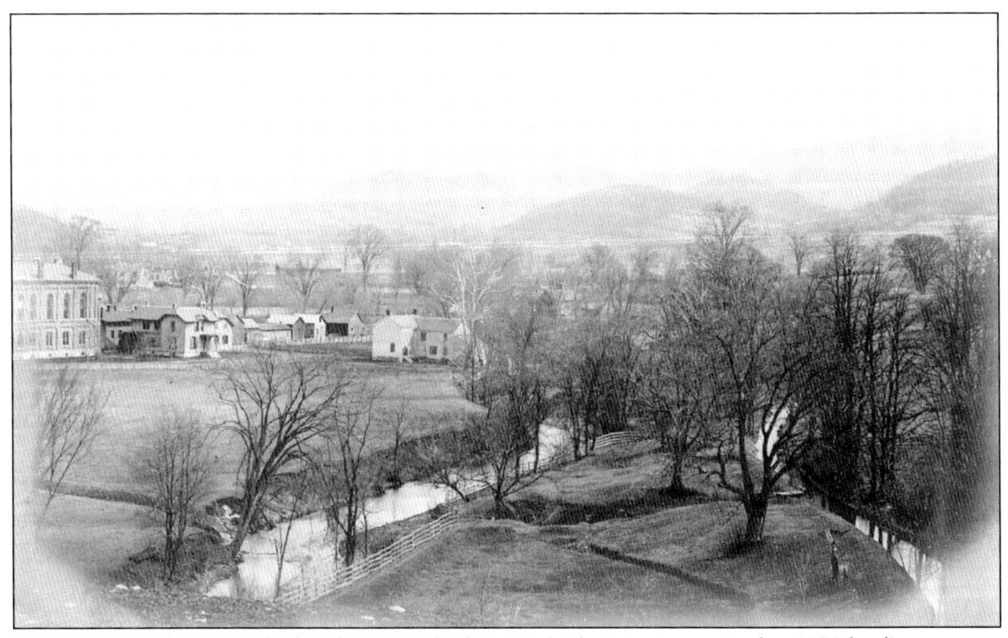

In addition to the Battenkill, White Creek also supplied waterpower. In this 1870 bird's-eye view, Williams's Canal (right) is shown making its way to Williams's Gristmill and Sawmill on Mill Street (Park Place). Gen. John Williams was a strong supporter of canals, and tradition has it that his method of sealing a canal with clay was used in building the Champlain Canal from Albany to Lake Champlain.

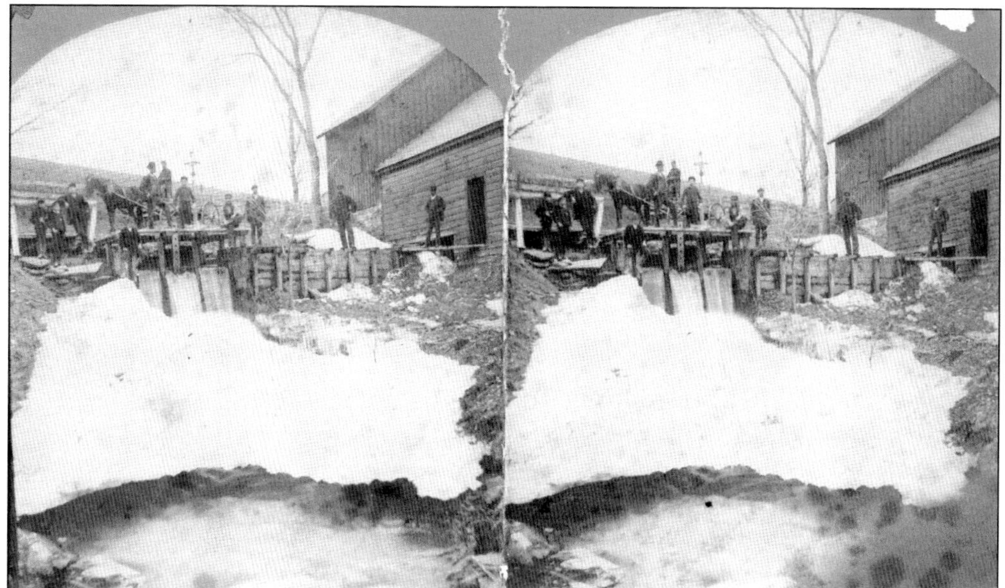

This stereoscopic photograph by Salem photographer B.C. Kinney shows the stock pen and workers at the Williams's Gristmill. The canal ran under Main Street on Mill Hill, where it was directed to the waterwheel of the gristmill and sawmill. The water outlet from the mill ran behind the houses on Mill Street and then under the road to White Creek.

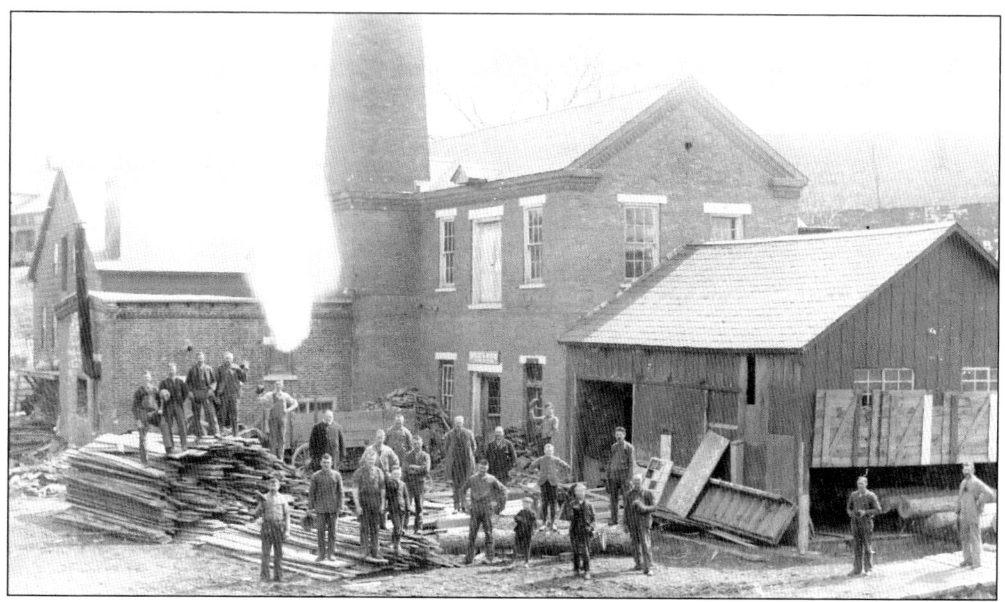

This 1892 photograph shows the brick Salem Steam and Sawmill that replaced the original Williams's Gristmill. The steam-powered sawmill sold housing supplies, flour, plaster, and cement until 1899, when it became part of the Manhattan Shirt Company building. "Salem Steam Mill," spelled out in slate on the south side roof, reminds passersby of the building's original use.

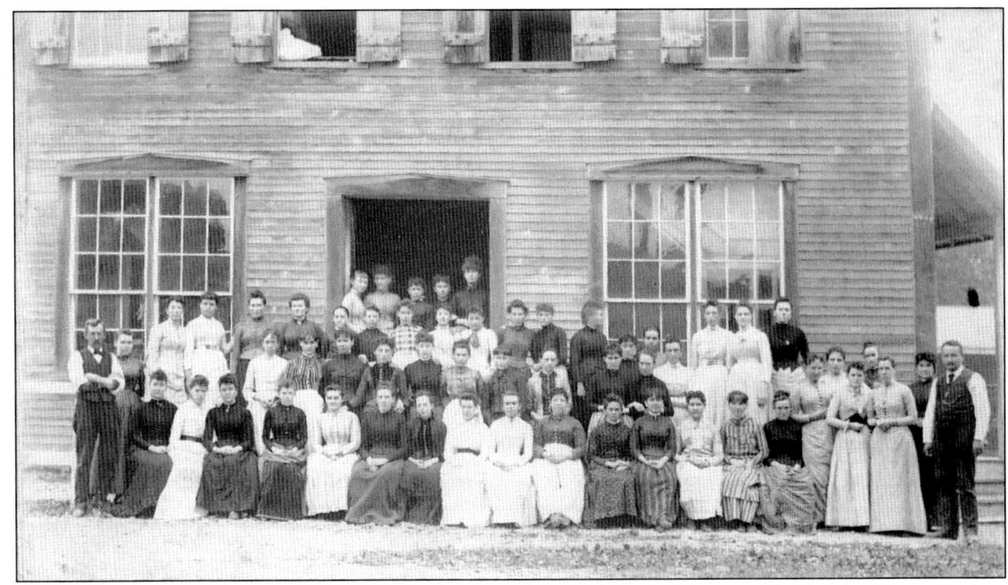

This 1899 photograph shows the shirt shop and workers on Mill Street (Park Place) just before it closed and moved into the 1899 Manhattan Shirt Shop, built by John M. Williams on the old mill site. Manager Henry Spallholz is seen on the far right. The old wooden building was moved across the street and became a boardinghouse for the workers.

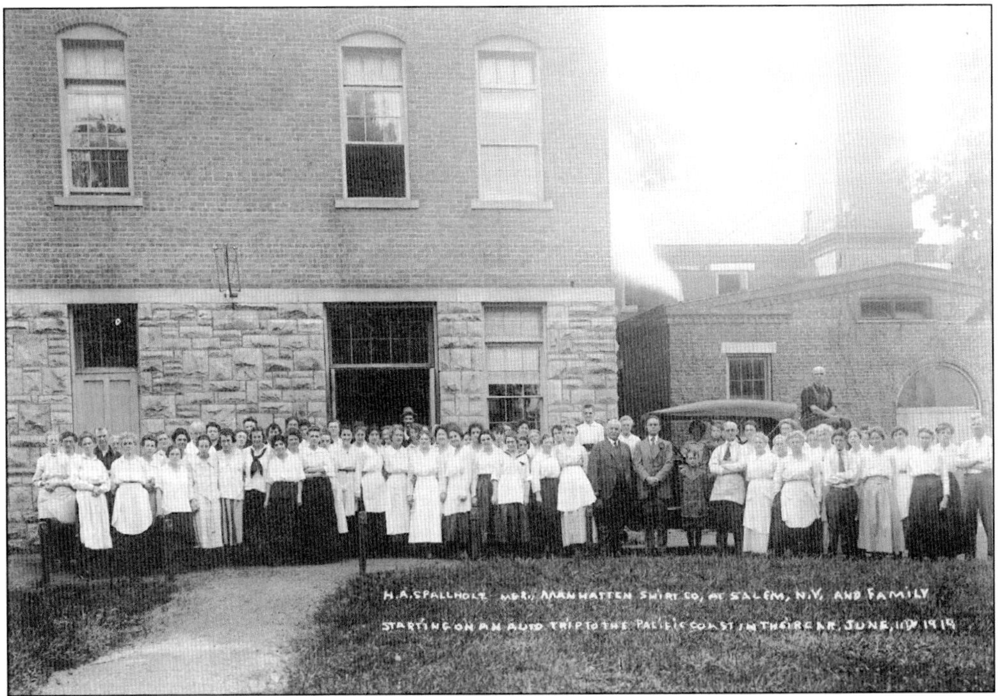

This July 11, 1919, photograph shows the Manhattan Shirt Company employees bidding Henry Spallholz (the younger man at center) and his family good motoring on their trip to the West Coast. The 1899 building with its heavy interior beaming, limestone, and brick construction attached to the steam mill made an impressive picture. The building contained one of the three elevators in the village.

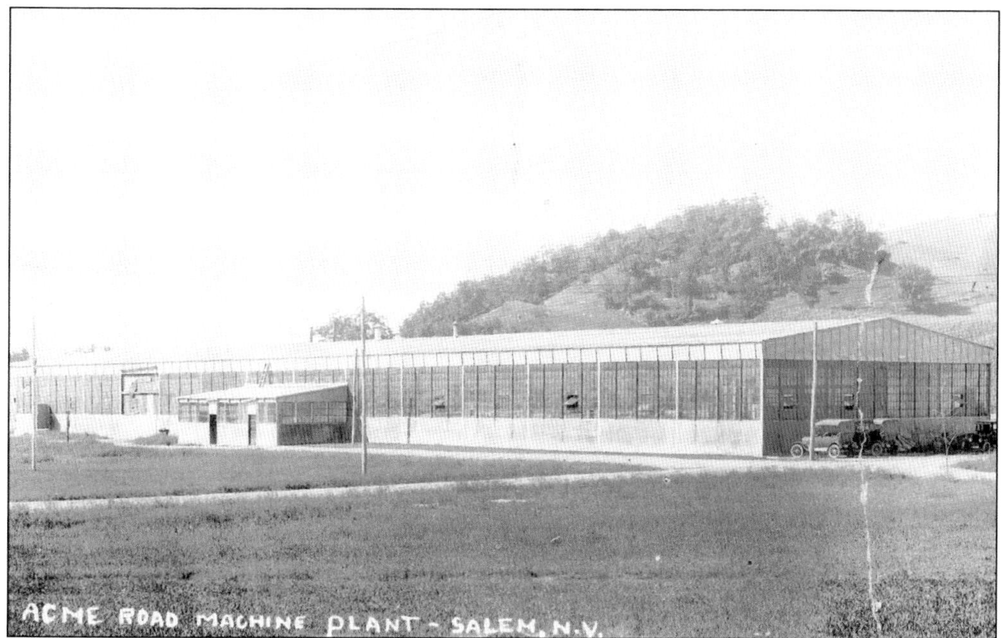

Beginning in 1924, one of Salem's heavy industries was the Acme Road Machine Plant. This 1925 photograph shows the extent of the manufacturing facility, where horse-drawn rollers, rock crushers, gravel screeners, road graders, bins, wagons, and road-making machinery were produced. In 1927, the business produced a new gasoline-powered grader called the Salem Grader.

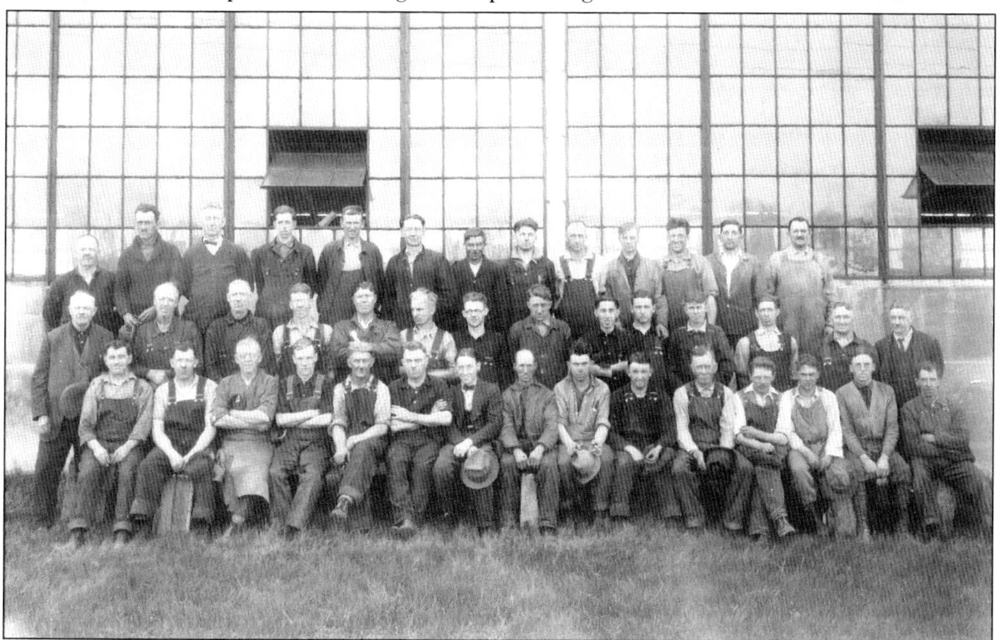

In 1925, the Acme Road Machine Plant employed 60 workers. They had to endure difficult working conditions in the winter because the only heat in the building was provided by forges, for heating and shaping metal parts, and kilns, for drying lumber for wagons and other pieces of equipment. In 1941, after the machinery plant closed, the building was used by the Gotham Tissue Corporation.

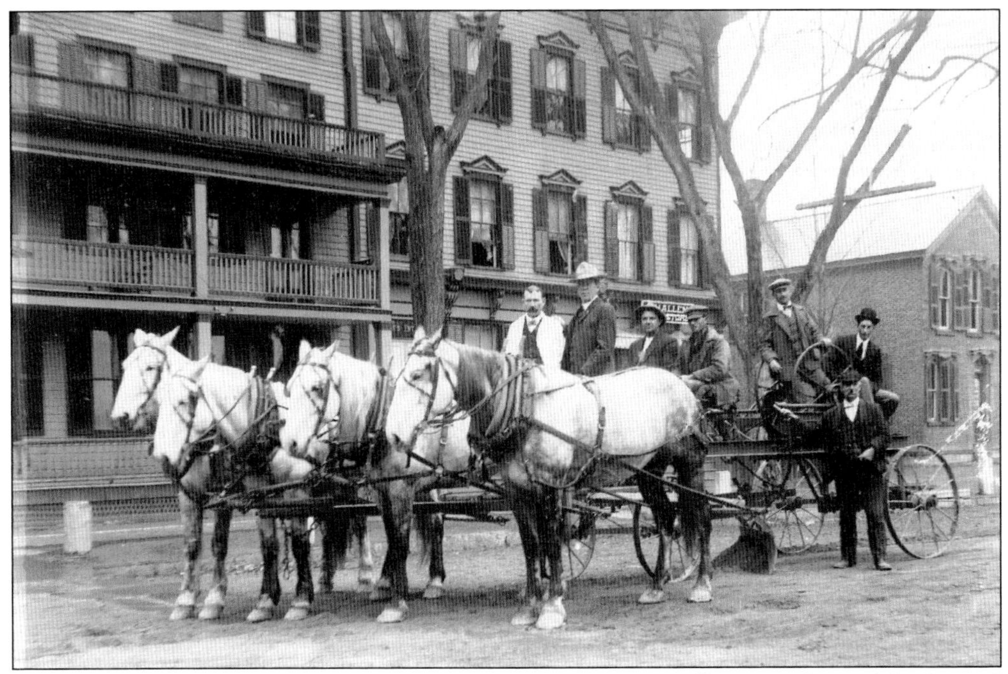

Before gasoline engines, this c. 1910 photograph shows two teams of horses in front of the Central House pulling a street grader. Main Street became part of the Northern Turnpike in 1814, and maintaining the road north to the Adirondacks was important. The men, dressed in business clothes, were perhaps demonstrating the grader.

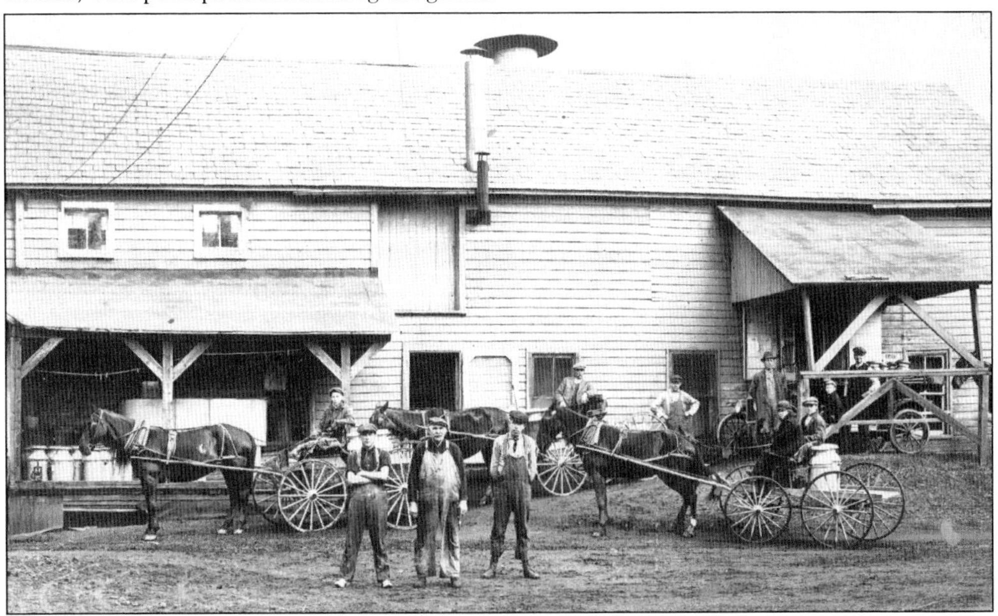

Dairy farming was an import part of the Salem agricultural economy, and farmers sold their milk to the H.P. Hood & Sons plant, which was located adjacent to the railroad yard. This 1910 photograph shows milk plant workers and farmers with their milk wagons. Under the shelter at right is an automobile with milk cans in the backseat. The milk was loaded on the morning Delaware & Hudson milk train going to Albany and Boston.

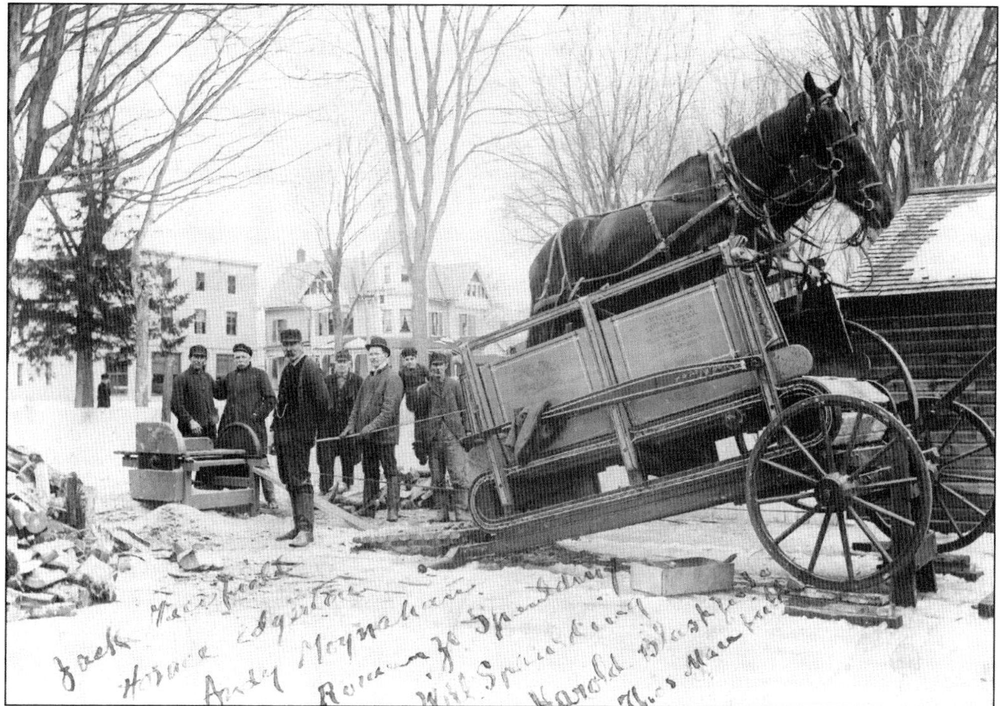

Here is another example of horse-powered mechanical equipment. The sign on the machine powering the saw says, "A.W. Gray & Sons, Horse Power, Patented and Manufactured by A.W. Gray & Sons, Middletown Springs, VT." Taken in 1891, this Williams Street photograph shows William Blashfield's furniture building and his Queen Ann–style house in the background.

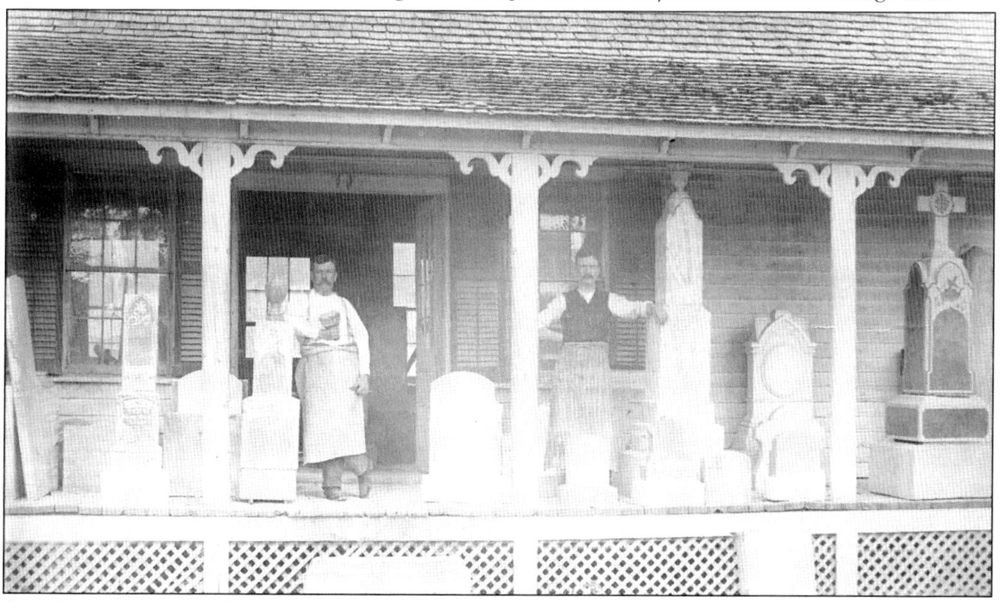

On the same street, the Oatman Monument Company sold marble monuments for cemeteries and gardens. This 1888 photograph shows Isaac Oatman (left) and his brother amidst their carved stones. The raw stone was shipped to Salem over the Delaware & Hudson Railway from the marble quarries in Rutland, Vermont.

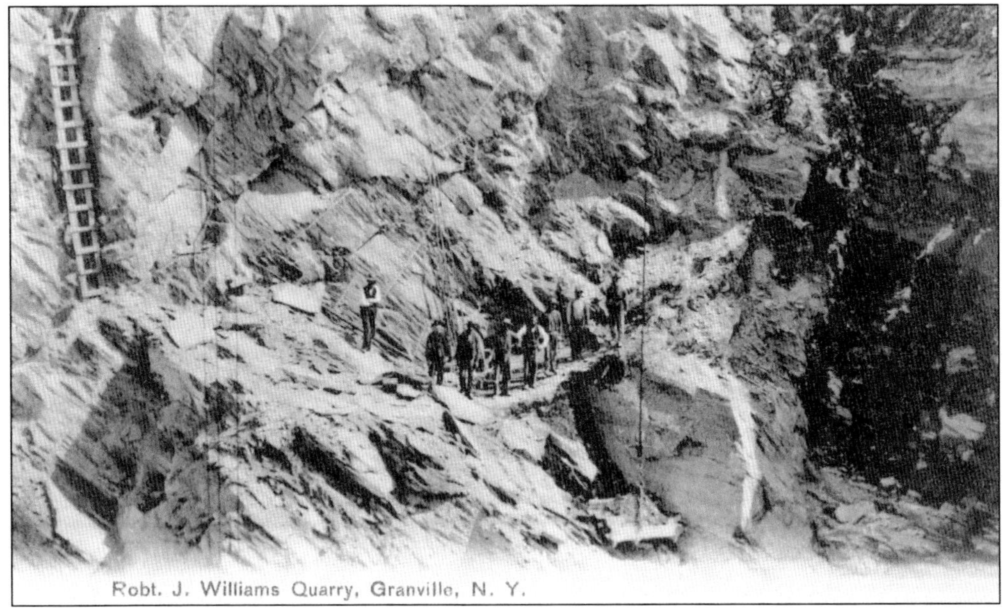

In the Slate Valley, cradling State Route 22 from Salem to Granville, numerous slate quarries, such as the Excelsior Quarry on Quarry Road in Salem, produced roofing slate. The labor-intensive slate quarry work required special skills; therefore, most of the quarry workers in the valley were experienced slate-mining immigrants from Wales. This early-1900s photograph shows the Williams Quarry in Granville.

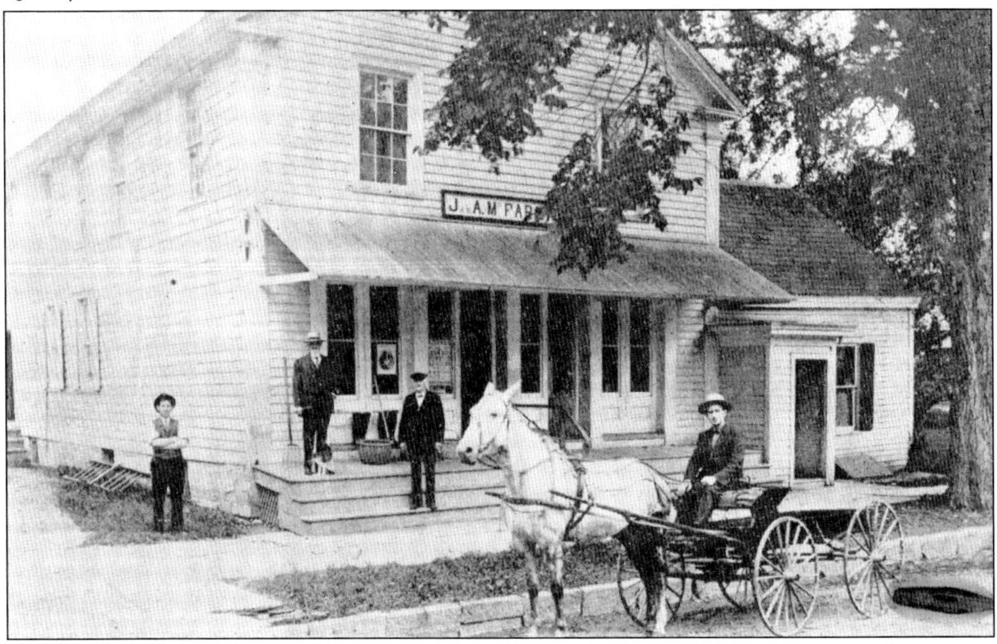

Merchants serving the farming community were always in demand. A popular general store was J.A. McFarland's Old Country Store, on the corner of South Main Street and East Broadway. Shown in this 1890 photograph are William McFarland (porch), James A. McFarland (steps), and James McFarland (wagon). In later years, the building housed the Grange Hall, Moore's Gulf station, and Evan's Grill.

Six

Community Life

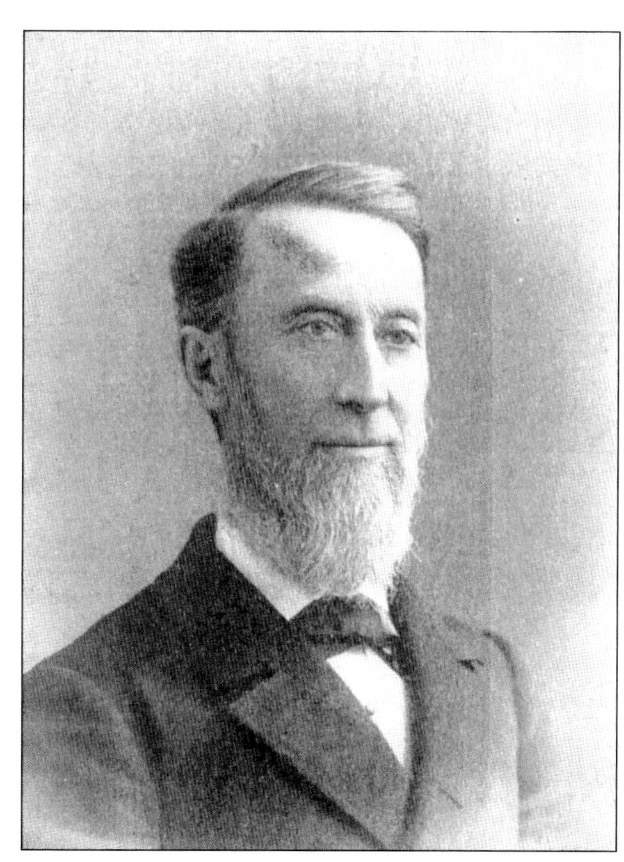

Doctors, who made home visits at all hours of the day, were an important part of country life, and Salem had many doctors over the years. One of them was Dr. John Lambert, a nationally known gynecologist who practiced in Salem for 55 years. He was a graduate of Bowdoin College and came to Salem in 1856.

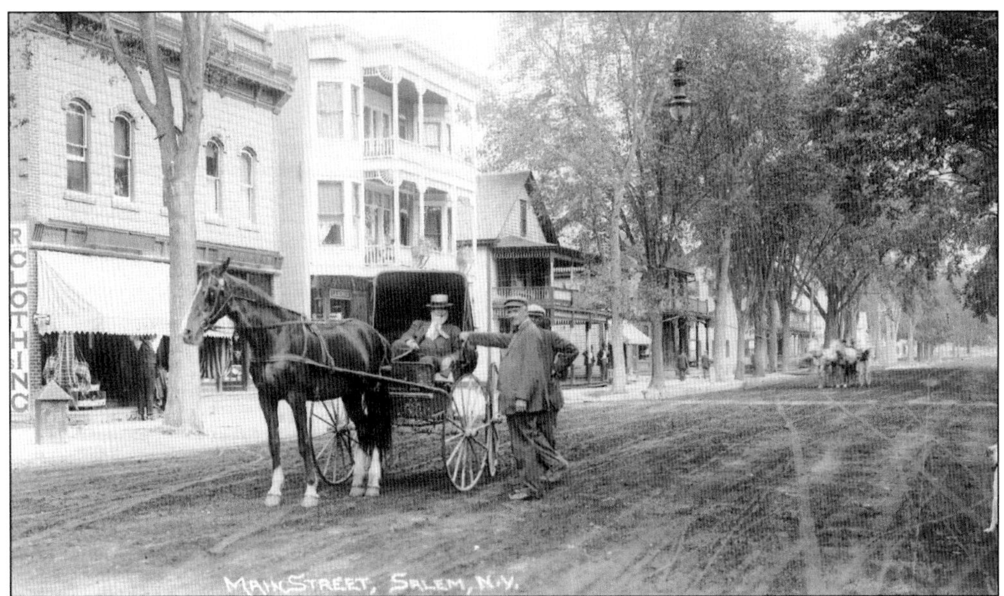

House calls were the norm, and horse-and-buggies, owned or rented, were necessary tools in a doctor's life. Seen around 1910, Dr. Albert M. Young is in his buggy on North Main Street, speaking to Fred Cleveland. Dr. Young came to Salem in 1875 after the deaths of Salem doctors Charles H. Allen and Charles O.T. Gillman. Dr. Young was influential in raising money for the Proudfit Building.

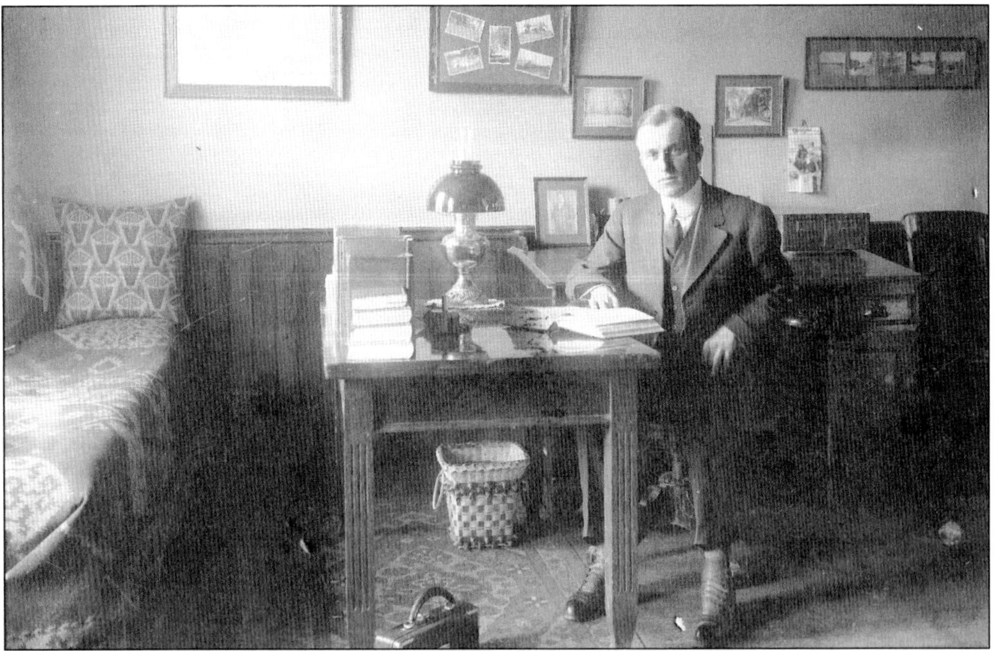
One of Salem's most popular doctors, Dr. Zenas V.D. Orton, is shown in his North Main Street office in 1911. This formal photograph shows the trappings of his profession, including his medical college diploma in Latin displayed on the wall, his medical bag on the floor, his day couch, his medical books at the ready, and his sartorial dress. He became the personal physician to Maria Audubon.

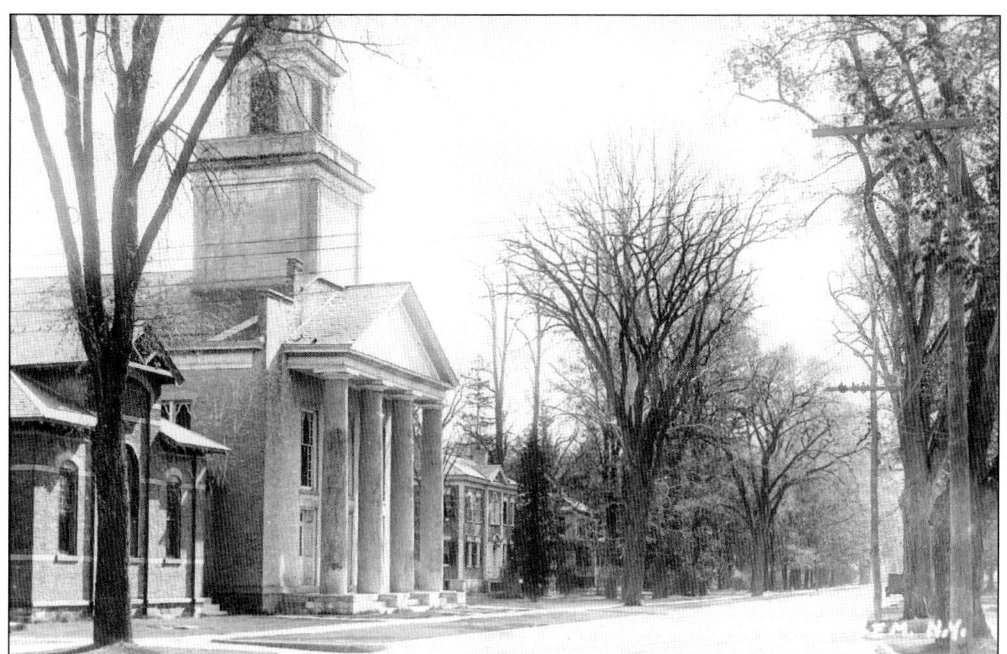

The New England pioneers of 1764 were Presbyterians who organized the First Incorporated Presbyterian Congregation Church. The original wooden church, built in 1777, was made into a fort, in reaction to Gen. John Burgoyne's threat to sack the town of Salem. When the militia and citizens abandoned Salem, the Tories and Indians burned Fort Salem to the ground. The existing brick church, now a theater, was built in 1840.

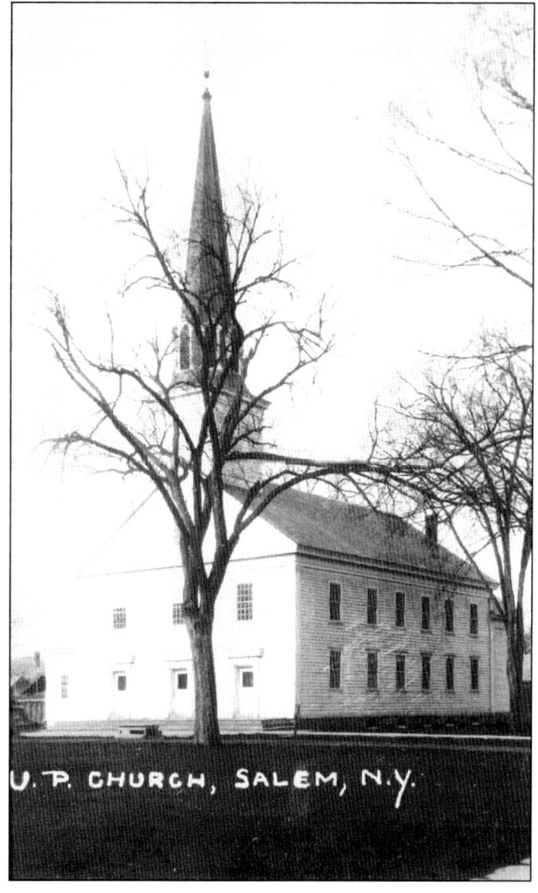

Known locally as the White Church, the First United Presbyterian Church, with its Scotch and Irish congregation, was organized in 1767 by Dr. Thomas Clark and his followers. Escaping religious persecution, they emigrated from Scotland, through Ireland, and, eventually, joined the New England pioneers who came to Salem in 1764 from Pelham, Massachusetts. The current church was built in 1797, and the spire was added in 1877.

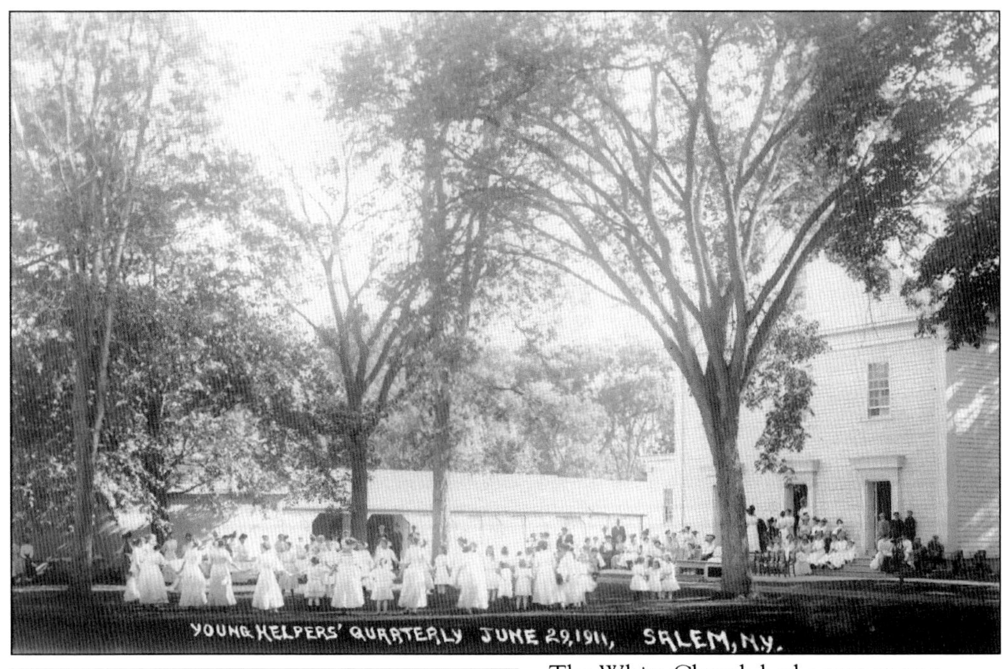

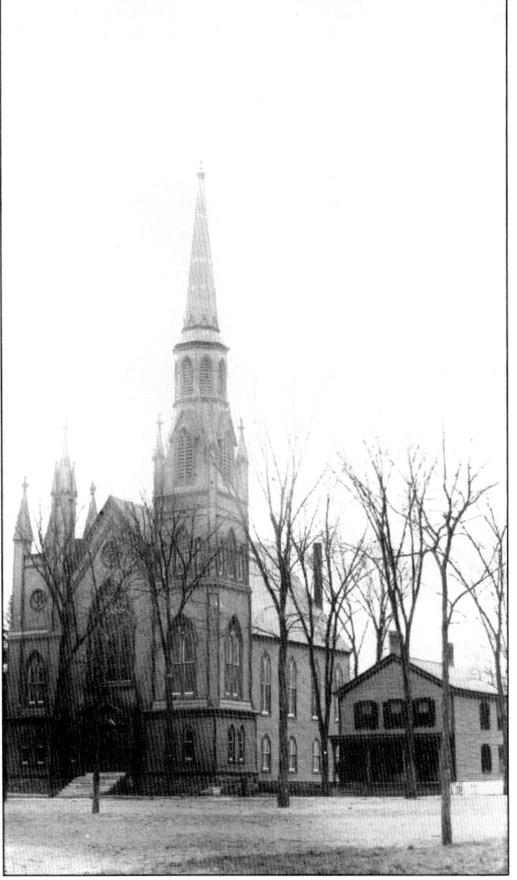

The White Church had a very strong church community, involving children and young men and women in Bible education. Organized by Harriet Williams, the great-granddaughter of Gen. John Williams, the Young Helpers' Quarterly brought church members together for social events. White clothing for the women was the fashion for these events. Note the extensive carriage barns to the left of the church in this 1911 photograph.

Other religions evolved as people immigrated to Salem. Minister Philip Embury, considered the founder of Methodism in the United States, and his followers came to Salem in 1770 to pioneer a tract of land in Camden Valley, outside of Shushan. From this movement, two Methodist Episcopal Churches arose. The Shushan church was built in 1847. Shown here is the Salem Village church, rebuilt in 1892.

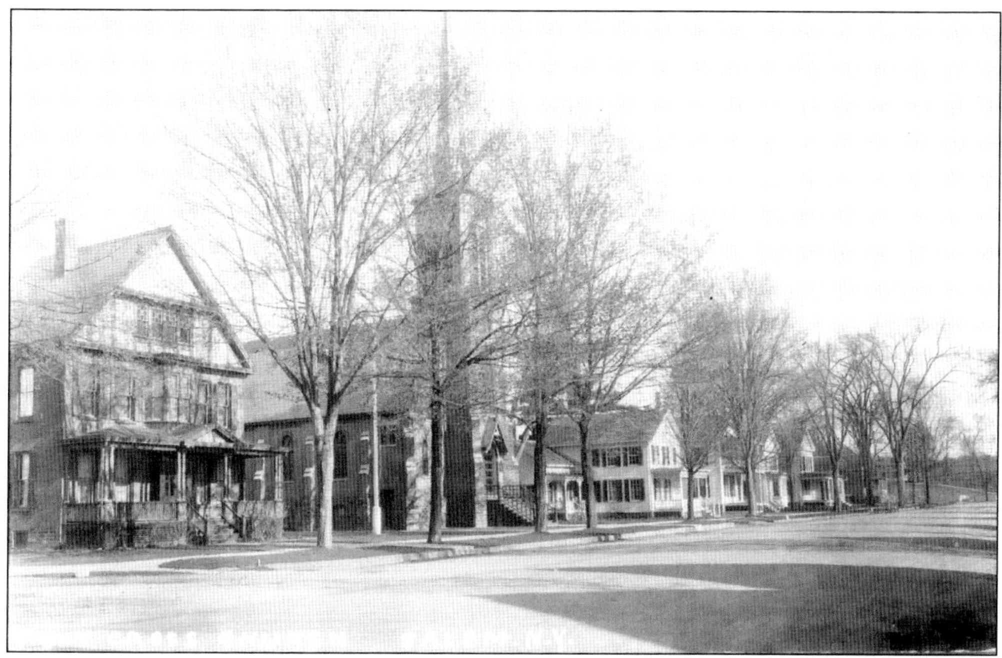

In 1859, Irish immigrants who escaped the 1840 potato famine built the first Holy Cross Catholic Church of wood. They came to the Salem area to farm the land and, later, to work on the Troy & Rutland Railroad. This 1942 photograph shows the 1889 brick church and brick parish house that replaced the wooden church.

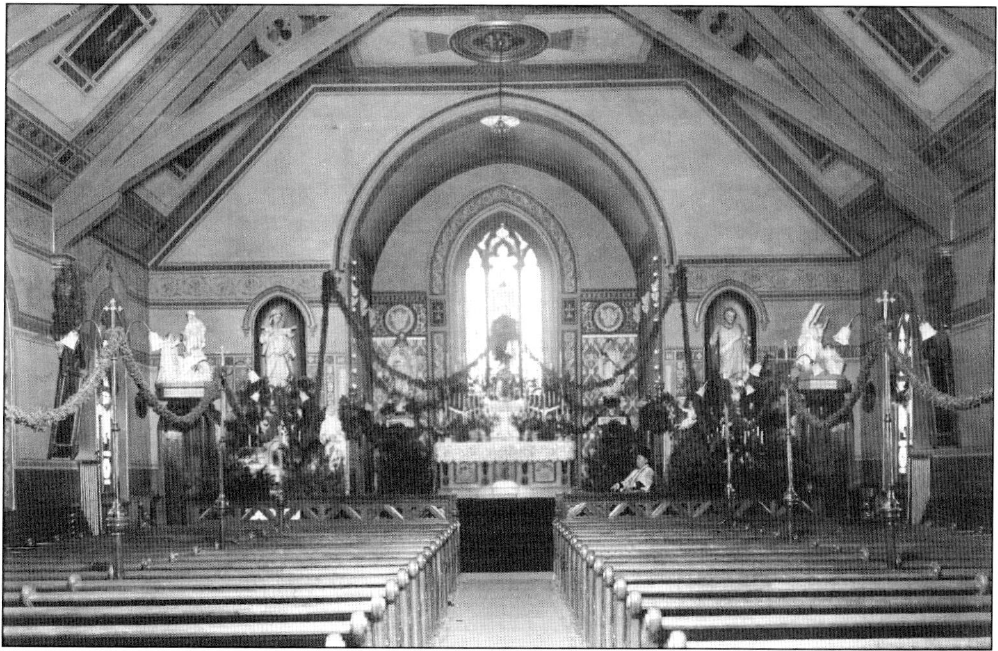

This 1932 photograph shows the newly decorated interior of Holy Cross Church at Christmastime. Fr. John Ready, who oversaw the interior decorating, sits to the right of the altar. Religious artwork and statues of Catholic saints embellish the interior, and stained-glass windows depict scenes from the scriptures. The 130-foot church steeple and spire dominate the north end of the village.

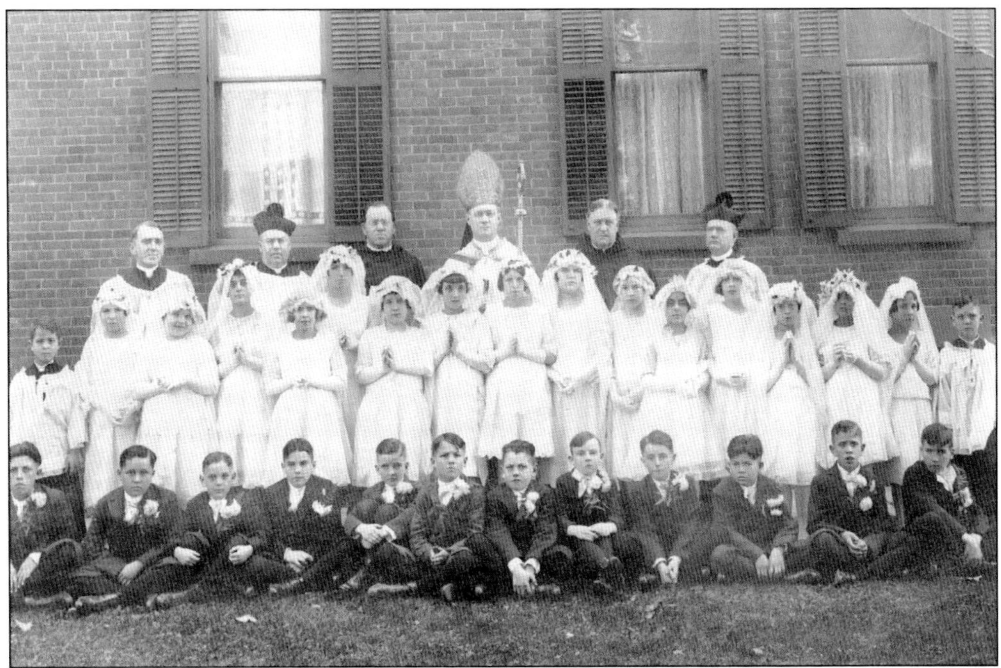

First Communion in the Catholic Church was a memorable event in the lives of the parish children. This photograph shows the First Communion class of 1925, with Bishop Edmond Gibbons (center) and Holy Cross pastor Rev. Thomas Delaney (far right) in the back row. Communion garb of white with lace headwear for the girls and black suits for the boys was the norm for the occasion.

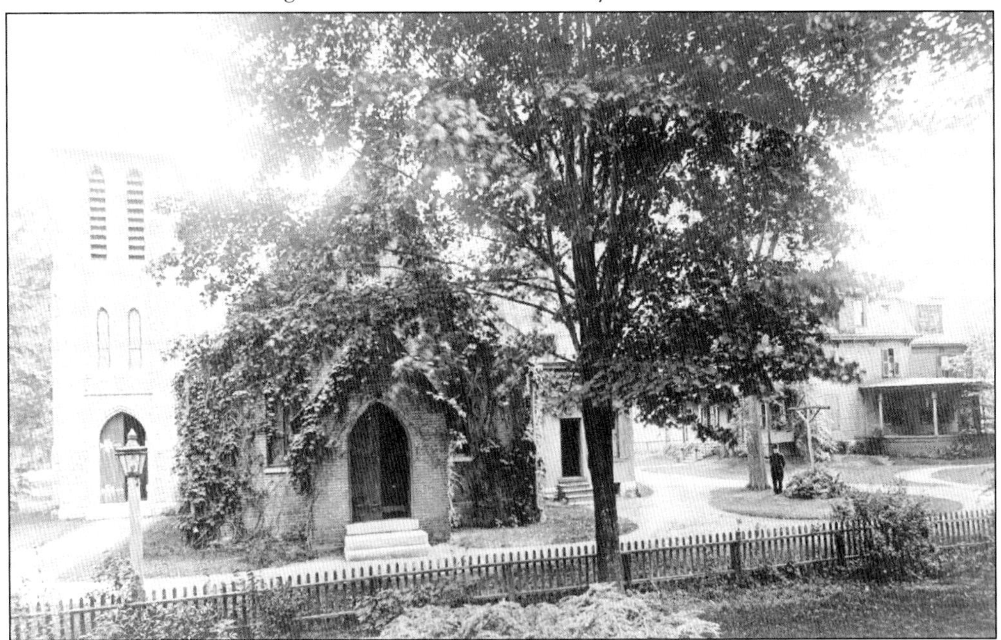

St. Paul's Episcopal Church was built of brick in 1860. Later, in 1895, it was enlarged with a limestone north transept and tower fronting East Broadway. The entrance doors for the nave and tower were painted traditional red. Tiffany stained-glass windows were installed in 1890. Shown standing next to the cross in this early-1900s photograph is the Rev. Harry C. Rush.

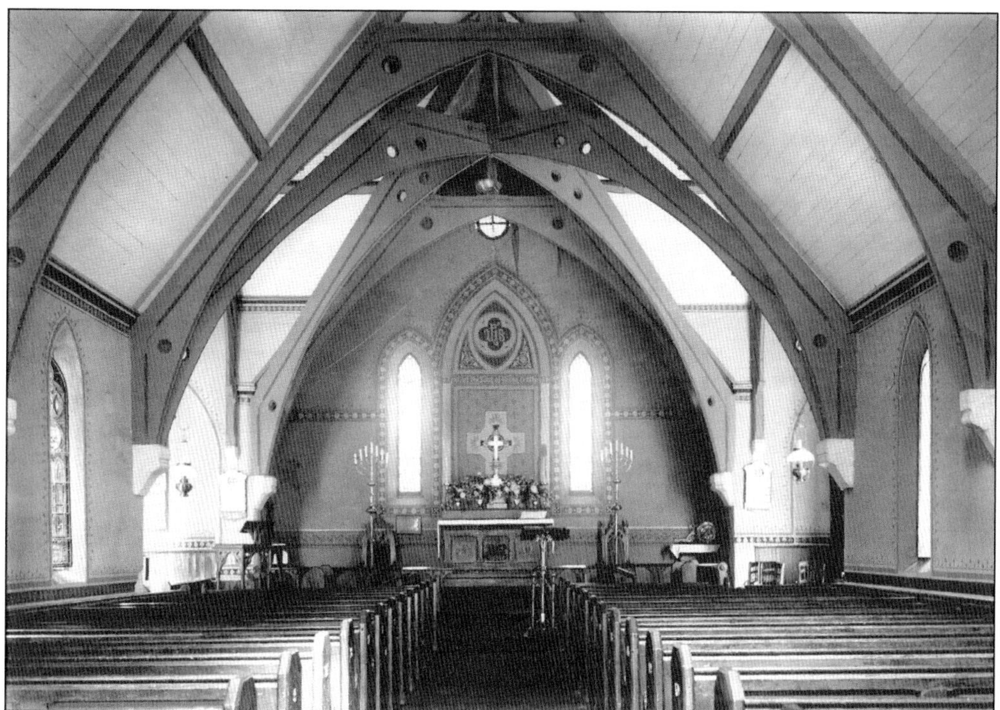

The interior of St. Paul's Episcopal Church reflects English Tudor craftsmanship. The exposed beams for the vaulted ceiling lead the eye to the altar and the Gothic-arch stained-glass windows on each side. An E&GG Hook organ (Opus 189), built in 1855 and installed in 1890, was purchased for $1,000 from the Unitarian church in Dorchester, Massachusetts.

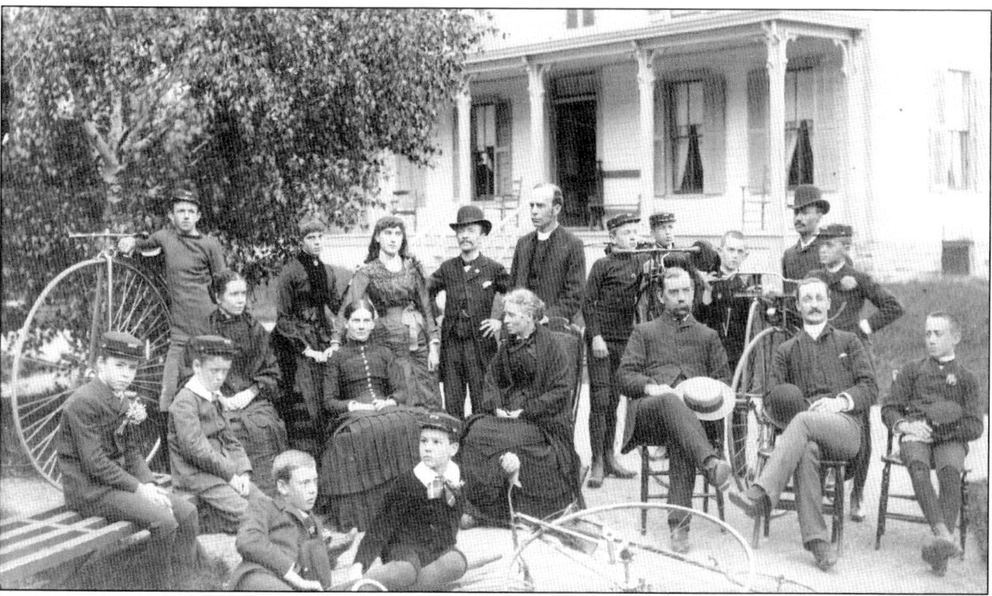

From 1882 to 1893, St. Paul's Church ran a private school known as St. Paul's Hall. This 1886 photograph shows the Rev. John Henry Houghton (center), members of his family, teaching staff, and other occupants of the rectory. High-wheel cycles were the travel mode for the adventurous in this group.

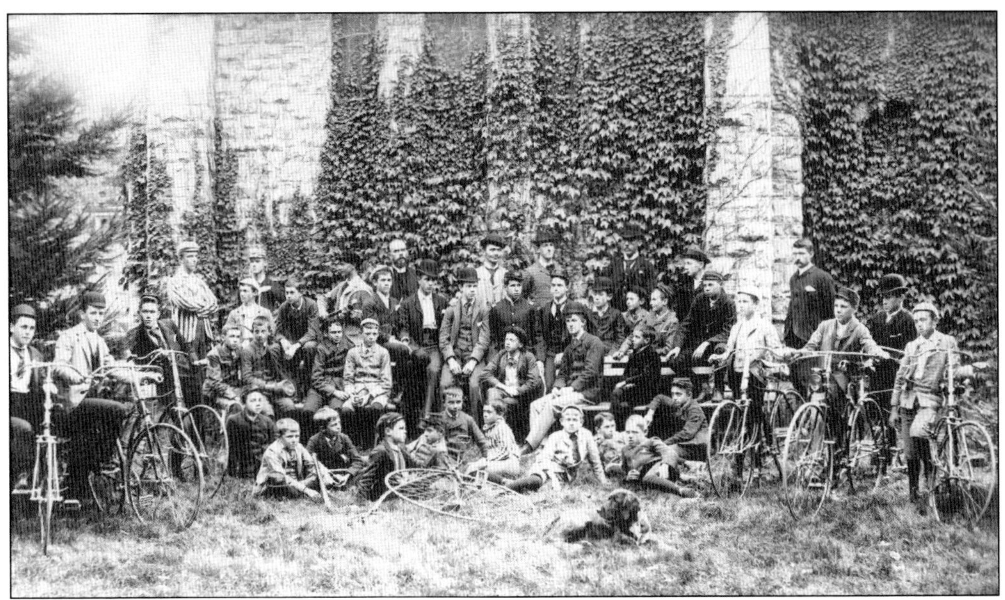

In 1887, Rev. John Houghton (center left), teaching staff, and 33 students posed in front of the north tower of St. Paul's Church. Baseball bats and bikes, both high-wheel and two-wheel, were popular in the 1880s. Living quarters for live-in students and staff were in a separate building connected to Burton Hall, where classes were taught. Local area boys and girls were allowed to attend as day students.

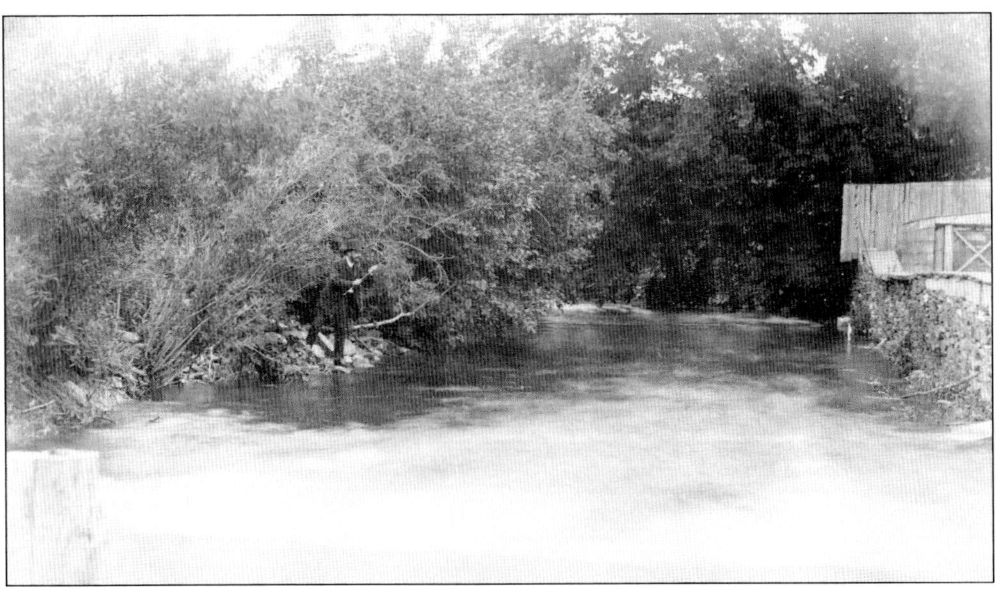

Fishing was a favorite pastime in the village. Salem was originally called White Creek, after the creek that ran through the village, which had plenty of native trout. White Creek ran to meet Black Creek and the Battenkill at Fitch's Point. Here, the Rev. John Houghton is shown fishing in back of St. Paul's Hall in this 1888 photograph.

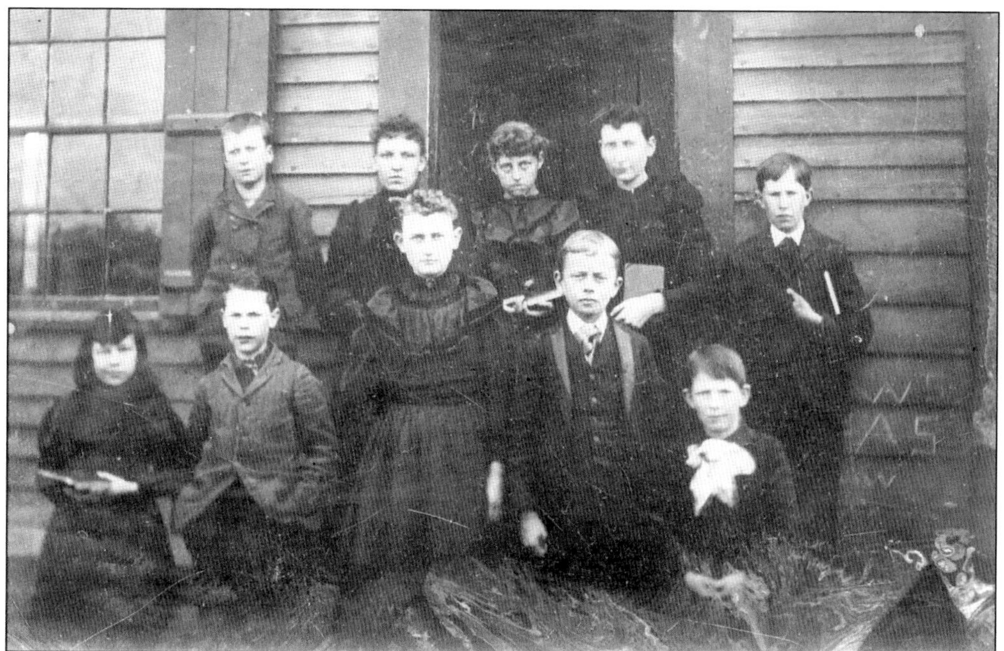

The Salem School District once consisted of 31 one-room schoolhouses located in the towns of Salem, Hebron, Greenwich, and Jackson. This 1893 photograph shows Rexleigh School teacher Minnie McQueen (second from left in the second row) with her students. They are, from left to right, (first row) Blanche Gilbert, William Searles, Mammie Anglam, Henry A. Spallholz, and Warren Hanks; (second row) Millard West, Lizzie McCordel, Fannie Blanchfield, and Hidey Searles.

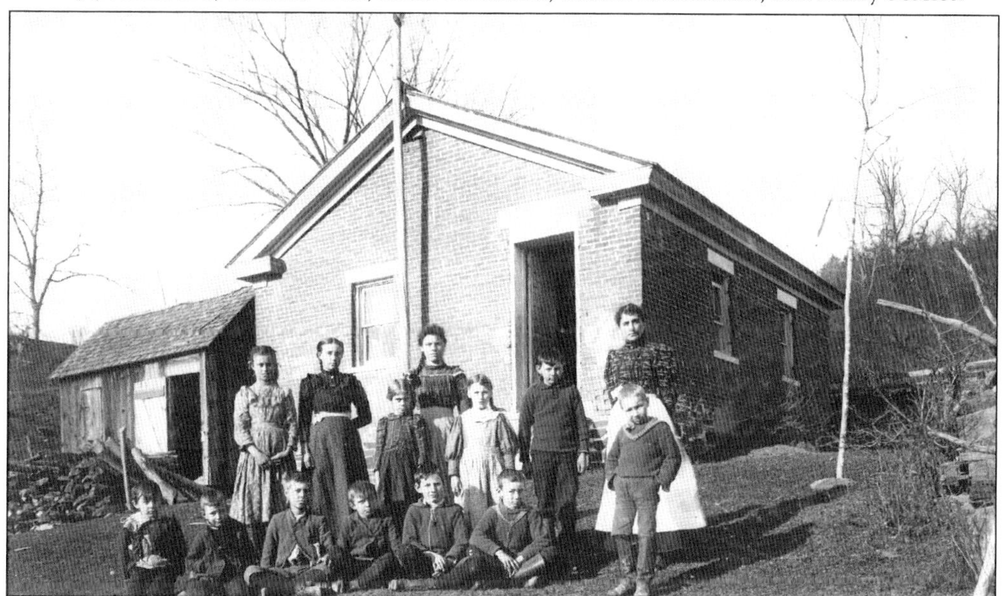

Some schoolhouses were constructed of brick, like the Frazier School on West Hebron Road. In this 1900 photograph, teacher Maggie Wadsworth is on the right. Her students were, from left to right, (first row) Hiley Keys, George Keys, Fred Burk, Albert Flowers, Lewie Glase, Leon Glase, and Stanley J. Burnett; (second row) Minnie Harriet Brown, Ida Grace Brown, Nellie Burnett, Laura Beatrice Brown, Sadie Burke, and Harrison Gove Brown.

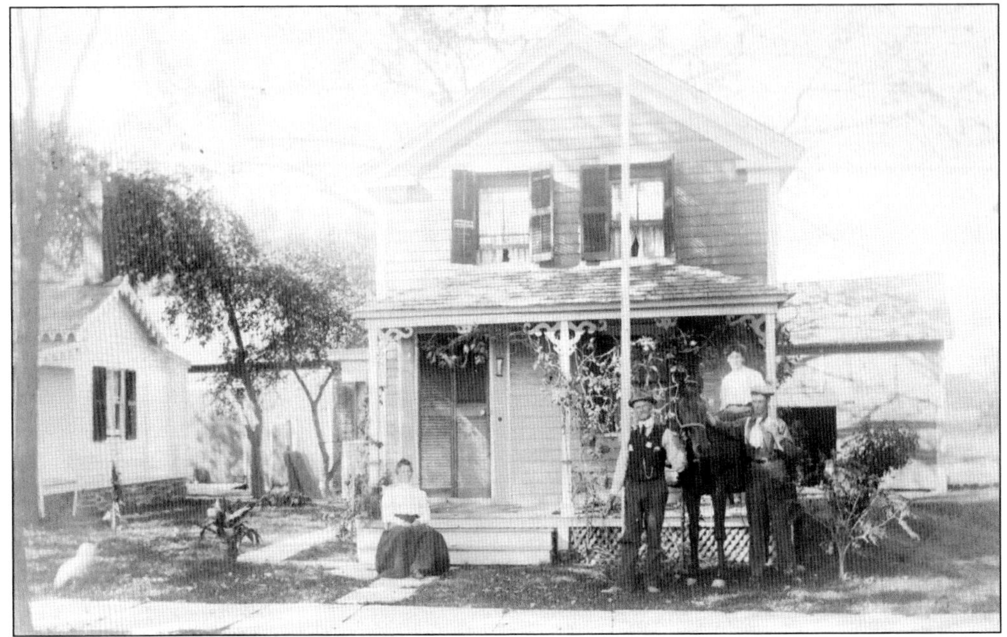

Self-sufficiency was the norm in rural areas, and, even in the village, many families had a barn with a horse or cow in the backyard. In 1910, the Cornelius A. Shipley family posed in front of their house on West Broadway. Shipley was an employee of the Delaware & Hudson Railway. Note the white chicken in the lower left corner.

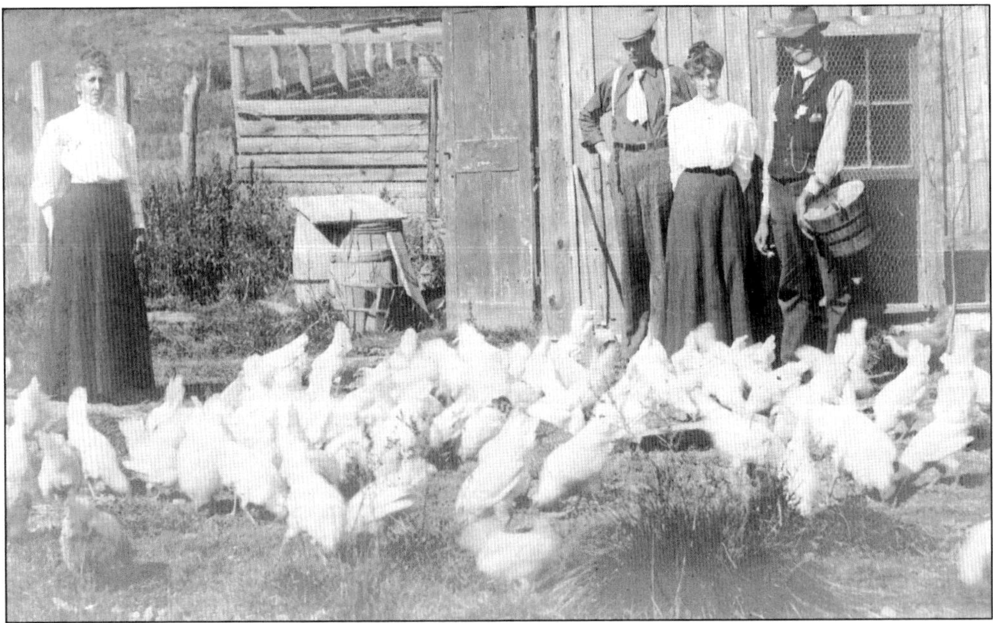

The Shipley backyard not only contained a horse barn but also a chicken coop. This photograph, taken on the same day in 1910, shows Shipley with a bucket feeding his white leghorns. Chickens were raised for their eggs, a cash crop, while roosters and non-laying hens became Sunday dinner. Vegetable gardens, common in most backyards, provided fresh food in the summer and preserved food for the winter months.

Salem had numerous publishers and different newspaper names over the years. Published in 1794 in Salem, the *National Courier* was the first in Washington County. This photograph shows Marian Lewis in the carriage and Helen Cruikshank standing in front of the old *Salem Axiom* newspaper's office in 1900. Today, the *Journal Press*, published in Greenwich, covers both Salem and Greenwich.

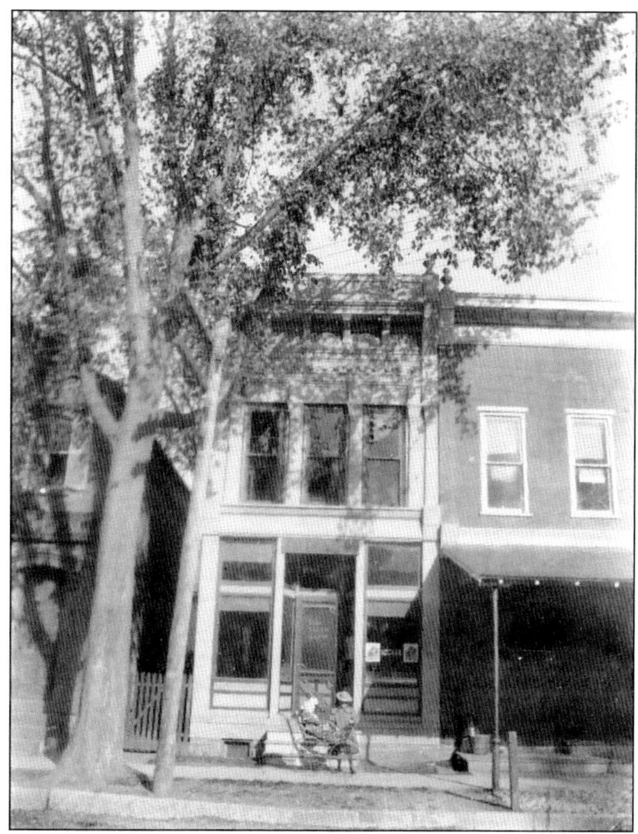

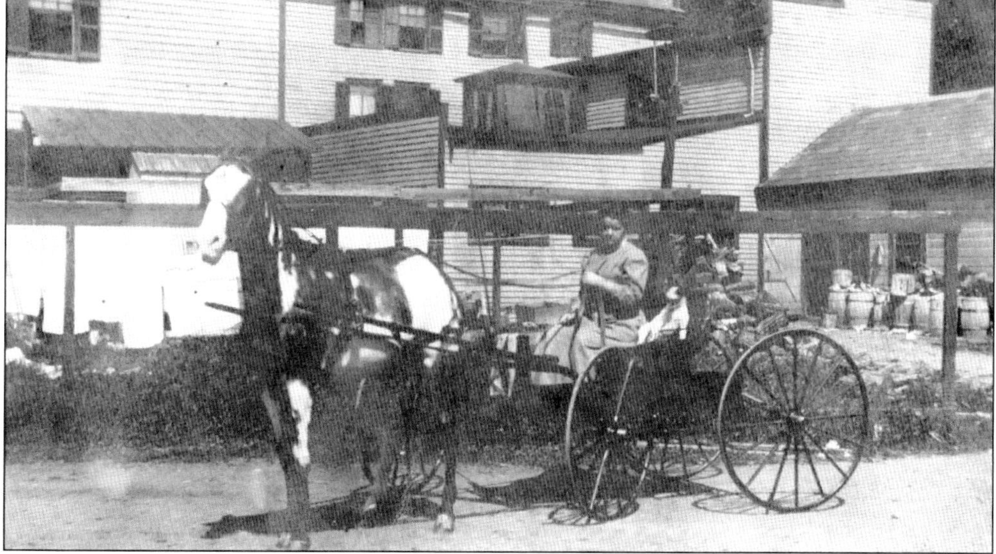

Before the automobile dominated transportation, people who did not own their own rigs would rent horses and buggies at Main Street liveries. This photograph shows Gretchen Lord Abbott in 1909 with a dog and a horse and buggy at the Central House stable. Situated across the street from the Delaware & Hudson depot, the Central House was a popular hotel for overnight travelers, long-term renters, and drummers selling their merchandise.

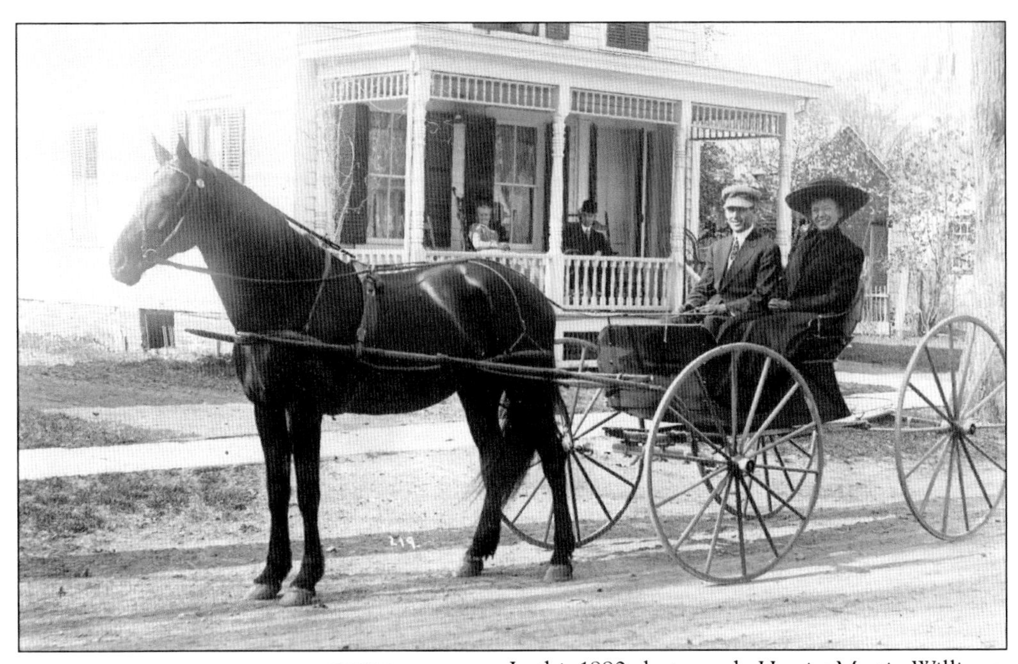

In this 1880 photograph, Harriet Martin Williams, with an unidentified driver, is shown with a horse and buggy on Nichol Street. Harriet was the great-granddaughter of Gen. John Williams. In 1896, she authored *The Salem Book*, a local history of Salem. She also wrote and had privately printed small books about nature to give her friends at Christmastime.

Dr. John Williams, a skilled surgeon, arrived in Salem in 1773 to help fight a smallpox epidemic. He soon became Salem's most influential and wealthiest citizen. Gen. Philip Schuyler appointed him colonel in 1775 to lead the Charlotte County Militia in the Revolutionary War. In 1786, he was appointed brigadier general of the county militia. He also served in the New York legislature and the US Congress.

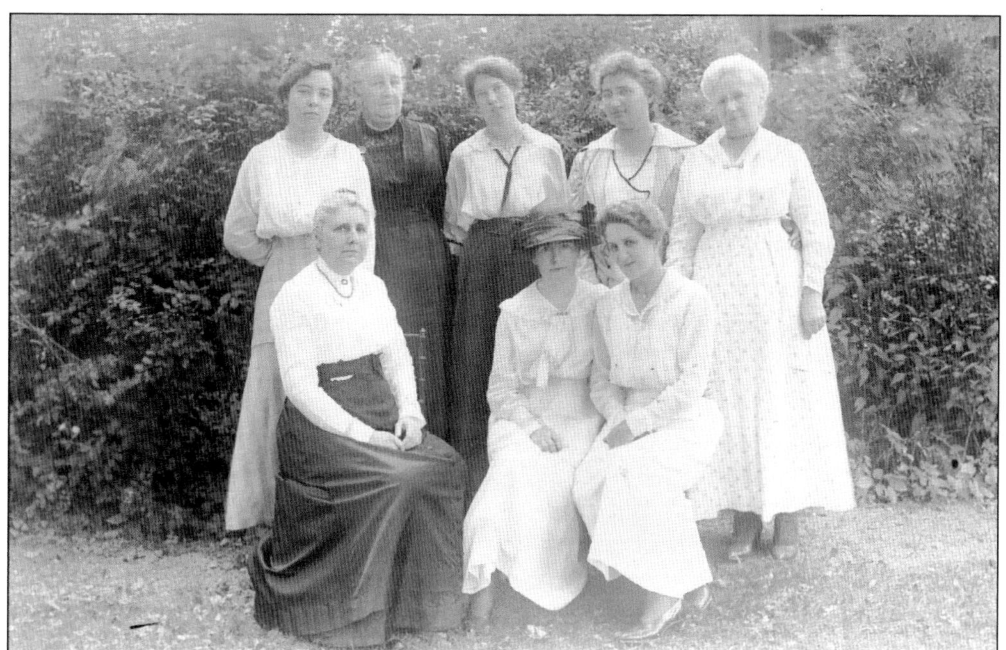

Neighbors to the Gen. John Williams family were the Audubon women: Caroline Audubon, daughter-in-law of John James Audubon, and her daughters Maria and Florence. This 1917 photograph was taken at the Audubon house at a birthday party for young Virginia Fortin. Maria Audubon is standing second from the left, Florence Audubon is sitting on the left, and Anna Fortin is sitting on the right.

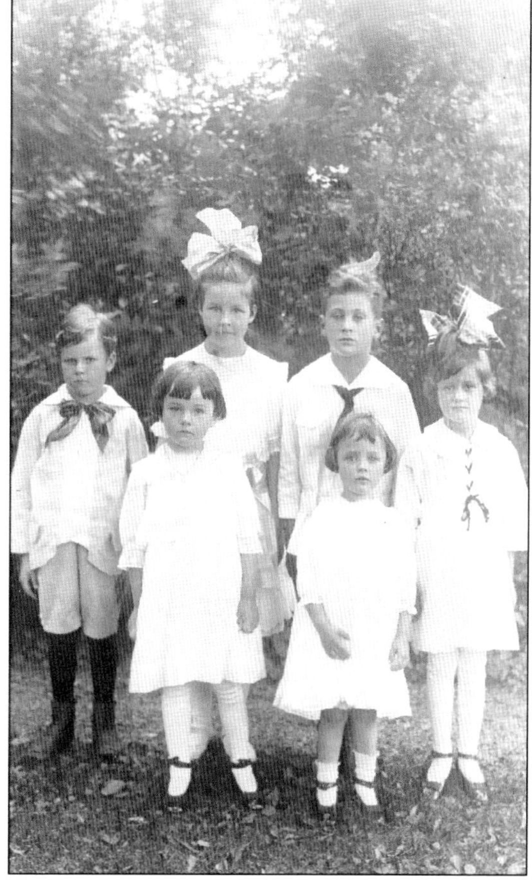

This photograph of the children at the 1917 birthday party at the Audubon house shows young Virginia Fortin with her friends. The children are, from left to right, (first row) Irene Hunt and Jean McKie; (second row) Arnold Close, Margaret Moulton, John Fortin, and Virginia Fortin. As usual, white dresses with hair ribbons for the girls and white shirts and ties for the boys were the fashion of the day.

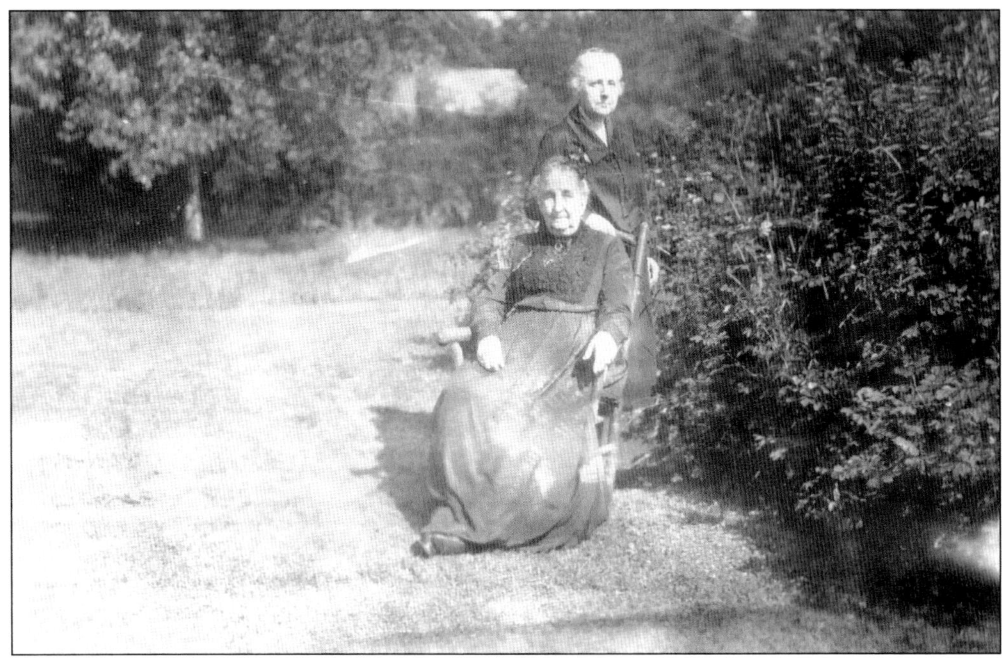

This 1925 summer photograph shows Audubon sisters Florence (standing) and Maria (sitting) in the backyard of the Audubon house. A few months later, Maria died, on December 22, 1925. Maria was best known for publishing her grandfather's diaries, titled *Audubon and His Journals*, in 1897. Before her death, Maria requested that Dr. Zenas Orton, her physician, purchase the house for his own family.

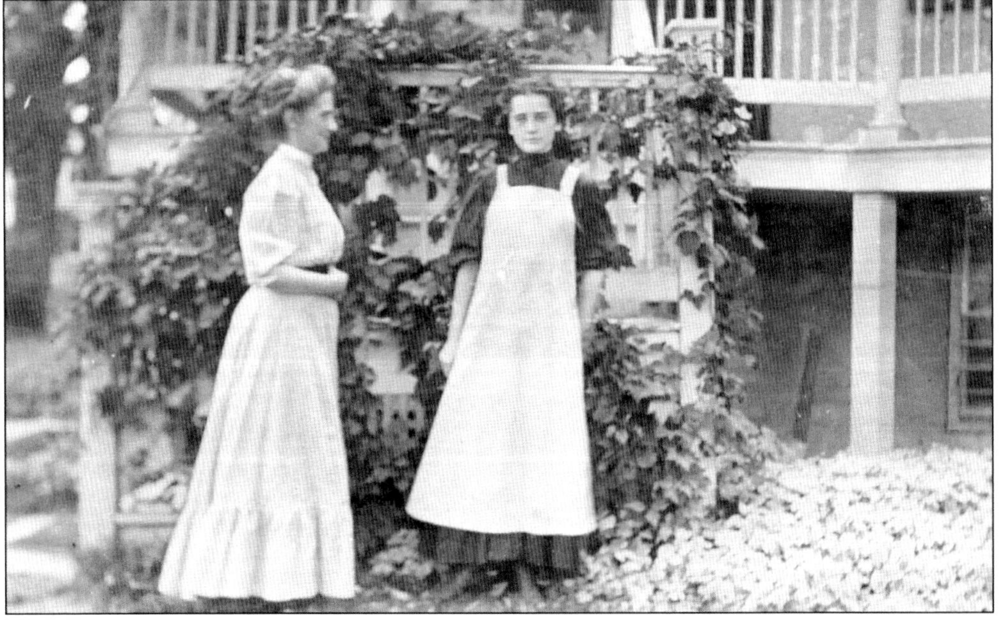

This 1909 photograph of two Audubon domestics, Maggie Quinn and Marion Baldwin, was taken in back of the Audubon house. Women domestics, working in private homes or at the village hotels and restaurants, were often Irish immigrants who came to Salem to escape the Irish potato famine or came with Irish railroad workers in 1852.

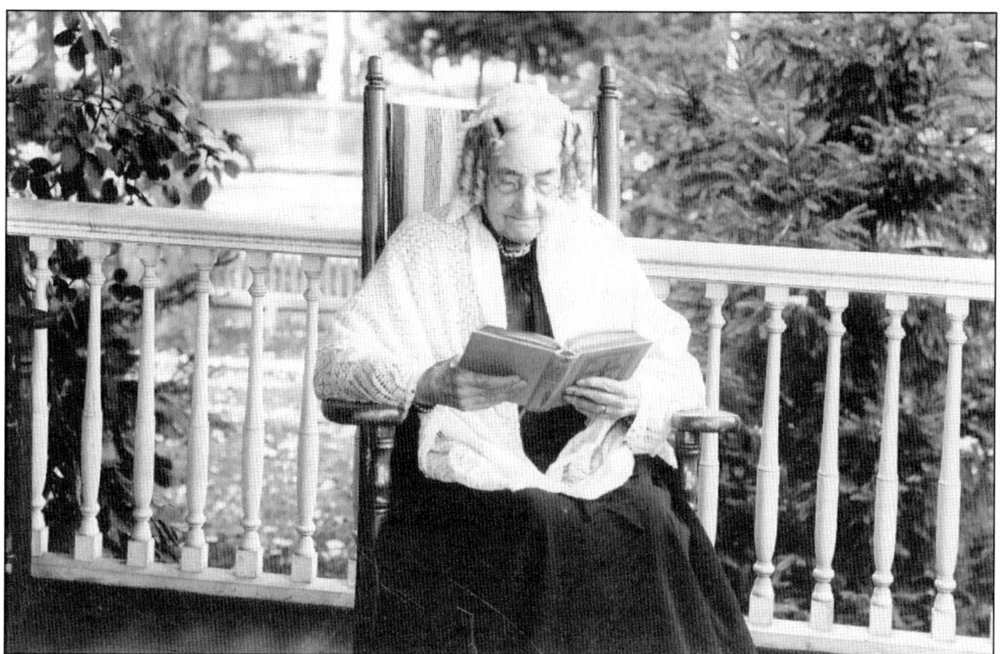

Caroline Hall Audubon, mother of daughters Maria and Florence and sons John and Benjamin, was the wife of John Woodhouse Audubon, the son of naturalist John James Audubon. Caroline moved into the Audubon house on East Broadway with her daughters in 1889. She is shown reading a book on the back porch of the house late in her life. She died on February 1, 1899.

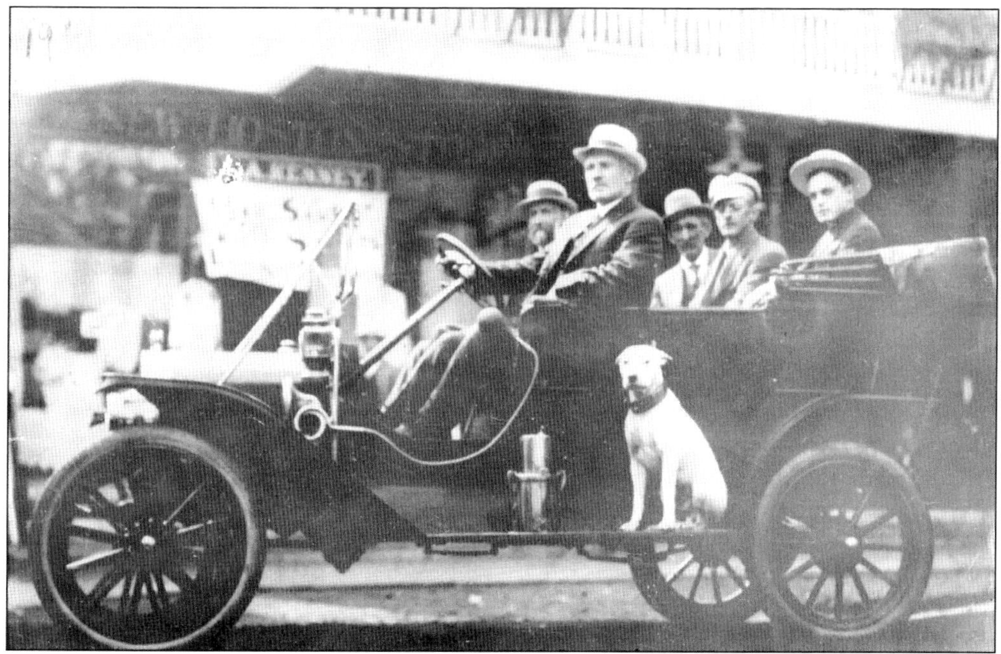

Thomas Lord, the Central House manager in the early 1900s, is shown with friends and his dog in his automobile in front of L.A. Kenney's Boston Store in 1914. Safety features seen on the automobile include a horn, a carbide gas generator for the headlights, and kerosene lanterns.

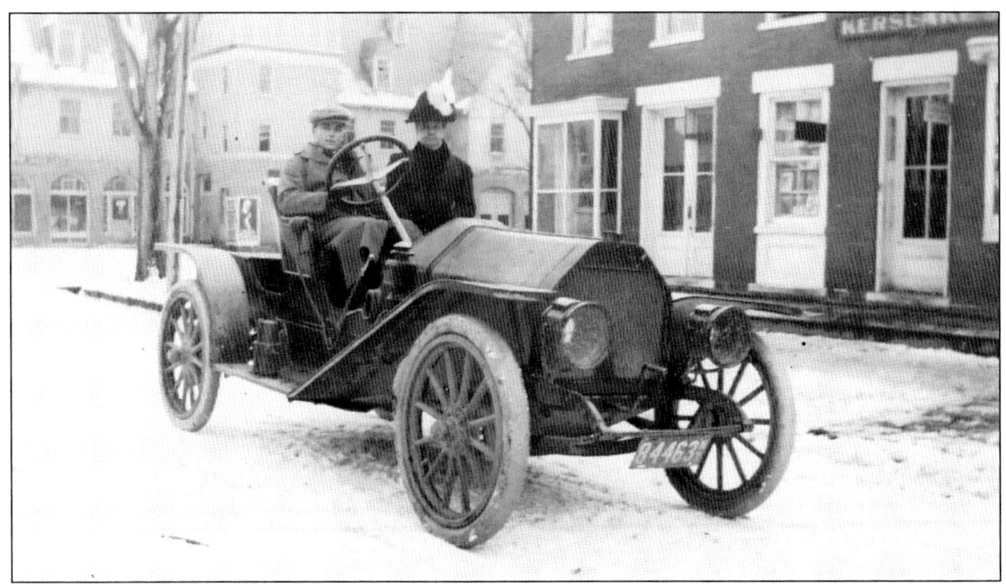

Andreas Lord, the son of Thomas Lord, is shown in an open-cockpit roadster with his mother, wearing a fancy hat and all, in front of the Red Store, located across the street from Proudfit Building, in this 1912 photograph. Before American automobile makers made the left-side steering wheel standard, many cars had right-side steering.

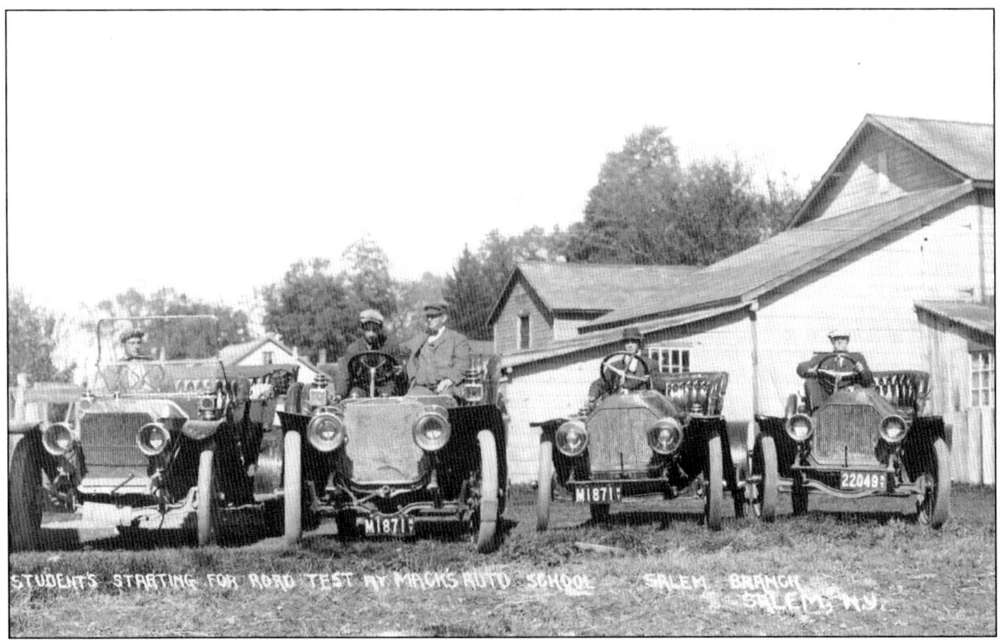

Automobile driving lessons and road tests for driving licenses were supplied by the Salem Branch of Mack's Auto School, shown at the ready on Archibald Street in 1910. All the early automobiles in this photograph had right-side steering wheels. The first woman in Salem to get her driver's license was Elsie Wright Rich, the daughter of Frank Wright, a Studebaker carriage dealer.

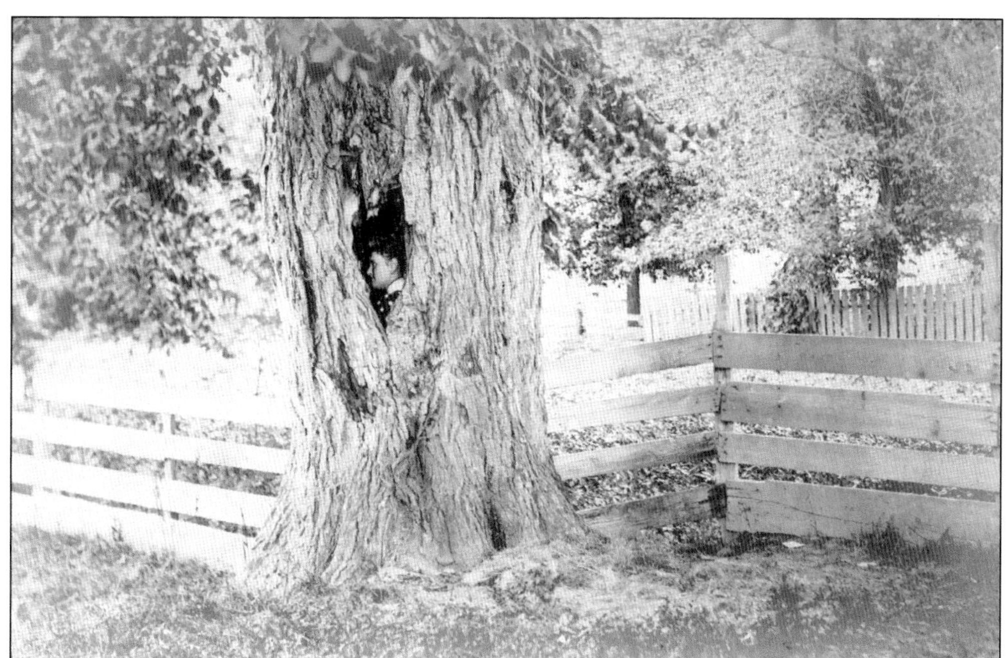

B.C. Kinney was a popular photographer with a studio in his building on North Main Street. When dry film plates and roll film made photography easier for photographers, candid shots, many of them joke shots, became popular. Here is a 1910 joke shot taken by B.C. Kinney of his wife, Jennie, who ran the dry goods store in the B.C. Kinney Block.

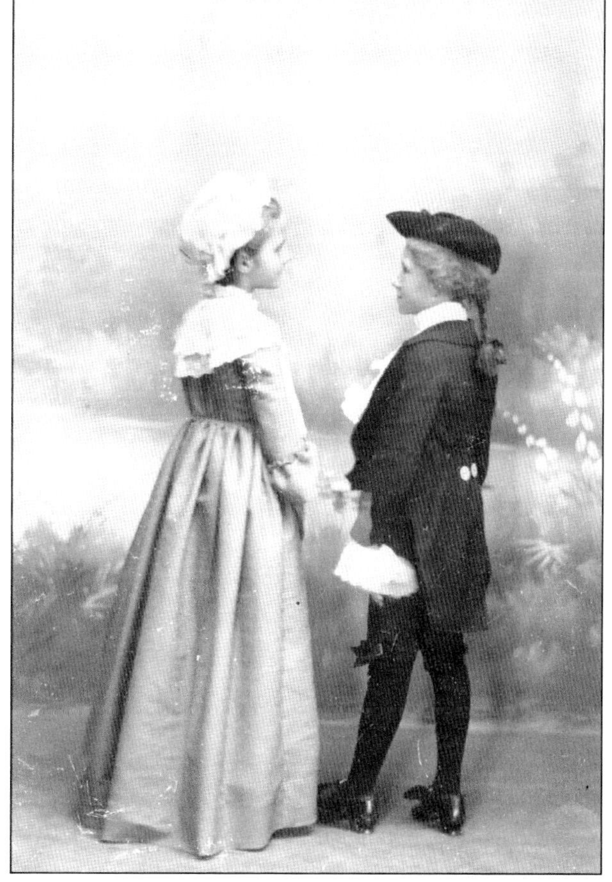

Jennie was not the only Kinney used by her husband. In this photograph, Clarence B. Kinney, their son, was the subject of a period costume photograph. Taken about 1900, the photograph featured him and friend Louise Goodrich in Colonial dress. Goodrich later became a teacher and taught English at Salem Washington Academy.

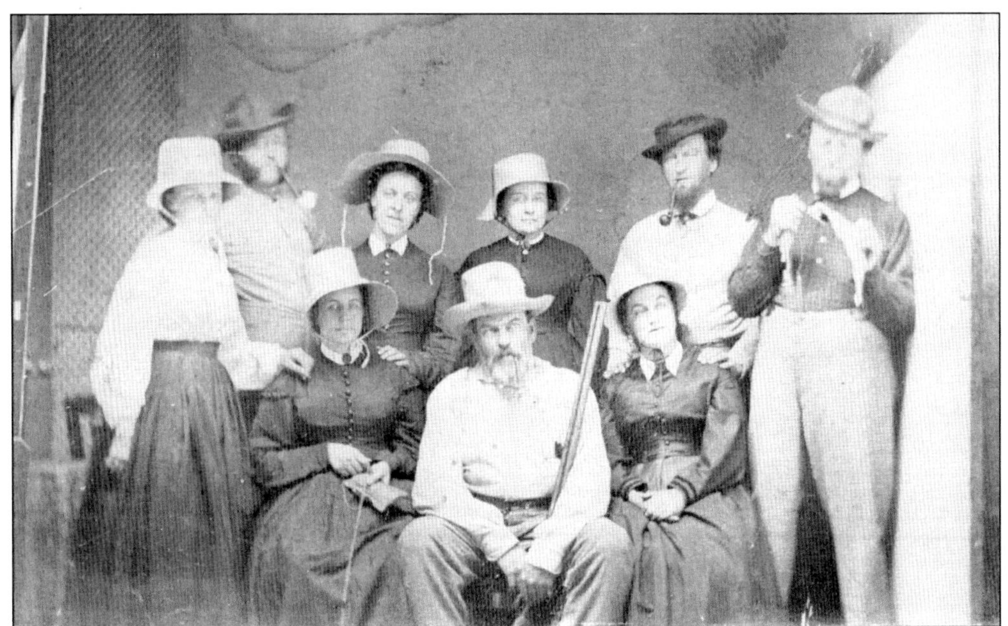

A group of Salem people on a fishing trip on Lake George in 1870 posed in their best woodsy clothing. Note the double-barrel shotgun in the center of the photograph, and the man on the right holding a fish. Pictured are, from left to right, (seated) Annie Austin, Dr. James Austin, and Jane A. Austin; (standing) Frances Austin, Henry Osborne, Sara Osborne, Eliza Freeman, Orrin Austin, and Harvey Freeman.

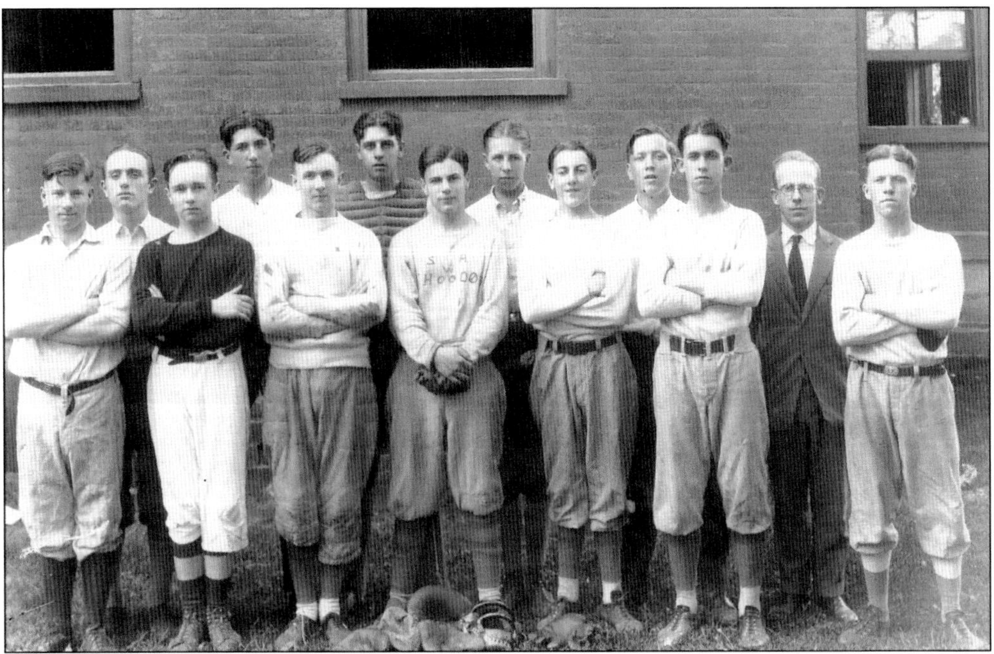

This 1926 photograph shows the baseball team and coach of the Salem Washington Academy on West Broadway. Those pictured are, from left to right, (first row) James Cowan, Lyle Bruce, Lawrence Bruce, Mike Gibson, Ken Greene, Bus Carrolan, coach Douglas MacCartee, and unidentified; (second row) unidentified, Jim Stanton, Bus Hedges, Doug McCarty, and John Lattenen.

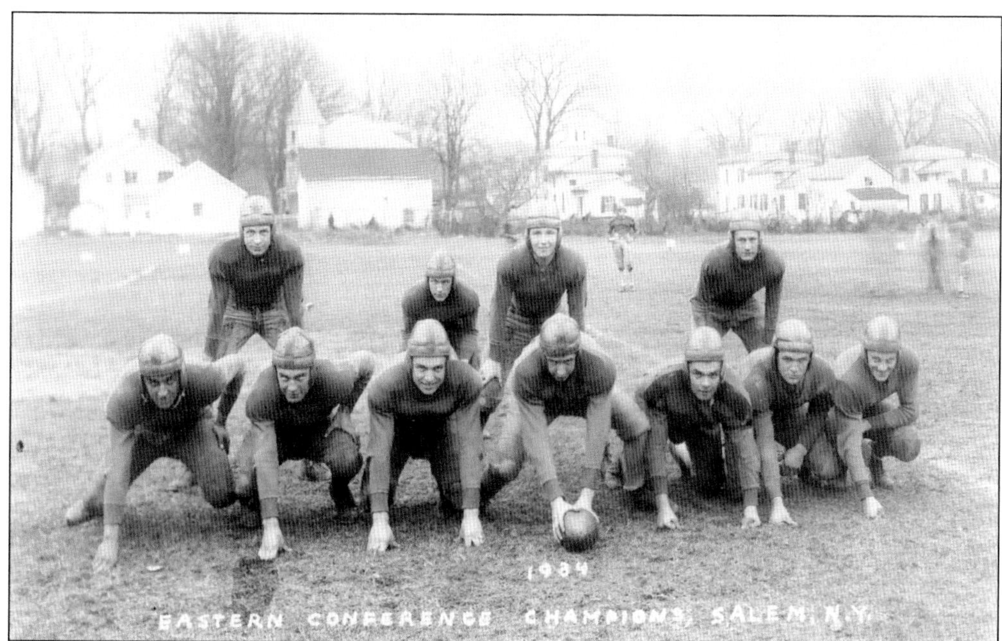

The Salem Washington Academy varsity football team won the eastern conference in 1934. The team members were, from left to right, (first row) Louis Capuano, David MacNeil, Carlos Cary, Leon Conety, Hugh McKinney, Donald Clement, and Gerald Gilchrist; (second row) Donald Hanks, Marius Hanks, James McIntyre, and Ralph Richter.

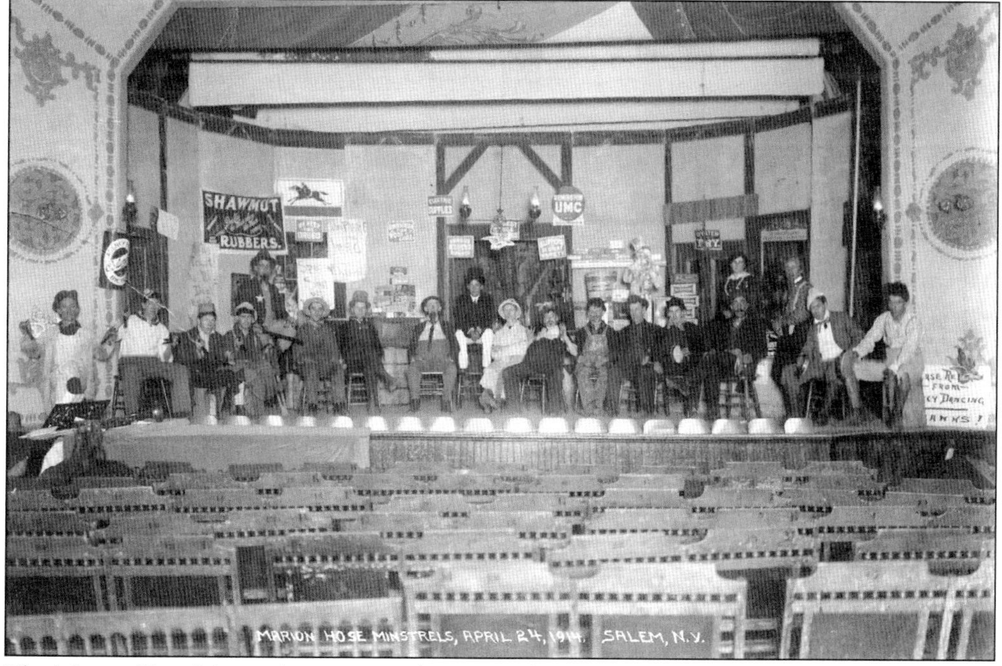

The Marion Hose Minstrels were one of many performing minstrel groups at Proudfit Memorial Hall. The fire hose company, named for Marion Williams, who gave the money to purchase the hose cart, appears to be putting on a rube minstrel show in 1914. Rube dances and shows were popular in the early 1900s, as Salem folk parodied rural folk, to the delight of the audience.

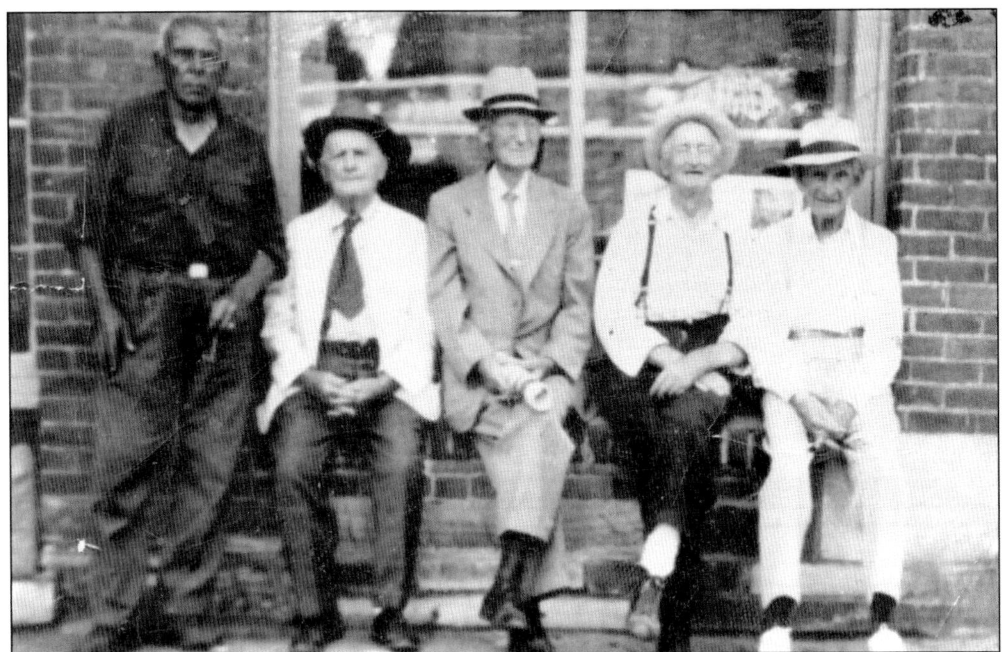

Main Street in Salem Village was a hub of activity and provided entertainment for any who wanted to loiter on the Proudfit Building's corner. Here, in the summer of 1940, Salem senior citizens spent their time watching the world pass by. Shown sitting on the windowsill of the building are, from left to right, Jake Wagner, Ollie Bebee, Charles Beattie, James Layden, and Dan Lasher.

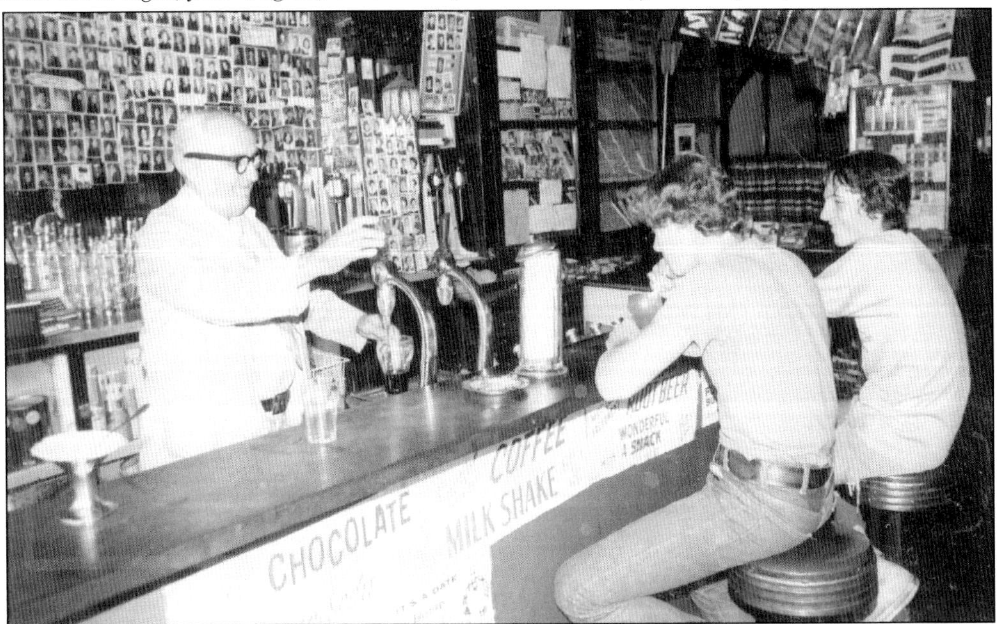

One of the most popular places with Salem Washington Academy students was "Jacko" Tomasi's Ice Cream Parlor, with its jukebox and pool table. Starting in the early 1960s, Jacko would paste a photograph of a graduating senior on the mirror behind the soda counter. By the time he died in 1982, the mirror was full. In the photograph are Jacko and high school students Bob Cormier (left) and Peter Hartney.

Seven

Hard Times

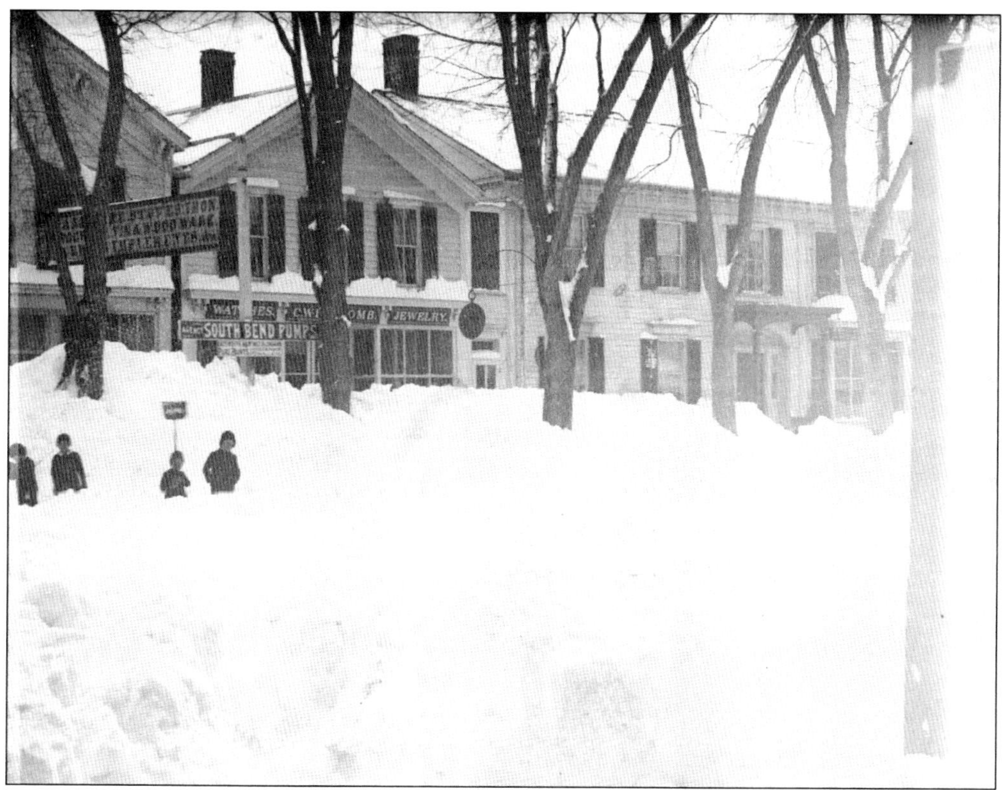

Life was sometimes interrupted by the unexpected. The great blizzard of 1888 brought life to a standstill in Salem and the surrounding area on March 12, 1888. Trains were stranded in snowdrifts, and highways were completely blocked for days. This photograph shows the east side of North Main Street in the Salem Village.

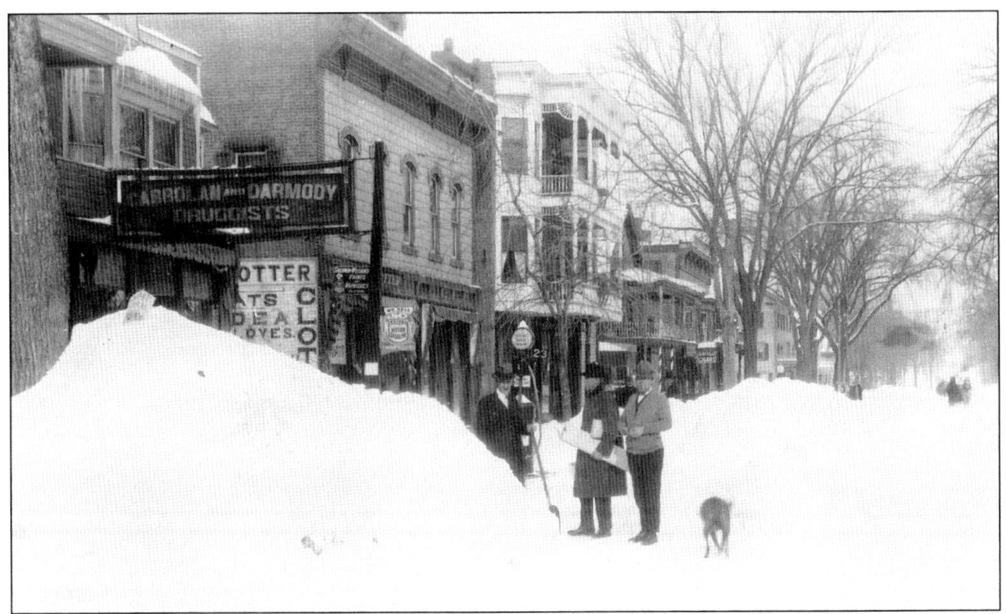

Another photograph shows the west side of North Main Street the day after the March 12, 1888, blizzard. Sleighs, like the one coming down the street in the distance, were the only way to travel the snow-covered roads. William Bruce, who worked as a railroad flanger, related that it took until March 16 to open the entire railroad line.

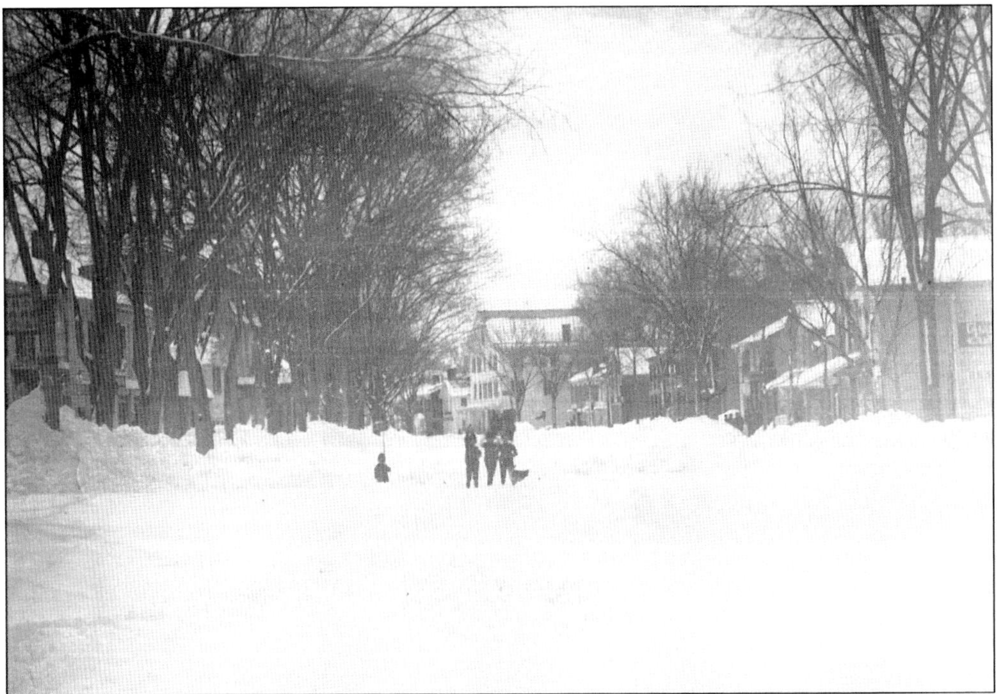

This North Main Street photograph looking south shows the extent of the 1888 blizzard. The roads were not entirely clear of snow until March 20, when the last of the historic snowstorm melted. The large white building in the center is the Fairchild House, which would burn to the ground a year later.

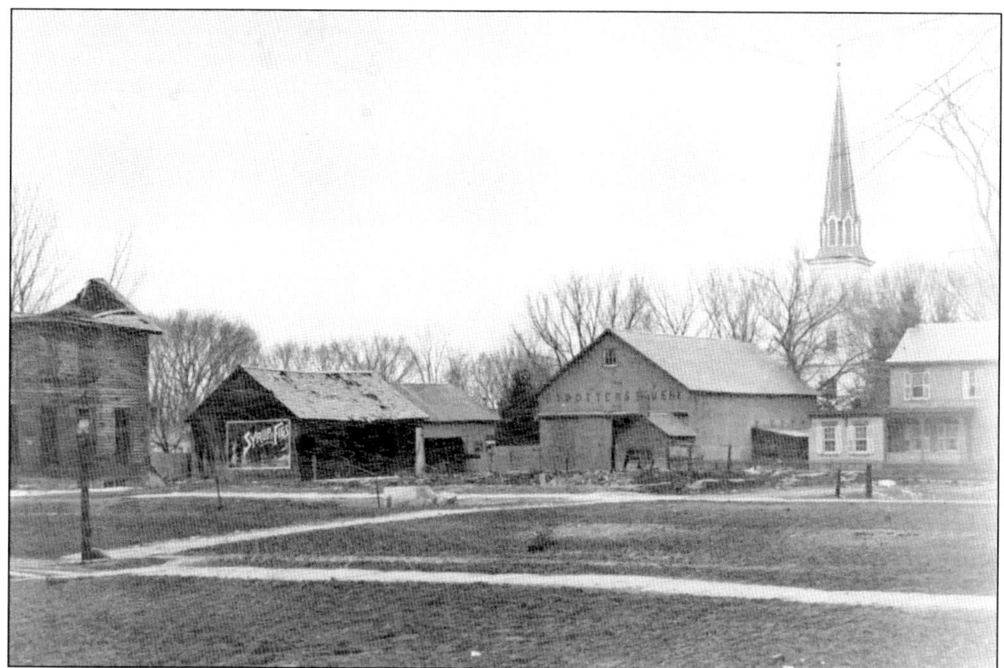

The burning of the Fairchild House, on February 27, 1889, destroyed a general store, law offices, and a roller-skating rink. Ruined buildings west of the Fairchild House included a meat market, a hardware store, and a marble shop. This 1889 photograph shows the damage to Potter's Livery and an adjacent building (left), which, at that time, housed the *Salem Review-Press* office.

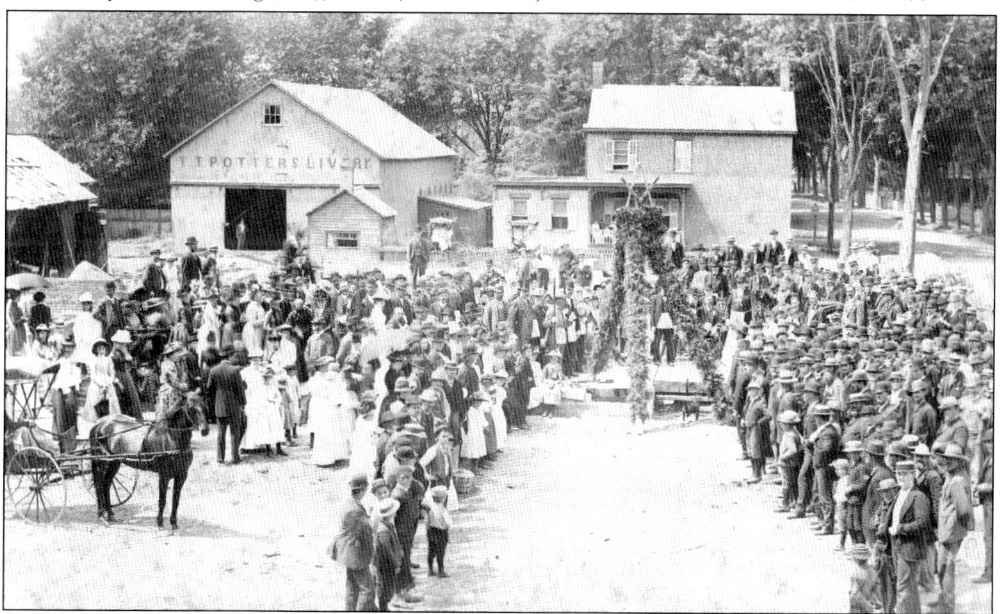

On July 30, 1890, members of the Salem Masonic Lodge laid the cornerstone for the Proudfit Building on the former Fairchild property. The building was to house an opera hall, a library, a clock and bell tower, offices, a public room, commercial rooms, and fire department rooms. Fanny R. Fairchild, the daughter and executor of her late father's will, donated the property to the village.

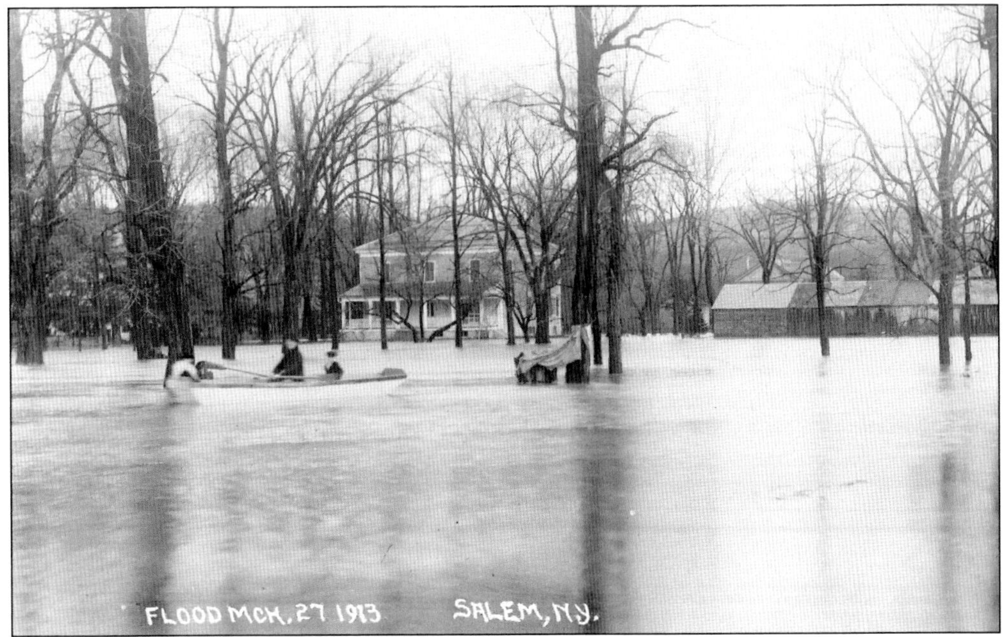

Floods were not uncommon, and White Creek, flowing through the village, flooded more than once. This 1913 photograph shows the field in back of the house at center, built by Gen. John Williams as a wedding gift for his daughter Maria and her husband, the Hon. Anthony James Blanchard, in 1796. To the right are the extensive carriage sheds of the New England Presbyterian Church (Brick Church).

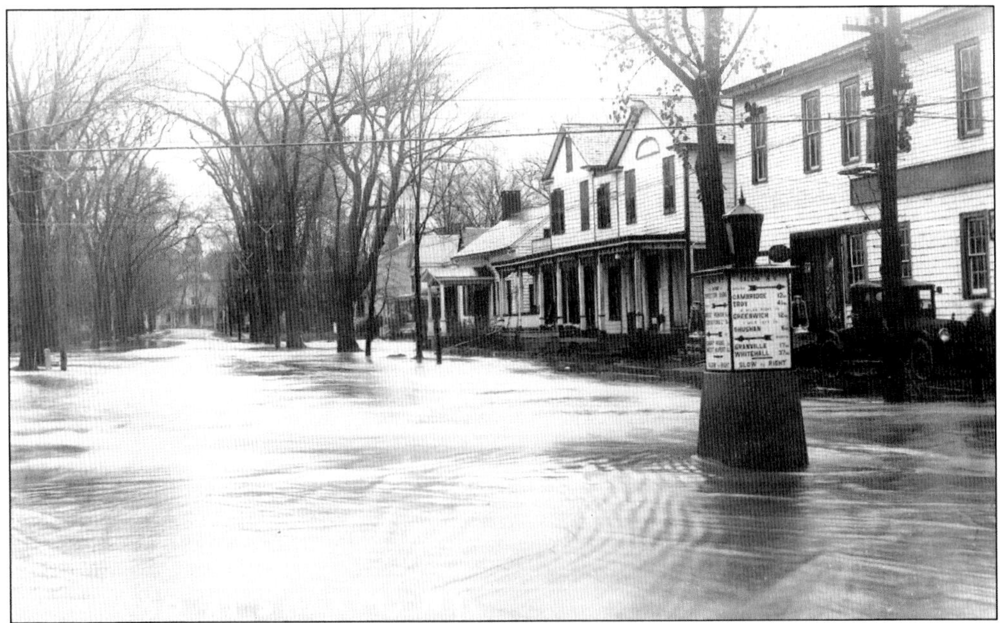

This 1927 photograph shows all of East Broadway underwater. In fact, most of the southern part of the Salem Village was submerged. The courthouse can be seen at the end of East Broadway. Note the improved mileage island in the center of the village—a sign that automobile travel had arrived.

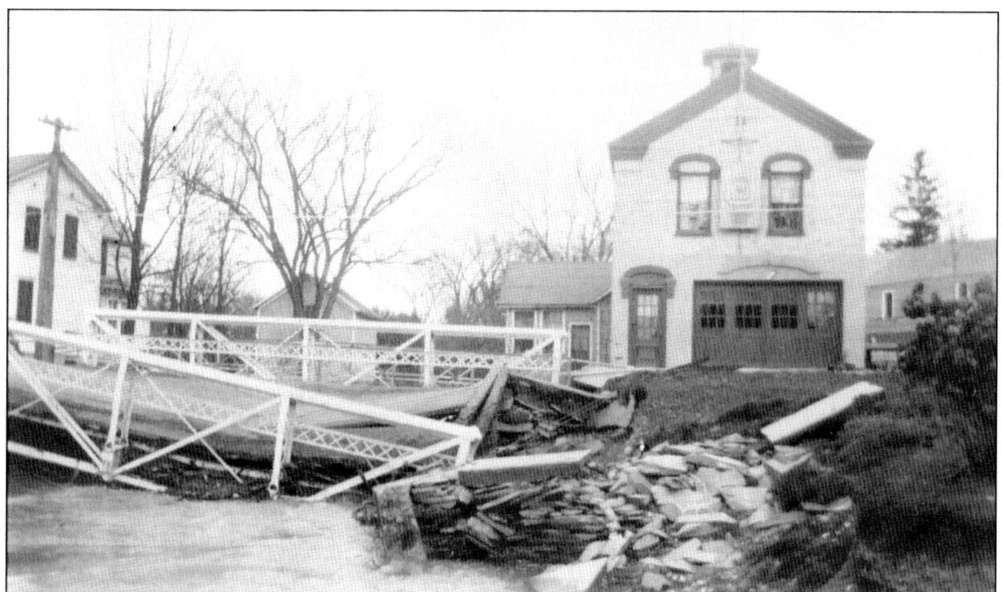

In 1927, flooding damaged property and roads in Salem Village. Here, the iron bridge on Main Street over White Creek was washed off its abutments, resulting in a more-modern iron bridge replacing it. The redbrick firehouse of Union Engine & Hose Company No. 1 (right) was undamaged.

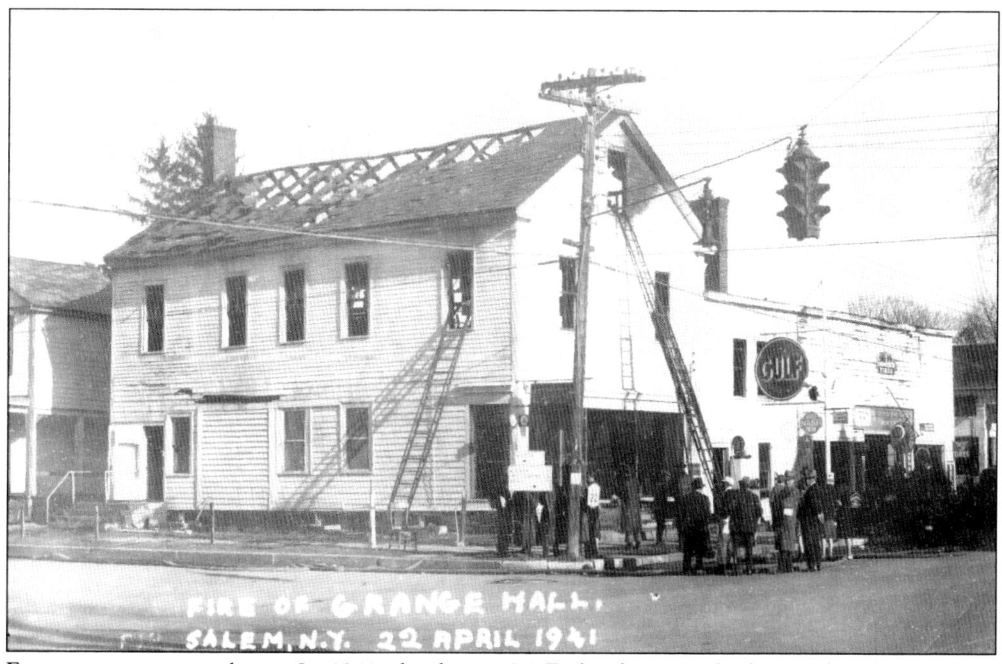

Fire was a constant threat. In 1941, the former McFarland store, which was then housing the Salem Grange, Evan's Grill, and Moore's Gulf station, burned. The building was not salvageable, and the Race Oil Company of Granville built a modern redbrick automobile station in its place. T.C. Moore & Son rented the station until 1978.

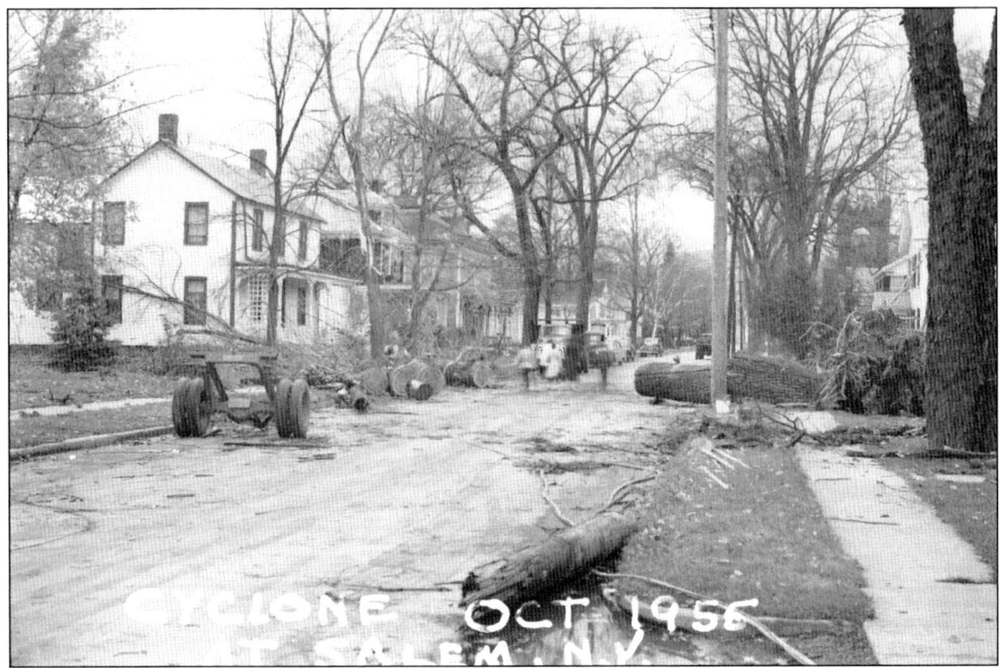

Water was not the only damaging element that hit the village. A cyclone in October 1955 toppled many elm trees in the village, causing serious damage to a number of homes and businesses. Telephone poles and electric and telephone wires were brought to the ground by the falling elms. West Broadway was hard-hit, as shown in this photograph.

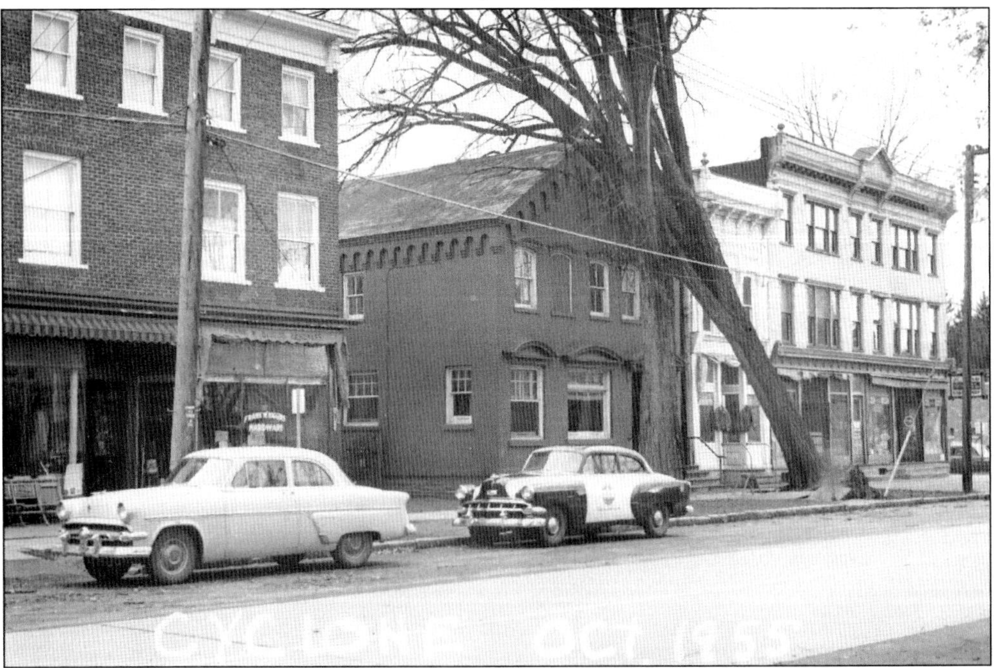

The huge elms on Main Street were also blown over in the 1955 storm. This elm tree rests against the Salem National Bank. The damage convinced the village trustees to cut down all the elms on Main Street in 1956, noting that Dutch elm disease had weakened the trees.

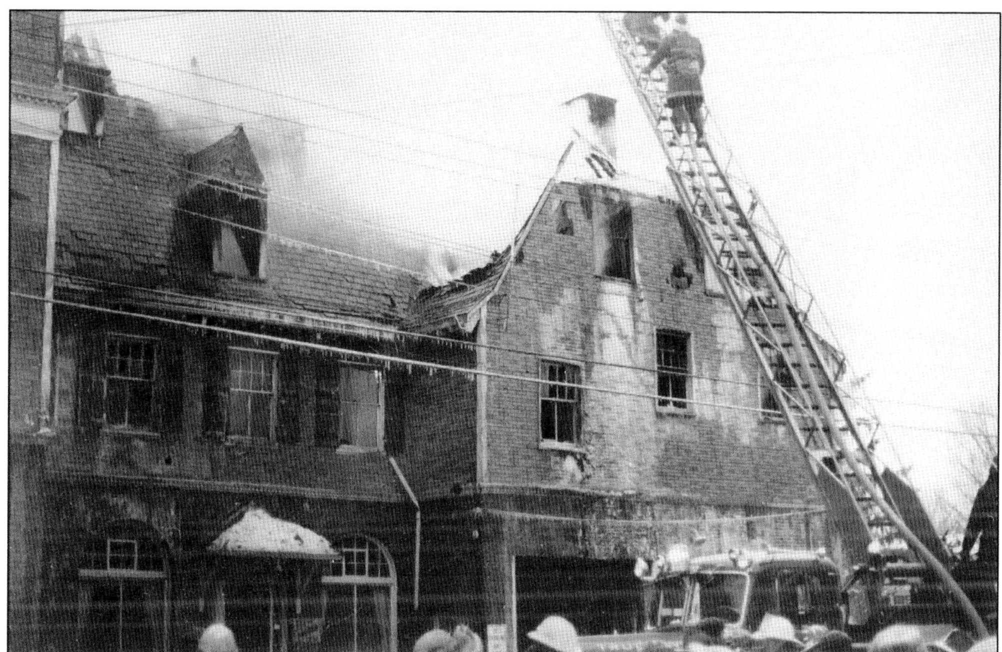

The Proudfit Building suffered the fate of all prior buildings on the West Broadway corner. On January 11, 1976, a fire destroyed all but the first floor of the building. Fire companies came from throughout the county to assist the Salem Volunteer Fire Department. The first floor was later restored for village use; it included Bancroft Public Library, a community room, the village office, and the fire department. (Photograph by William D. Cormier.)

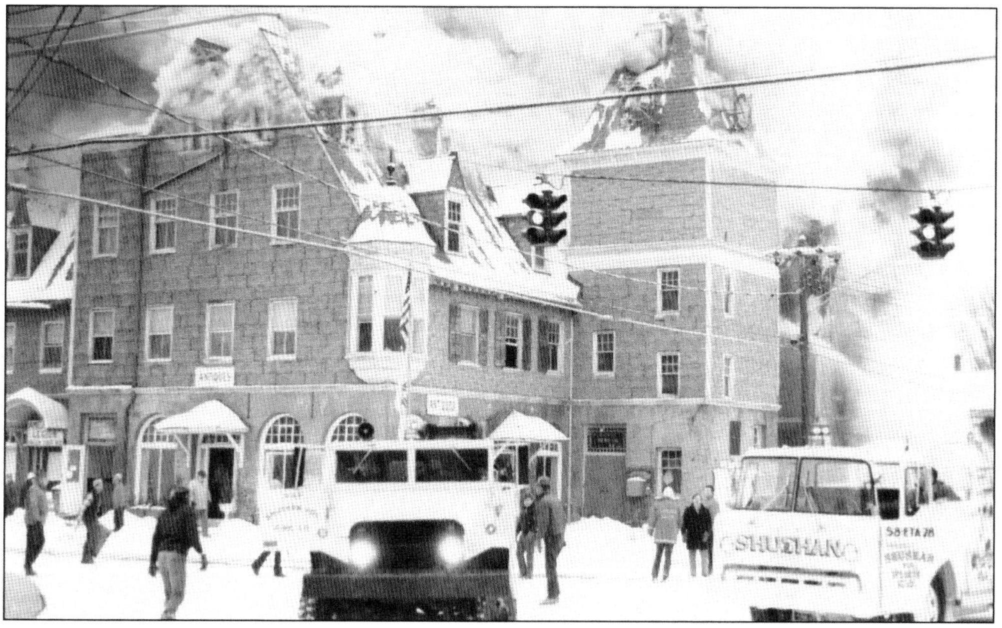

This 1976 photograph of the Proudfit Building fire shows heavy smoke pouring from the Irving Memorial Clock Tower. The clock's Maneely bell, made in Troy, New York, suffered a large crack from the heat, making it unusable. Today, the cracked bell is displayed at sidewalk level in front of Bancroft Public Library. (Photograph by William D. Cormier.)

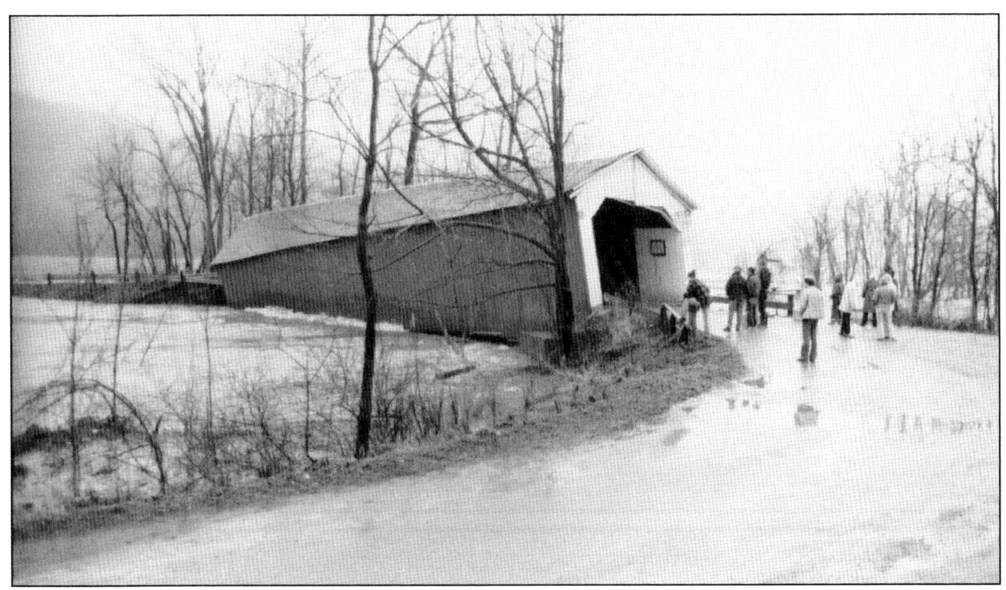

Another flood in the spring of 1977 knocked the 1858 Eagleville Covered Bridge off its abutments, badly warping the entire bridge frame and making the bridge impassable for traffic. The ancient Town's lattice truss, made with double-chord wood, could not withstand the power of the flooded river. (Photograph by William D. Cormier.)

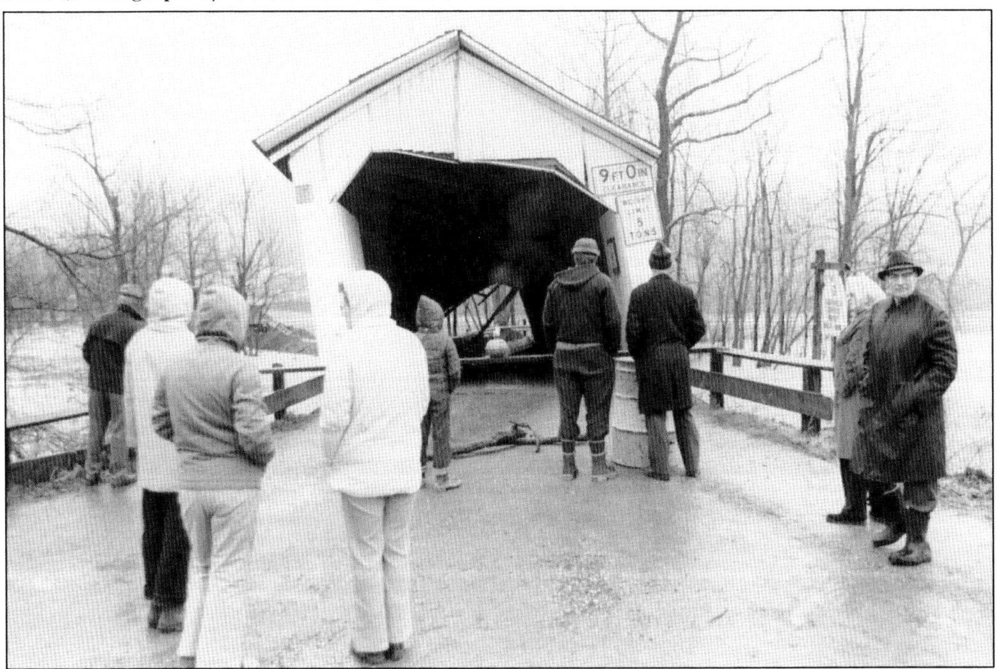

In 1977, the Washington County Board of Supervisors repaired the flood-damaged Eagleville Covered Bridge, but structural problems in the following years plagued the bridge, as well as the Rexleigh Covered Bridge. In 1994, the county, at the urging of Washington County Covered Bridge Advisory Committee, chose to properly restore the Eagleville and Rexleigh Covered Bridges. In 2007, the bridges, which are both listed in the National Register of Historic Places, were reopened to traffic. (Photograph by William D. Cormier.)

Eight

Parades and Patriotism

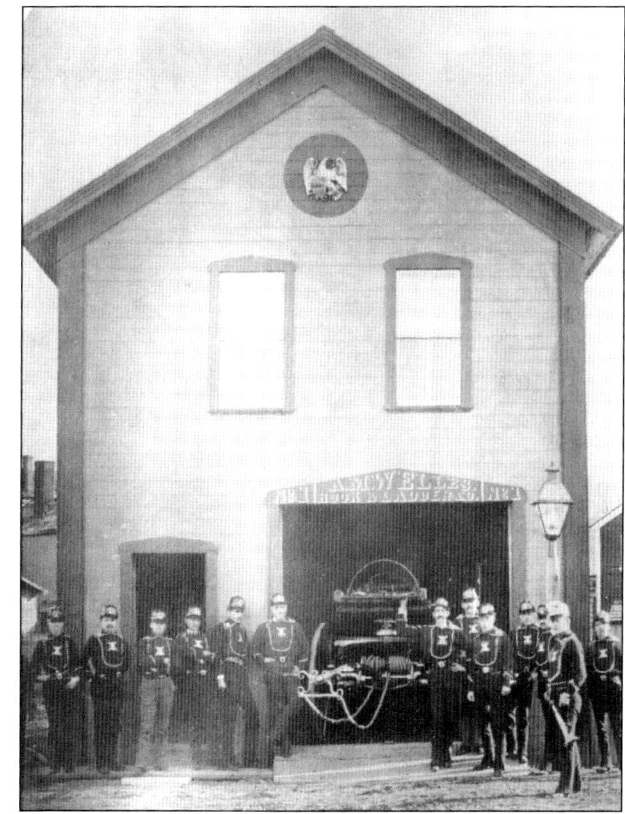

Members of the A.M. Wells Hook & Ladder Company No. 1 were ready to parade in 1890. The truck and ladders were purchased in 1875 from the Trojan Hook-and-Ladder Company No. 3 of Troy, New York, for $1,500. The truck was 55 feet long and had seven ladders, ranging from 15 to 55 feet. A new building was erected on Railroad Street to house the company.

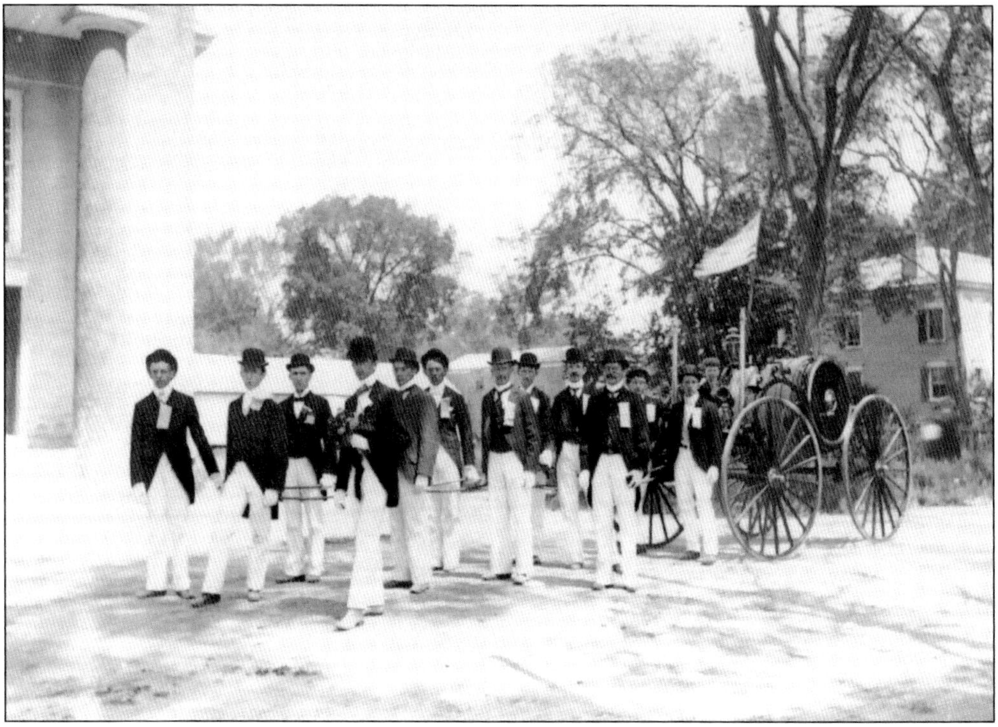

Members of the Marion Hose Company No. 2, organized in 1875, stand ready in their parade dress. The company was named for Marion Williams, the daughter of John M. Williams, who donated the money to purchase the equipment. This 1890 photograph was taken in front of the New England Presbyterian "Brick Church" on East Broadway. Today, the Marion Hose Company cart is on display at the Fire Museum of Maryland, in Lutherville, Maryland.

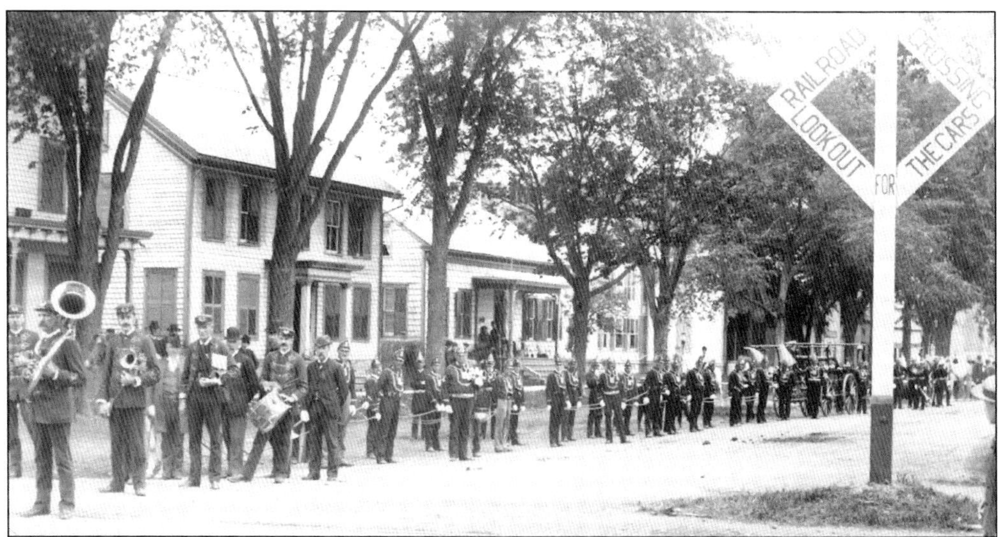

Members of the Salem Cornet Band and the Union Engine & Hose Company No. 1, in their parade dress, are lined up on North Main Street in 1890. The hand-pump engine pulled by the firemen was purchased in 1861. The hand pump was eventually housed in the redbrick firehouse, built on the south bank of White Creek in 1866, on land donated by John M. Williams.

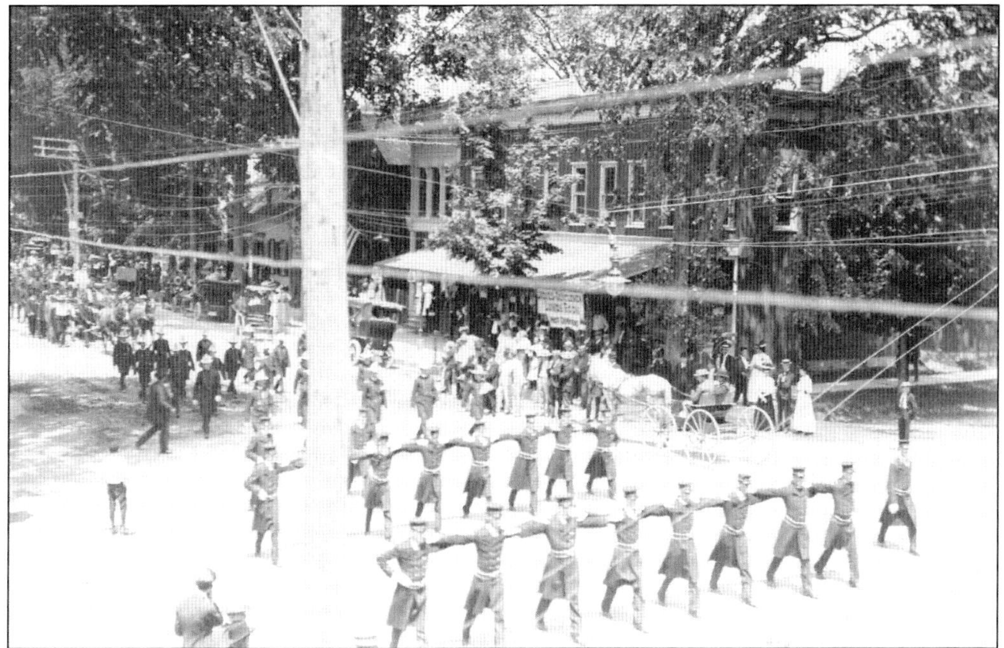

Held in a different town each year, the annual Tri-County Fireman's Convention was hosted in Salem in 1907. Fire companies came from far and wide to parade, show off their equipment, and participate in the hand-pump engine contest, measuring which hand-pump engine could throw a stream of water the farthest.

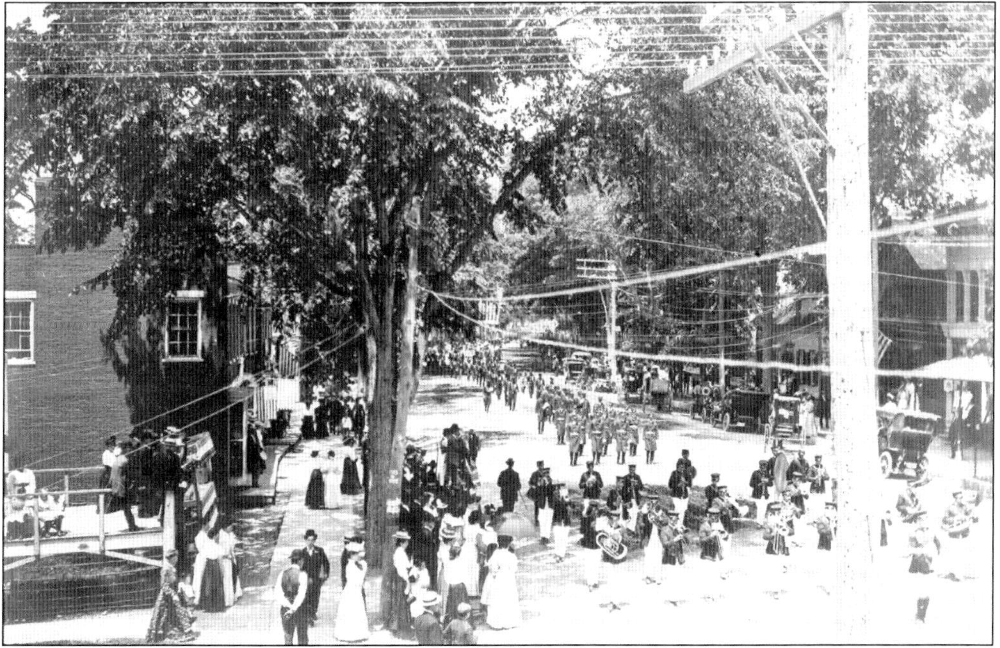

This scene of the 1907 Tri-County Fireman's parade shows the view from the Proudfit Building. A viewing stand is on the left, allowing a good view of the marching bands and fire companies in their dress uniforms. Horse-drawn buggies and motorcars lined the street for a closer view of the events.

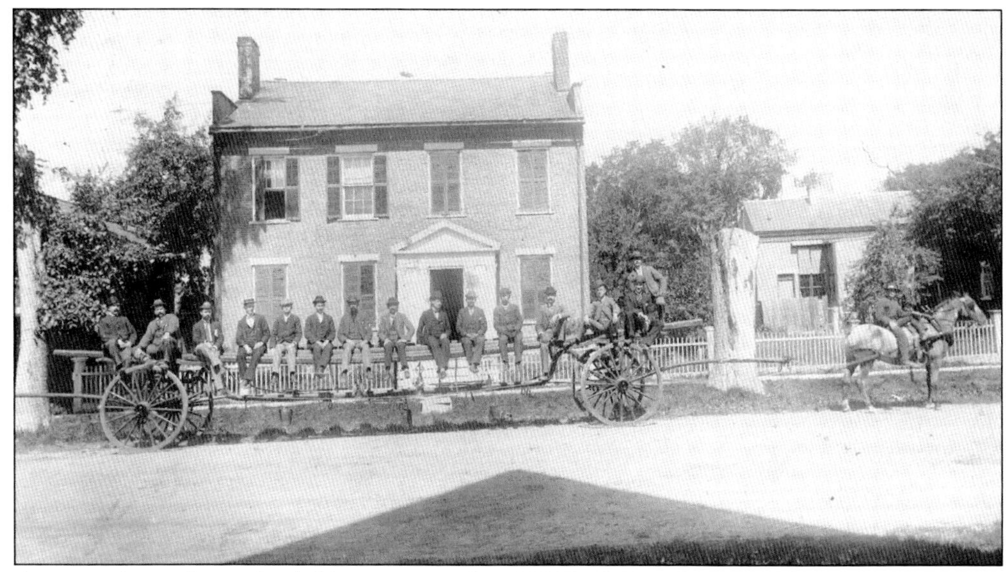

A visiting horse-drawn fire ladder wagon at the 1907 Tri-County Fireman's Convention is shown parked in front of a West Broadway brick house across the street from the Proudfit Building. The 15 men seated on the equipment give the reader an idea of the length of the ladders and the manpower needed to erect them.

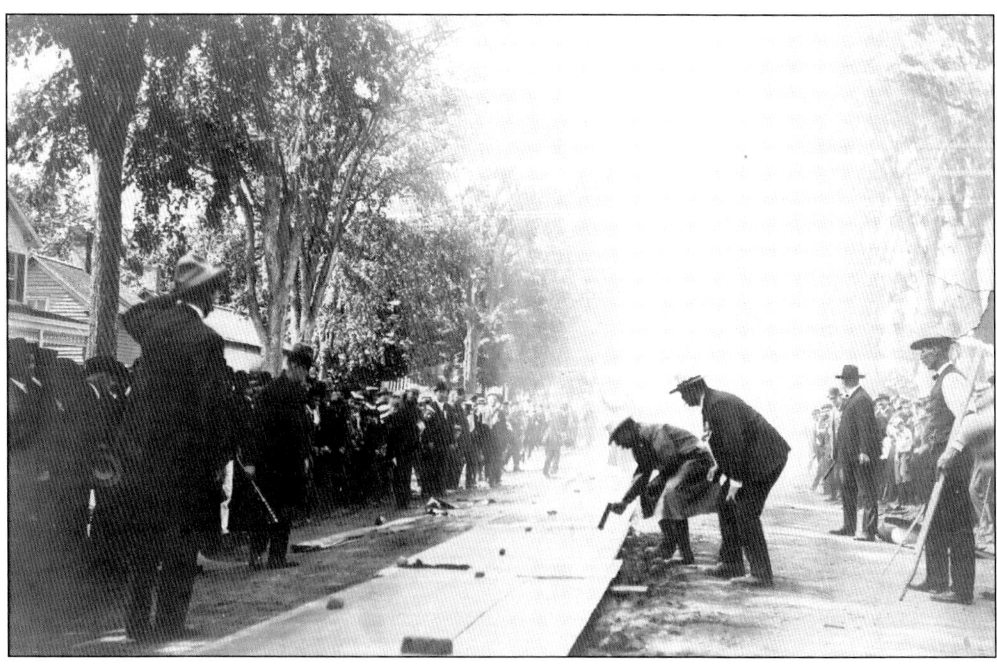

Judges are shown measuring the distance of a stream of water thrown by the hand-pump engines at the Tri-County Fireman's Convention. A total of $2,500 in prizes was awarded in 1907 for all events. Hand-pump prizes were $300 for first, $200 for second, $100 for third, and $50 for fourth.

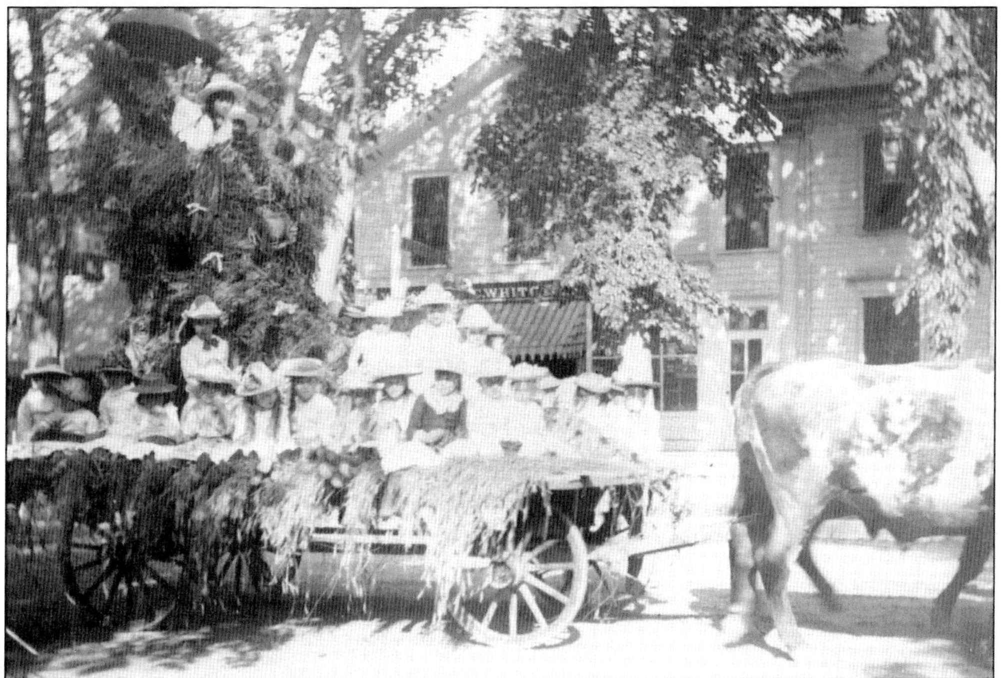

For many years, a "Harvest Home Parade," starting at St. Paul's Church, was held each fall in Salem. This 1884 photograph of the St. Paul's Episcopal Church float shows the children of the parish, decked out in their best festive clothes and hats, on a decorated wagon pulled by a pair of oxen.

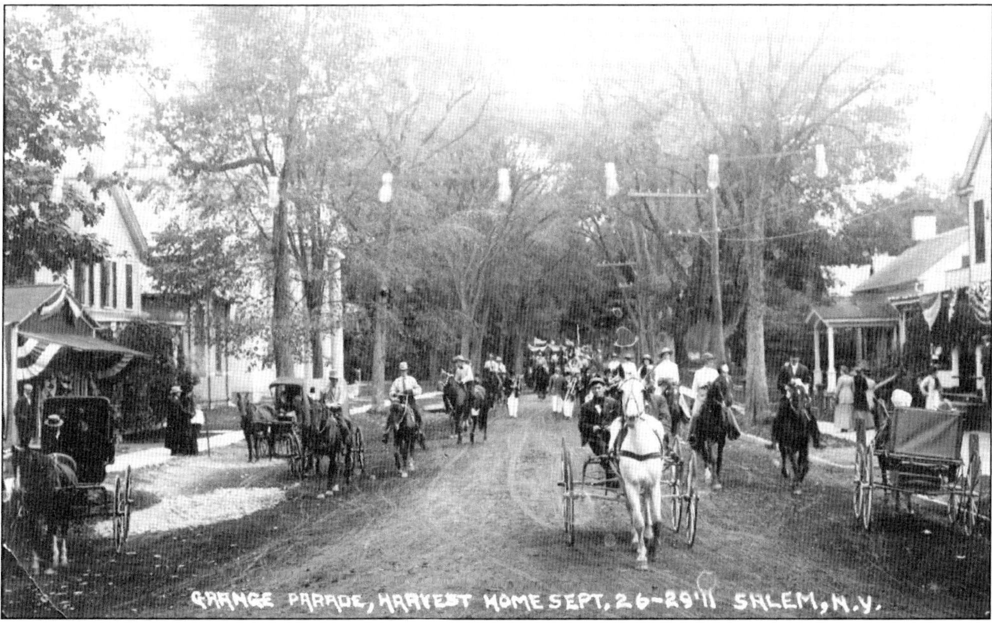

Salem Union Grange members, on horseback and buggy, parade down East Broadway in the 1911 Harvest Home Parade. The Grange was a popular nationwide farm fraternity organized in 1867 that promoted rural living, family life, animal husbandry, patriotism, gardening, and farming techniques. In addition to the Washington County Pomona Grange, most rural towns in Washington County had a Grange chapter.

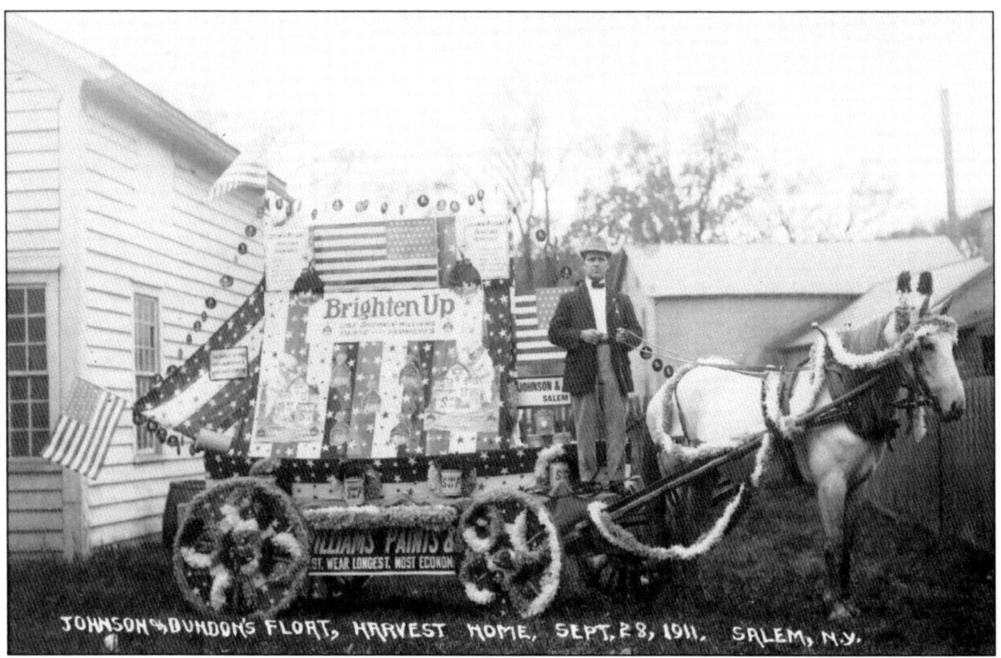

What better way to advertise than for Main Street merchants to have a float in the Harvest Home Parade? Johnson & Dundon Hardware Store encouraged all to brighten up their world with a new paint job for the house or barn. Sherwin Williams paints were featured. Even the horse appears brightly decorated.

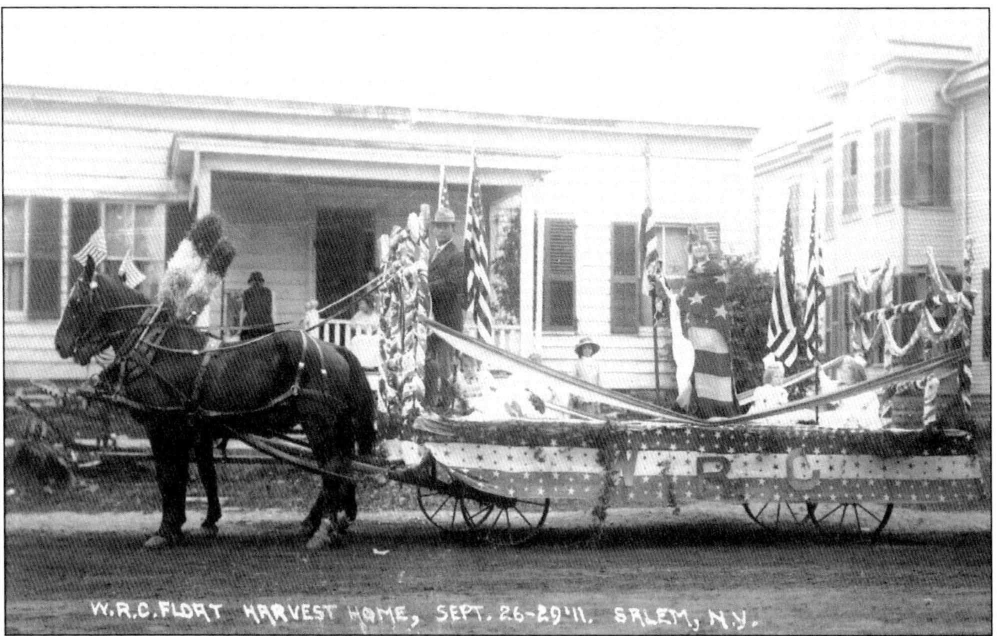

This 1911 float was decorated by the "W.R.C.," which appears to be an abbreviation for "Women's Rights Club." The women's rights movement was in full swing across the country, finally resulting in women's right to vote in 1920. The adult woman on the float is dressed as the Statue of Liberty draped in an American flag.

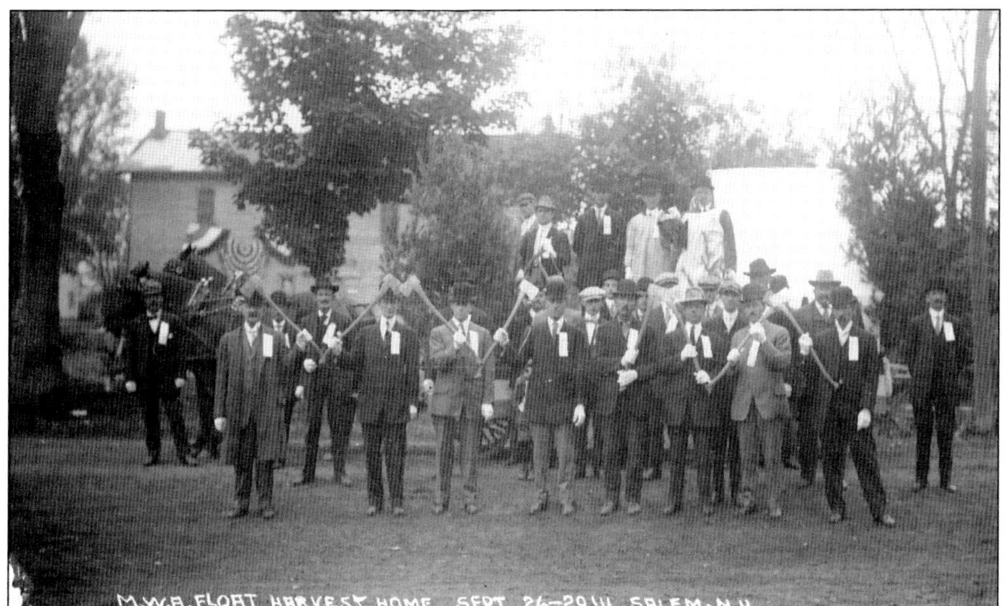

Members of the Salem Chapter of the Modern Woodmen of America, each carrying the symbol of their affiliation, posed in 1911 in front of their float in the Harvest Home Parade. Founded in 1853 by Joseph Cullen Root as a fraternal benefit organization, the Woodmen are today the third-largest fraternal organization in the United States. Salem's chapter has since disbanded.

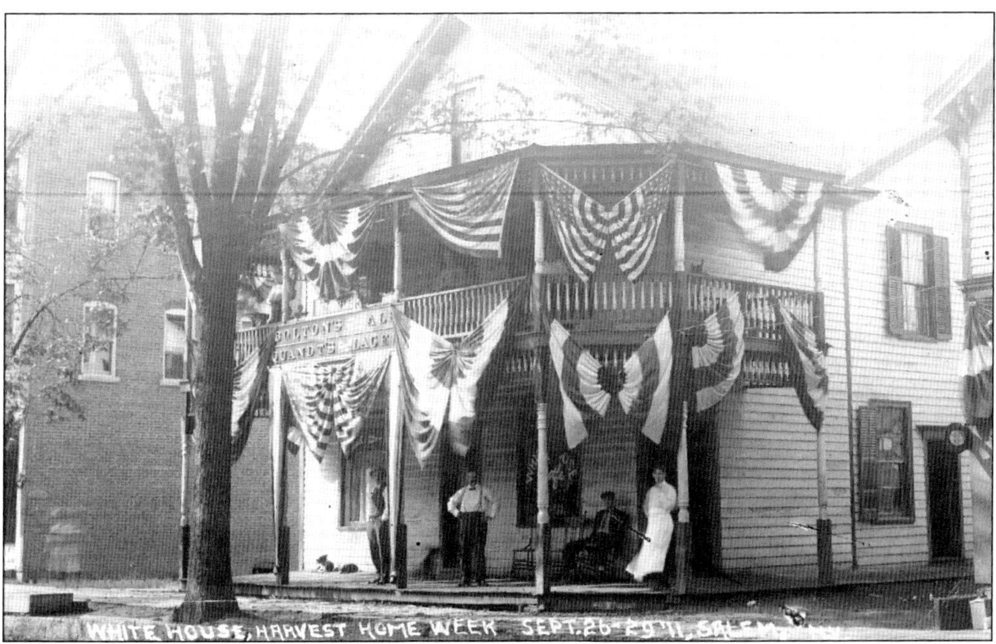

Buildings on Main Street were decorated for the 1911 Harvest Home Parade. The White House Café, owned by Charles Clark at this time, had rental rooms on the second floor. The beer signs on the building imply the more popular business. The building was destroyed by fire in 1940. In 1942, Vivian Sweet replaced the building with a brick structure that housed the Star Theatre, a movie house.

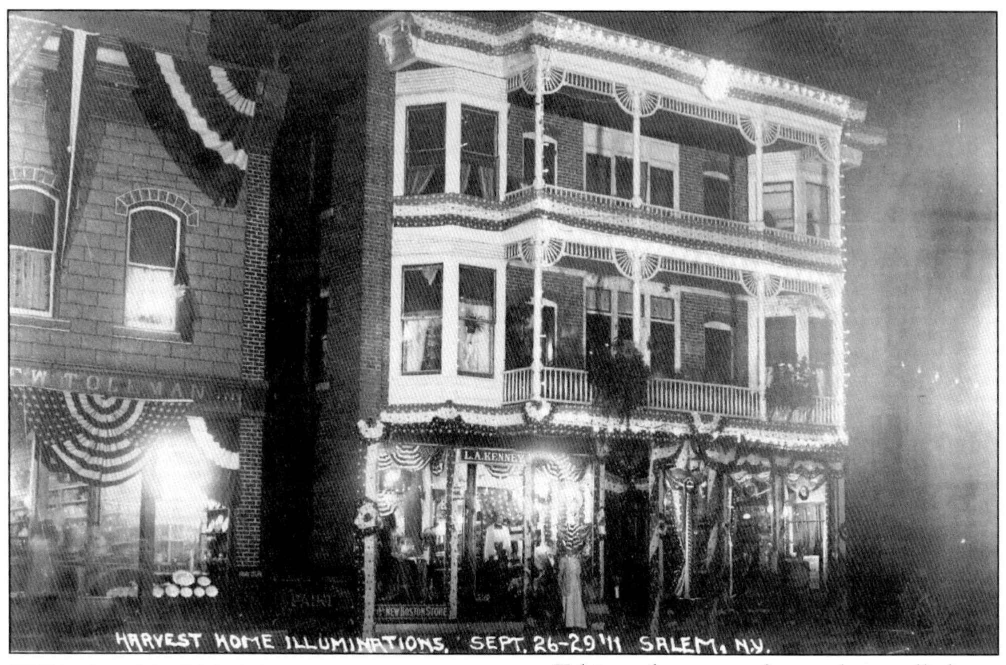

Taking advantage of recently installed electrical lines in the village, many buildings illuminated their businesses for the three-day September event. Lighted up are the F.W. Toleman store (left), L.A. Kenney's Boston Store (right), and the porches of the apartments on the second and third floors.

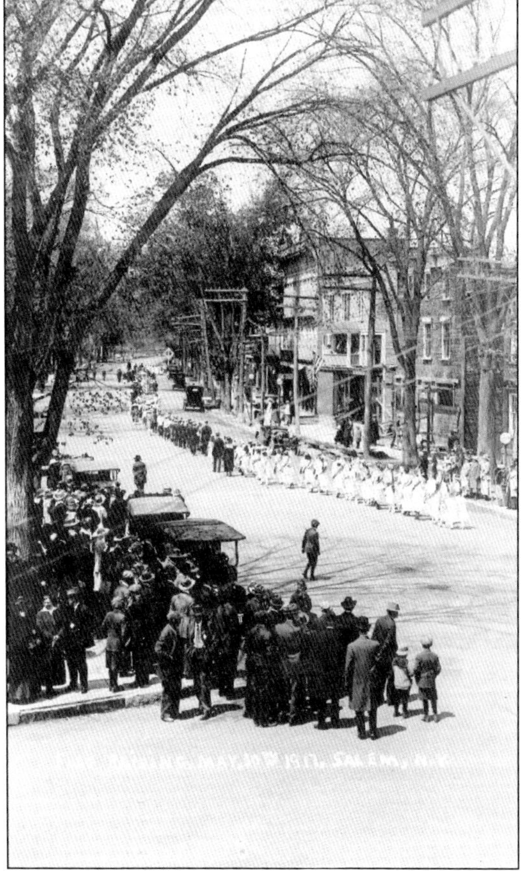

This 1917 parade is shown marching up North Main Street. After the Civil War, May 30 was designated as the day to remember the Union dead, and Grand Army of the Republic chapters decorated the soldiers' graves. May 30, 1917, was the last time Union soldiers alone were memorialized. After World War I, the federal government designated the day as a Memorial Day for fallen soldiers of all wars.

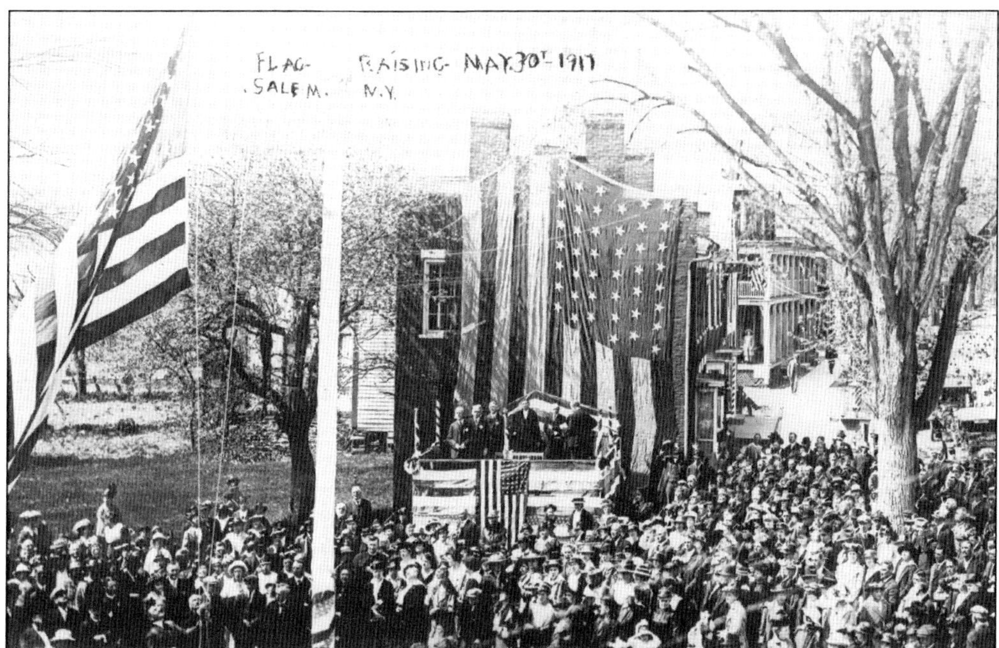

This photograph shows the flag being raised on May 30, 1917, in front of the Proudfit Building, while a large crowd watches the event. A larger flag is draped over the Red Store, across the street. Dignitaries are gathered on the speaker's stand in front of the building. The Ondawa Hotel can be seen in the background.

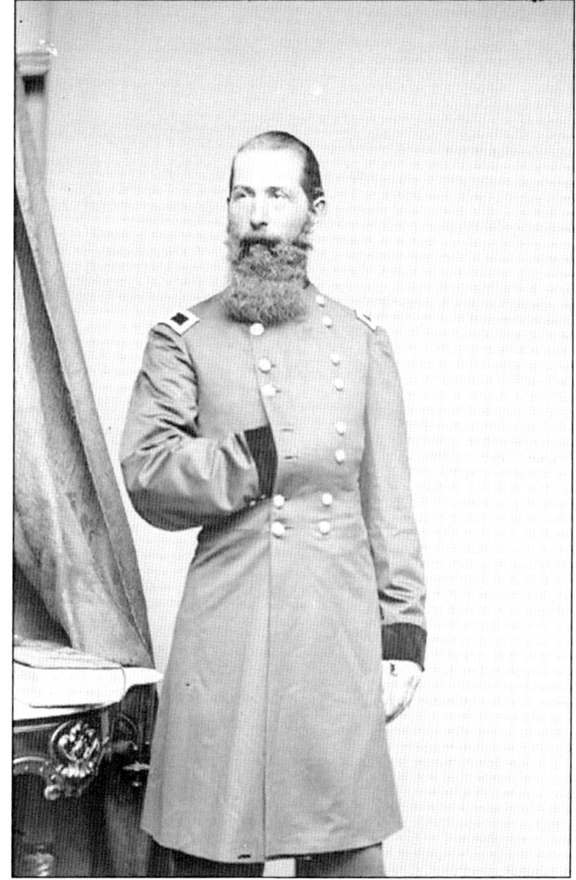

Gen. David Allen Russell, shown as a colonel in this photograph, was a graduate of Salem Washington Academy and West Point. Upon graduation from West Point, he went west to fight in the Indian wars with Philip Sheridan, who became a close friend. Russell, fighting with the 6th Army Corps in the Civil War, died in the Battle of Winchester on September 19, 1864.

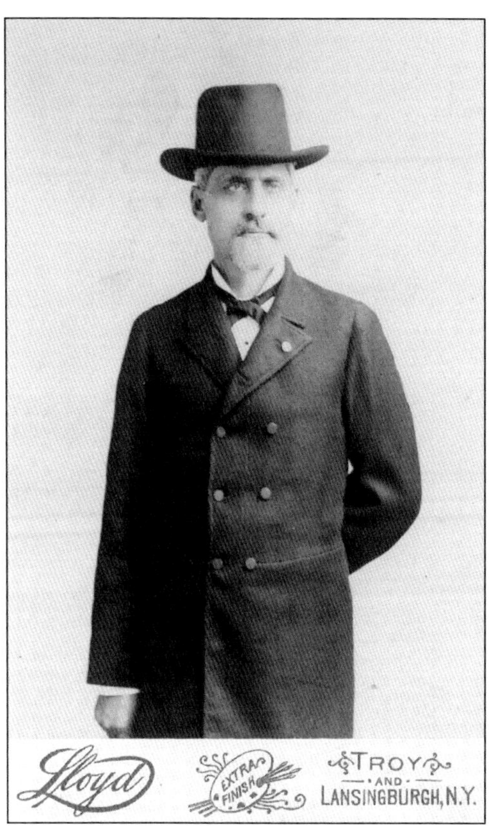

Col. Solomon R. Russell, shown in this 1891 photograph, enlisted in the Civil War on September 9, 1861, and served with a number of regiments during the war. After being severely wounded at the Battle of Rappahannock in 1863, he was assigned as adjutant to his cousin David Allen Russell of the 6th Army Corps. In 1916, he was elected commander of the New York Grand Army of the Republic.

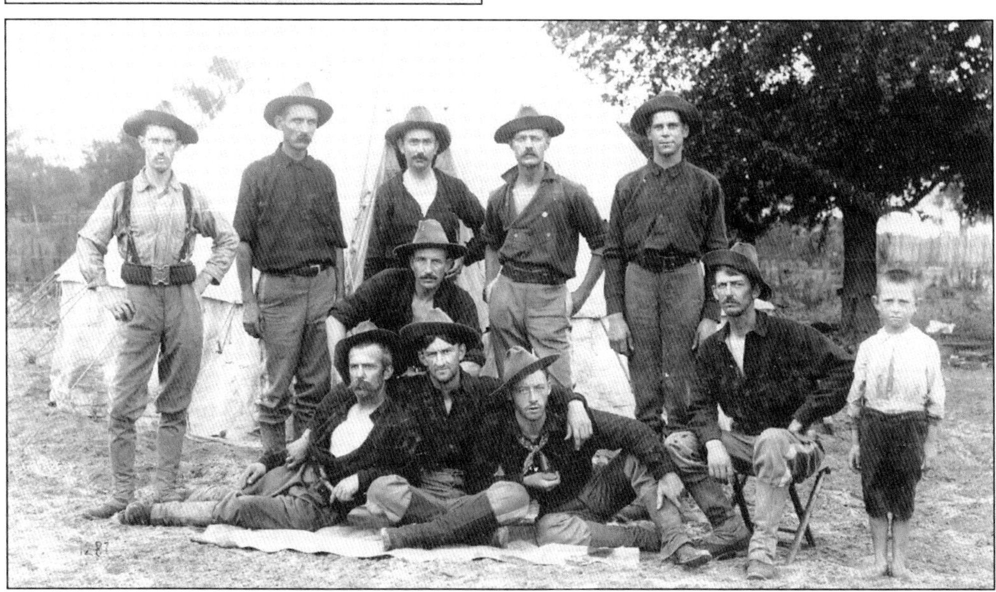

This photograph, taken in 1898, shows some members of Whitehall Company I, 14th Battalion, during the Spanish-American War. The photograph is identified as being taken in Sanford, Florida, where the men were perhaps waiting to be deployed to Cuba, if needed. Salem men in the photograph are (standing) George McCartee (left); a Mr. Baker (third from left), and Albert Davis Broughton (fourth from left).

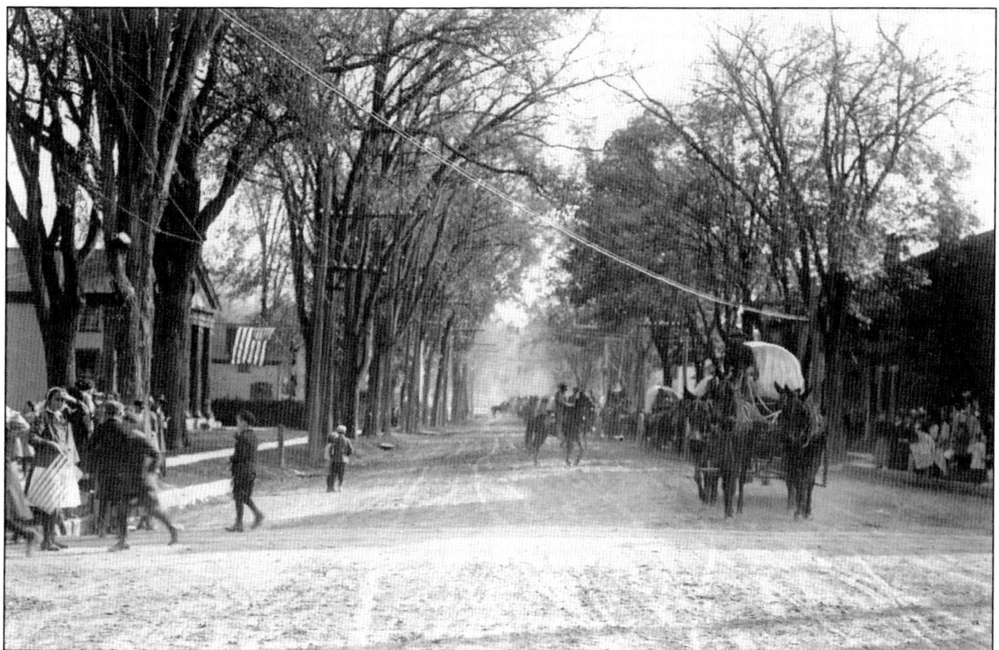

On more than one occasion, Congressman James Parker and his wife, Marion Williams Parker, invited the segregated 10th US Cavalry to bivouac in a pasture at the foot of Woody Hill, across the street from the Williams-Parker mansion. This 1912 photograph shows them entering the village after attending the dedication of the Saratoga Battlefield Monument in Schuylerville.

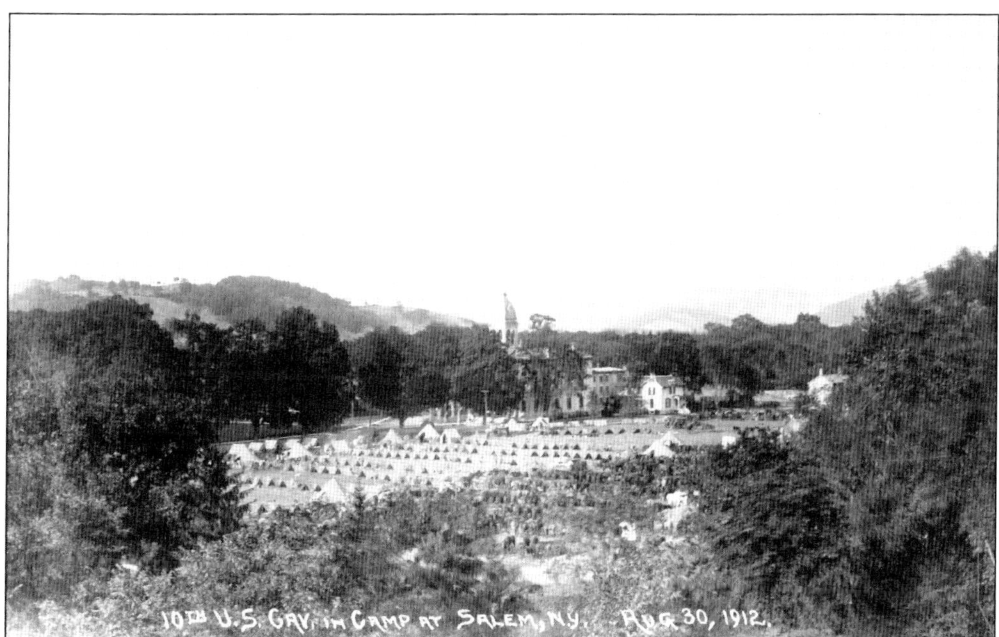

This 1912 view from Woody Hill shows the entire 10th Cavalry bivouacked in the pasture across from the Williams-Parker mansion. The Washington County Courthouse and Jail can be seen in the background. The "Buffalo Soldiers" were stationed at Camp Ethan Allen in Colchester, Vermont, where they were stationed for four years.

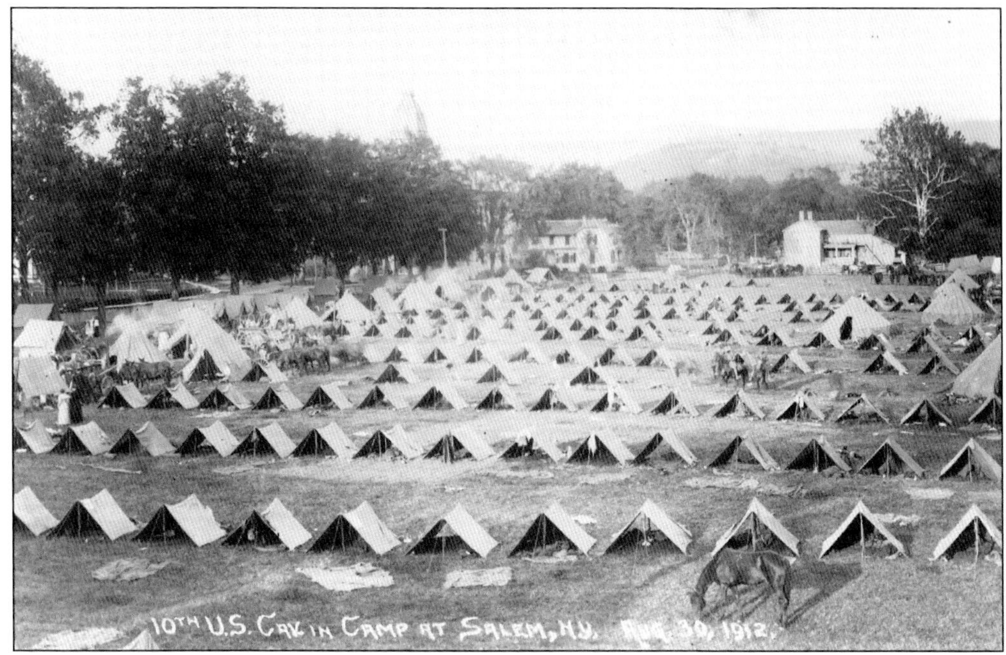

Two-man pup tents sheltered the Buffalo Soldiers from the weather. The Arizona Indians gave the 10th Cavalry the name "Buffalo Soldiers" because of their interaction with the buffalo herds on the prairie during the Indian wars. Note the grazing and saddled horses throughout the camp. The jailor's house can be seen next to the Washington County Courthouse and Jail.

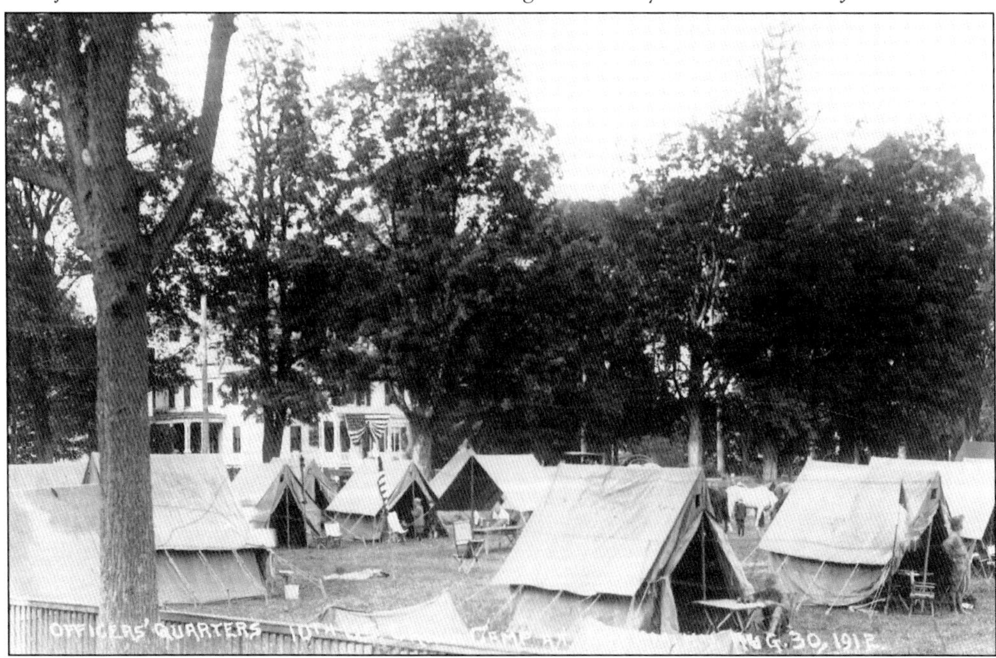

Larger, more-comfortable tents with tables and chairs made up the 10th Cavalry officers' quarters. Congress created the segregated 10th Cavalry on July 28, 1866, following the Civil War. The Williams-Parker mansion, draped with an American flag, can be seen in the background. The public was invited to view the campgrounds and attend a military band concert.

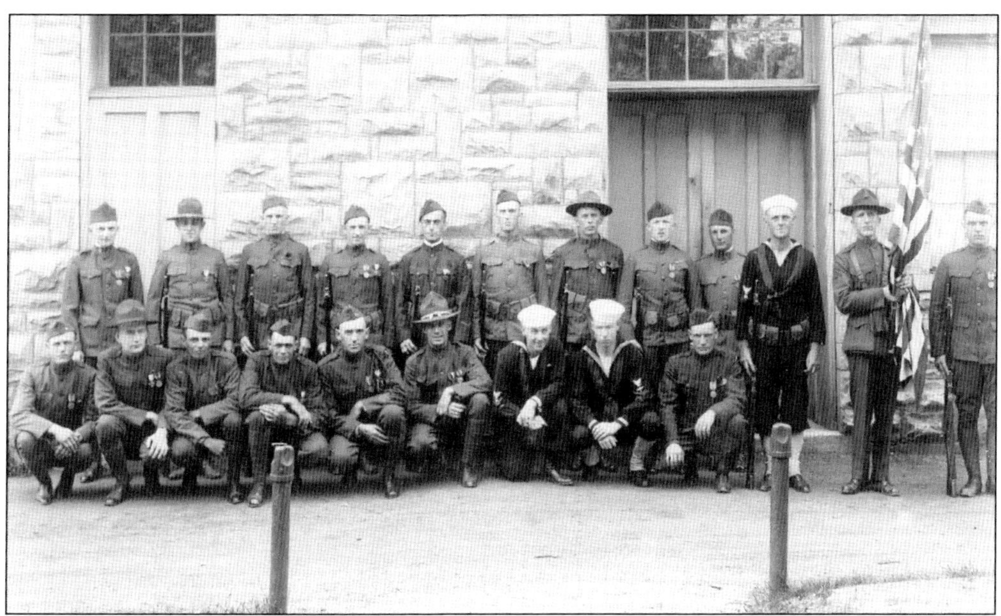

Returning World War I veterans posed for this 1918 photograph in front of the Manhattan Shirt Shop. Pictured are, from left to right, (first row) James Stewart, Gordon Dillon, Stewart Green, Joe Roberts, Bill Powers, Earl Toleman, George Roche, Carleton Sampson, and Alex Fisher; (second row) T. Orley Rogers, Mark Abrams, Jay Crosier, H. Rogers, Percy King, Cassie Lincoln, Ray Blanchfield, unidentified, Irving McNeil, and James Moore.

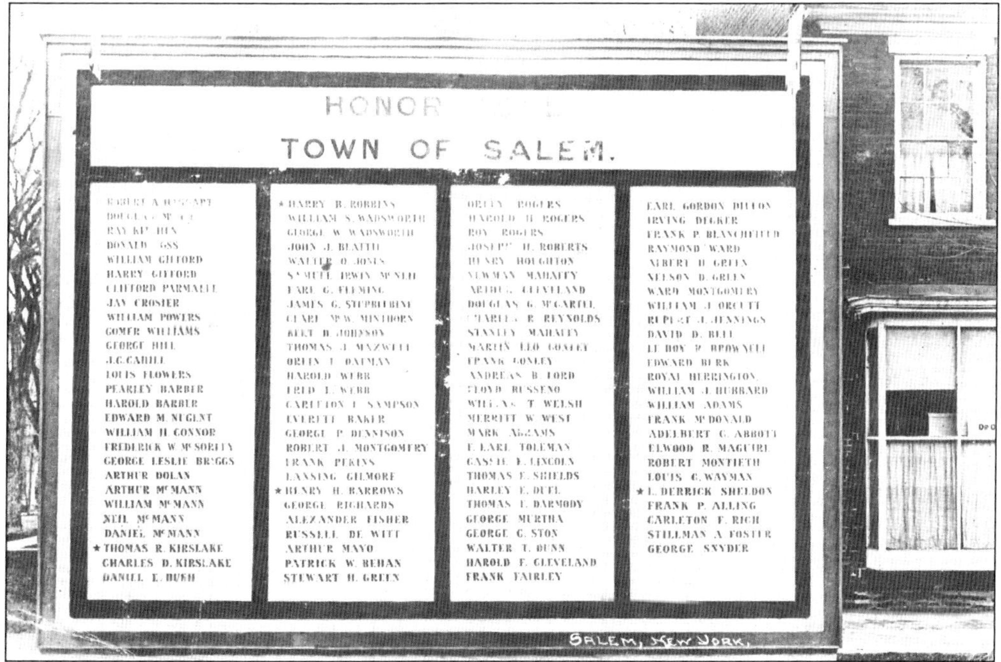

The World War I Honor Roll was displayed on Main Street. A total of 104 men served in the war, and four died during the war: Henry H. Barrows, Thomas R. Kerslake, Harry H. Robbins, and L. Derrick Sheldon. The *Salem Press* of January 24, 1918, announced that William Gifford of Salem fired the first American cannon shell in France.

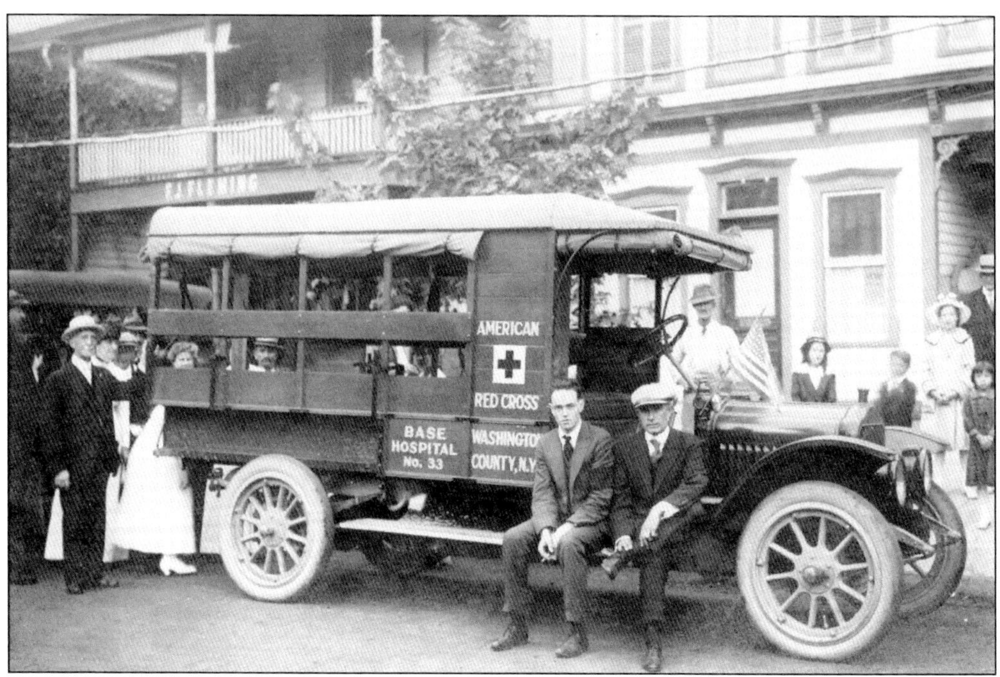

World War I Liberty Loan promotion quotas for the war effort were met by Salem citizens, who also contributed to funds raised by Washington County for the purchase of ambulances for the war front. The ambulance on display shows Dr. Orton and Dr. McSorley (cap) sitting on the running board. The Rev. David Stewart is seen on the left.

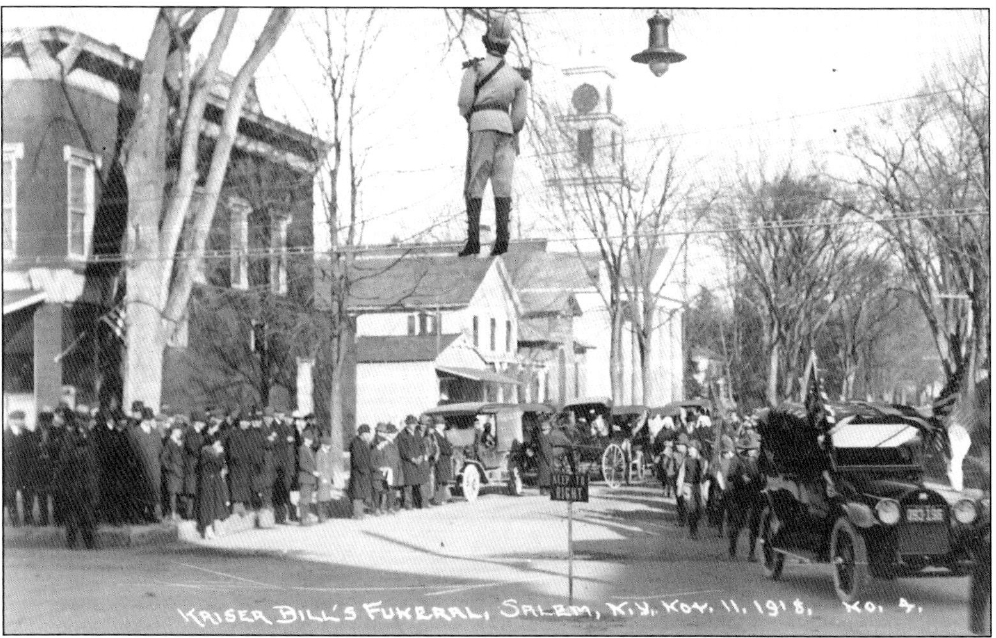

When the World War I armistice was signed on November 11, 1918, a spontaneous parade erupted on Main Street. Germany's Kaiser Wilhelm II was hanged in effigy, while church bells rang and adults and children cheered and blew horns. The *Salem Press* reported that 1,500 citizens attended the parade of bands, children, adults, automobiles, and Red Cross workers.

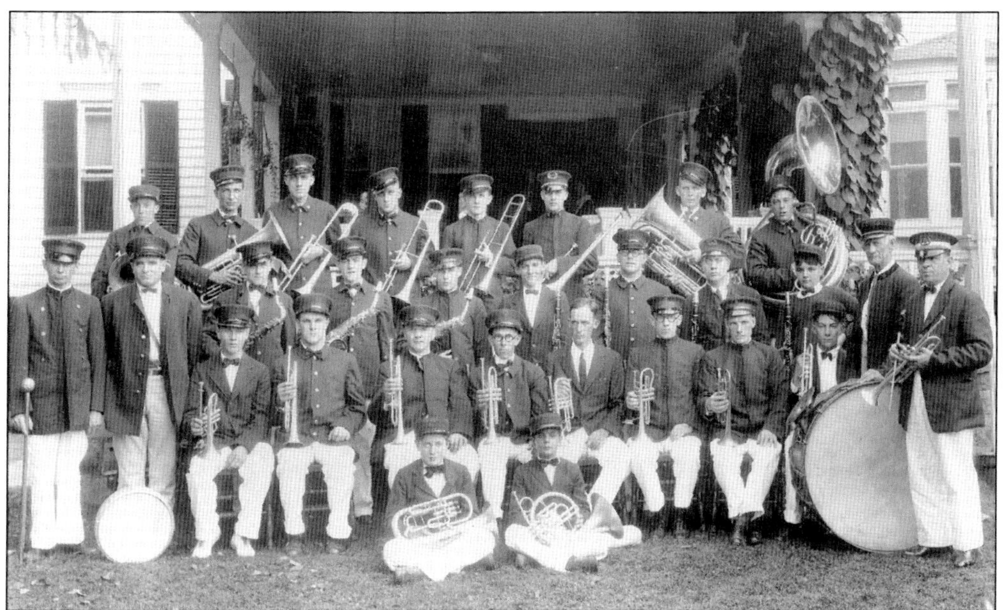

This September 25, 1926, photograph of the Salem Brass Band was taken in front of the Williams-Parker mansion. Congressman James Parker had requested that the band play for members of a Congressional committee on this day. The mansion is now the site of Salem Washington Academy and elementary school.

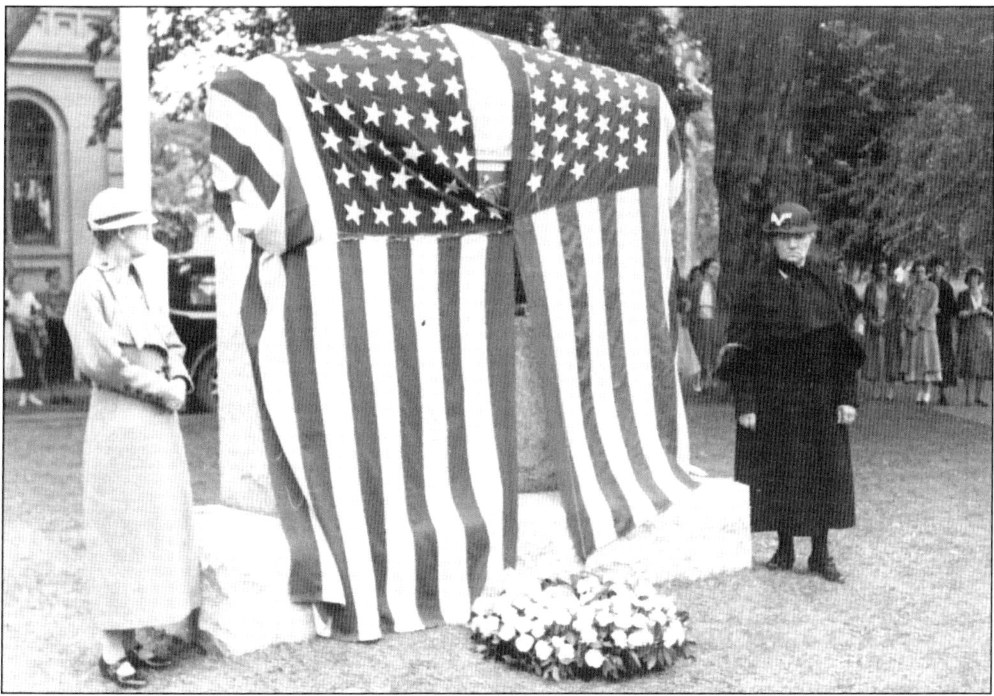

Years later, in 1934, the Women's Relief Corps dedicated a World War I monument on the green in front of the Washington County Courthouse and Jail on East Broadway. Shown here ready to unveil the monument are Kittie Kerslake (left) and Lottie Robbins, whose husbands were killed in the war. The names of 106 servicemen are listed on a bronze plate on the back of the stone.

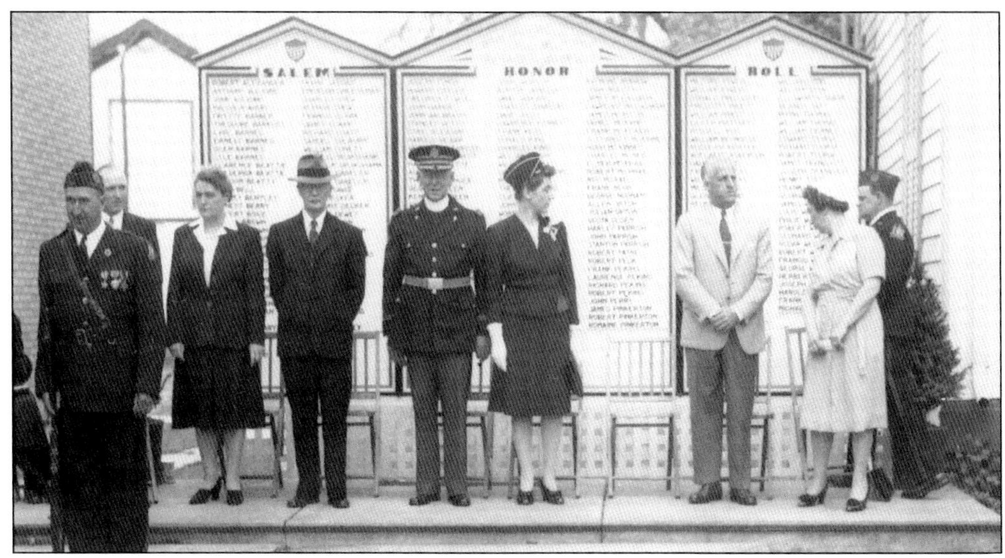

In 1941, World War II involved both men and women in the service of their country. An honor roll of 249 men and women military members was dedicated on May 26, 1944, on North Main Street. School closed for the ceremony, allowing the students and faculty to share the historic event with a large crowd of other citizens.

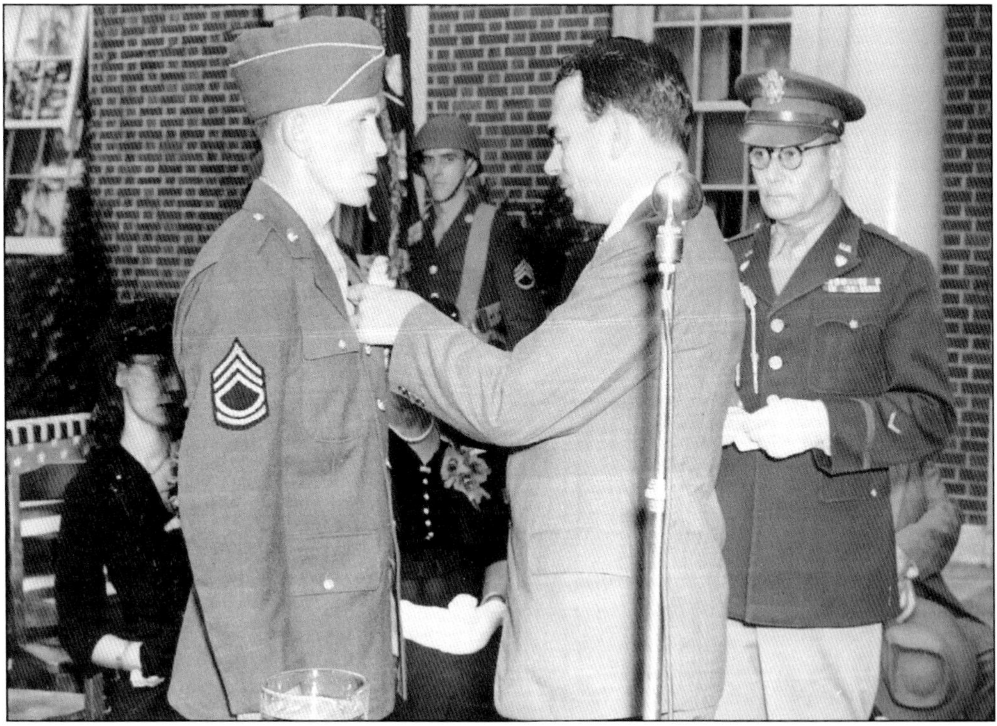

The most medaled Salem soldier in World War II was Sgt. Francis Clark. Here, on September 8, 1945, New York governor Thomas Dewey awards the New York State Conspicuous Service Medal to Sergeant Clark. A month earlier, Pres. Harry Truman, in a White House ceremony on August 23, awarded Sergeant Clark the Congressional Medal of Honor for heroism while fighting with Pennsylvania Company K, 109th Infantry, 28th Division.

Nine

NORTHERN EXPOSURE

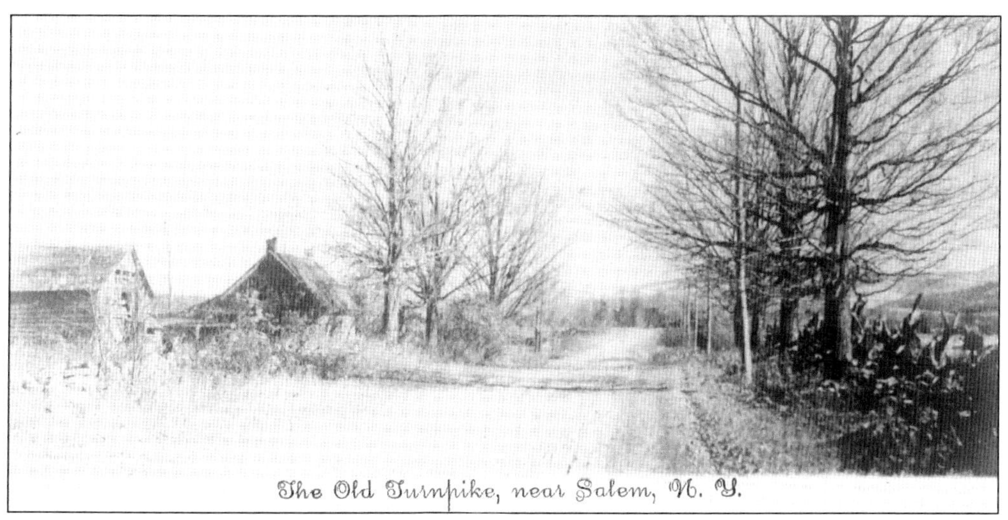

Travel north from the Battenkill, originally on old Indian trails north to Lake Champlain, was made easier by the building of the 50-mile-long Northern Turnpike from Lansingburg (Troy) to Granville in 1802. Marble markers notified travelers every mile of the distance from Lansingburg to Granville. In 1814, the Village of Salem approved a contract for $150 to allow the Northern Turnpike to run through Main Street.

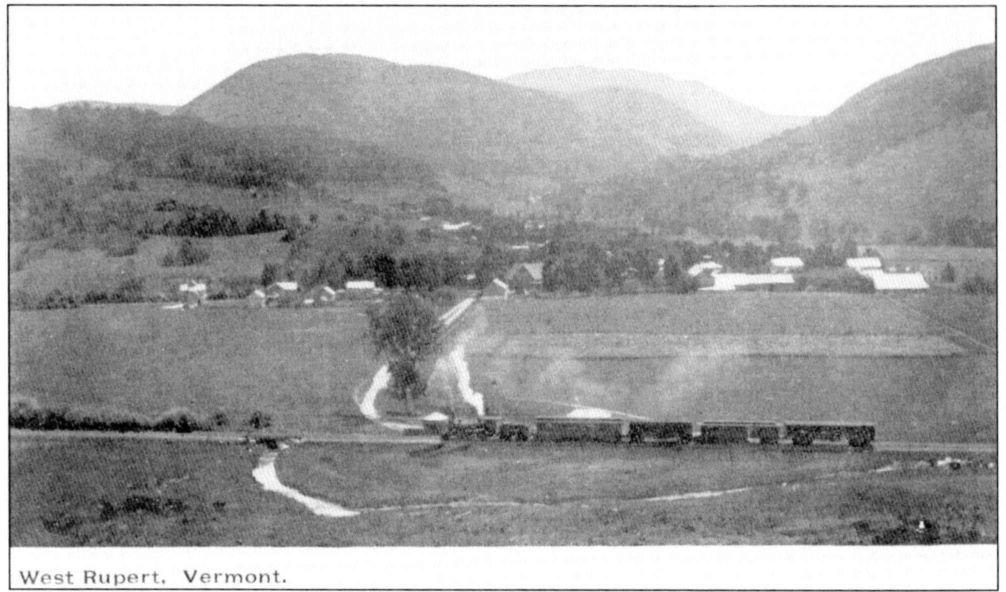

The 1852 Troy & Rutland Railroad paralleled sections of the Northern Turnpike, the Battenkill, and White Creek on its route through Salem to Rutland. Correspondingly, the Delaware & Hudson Railway ran from Albany to Whitehall and on to Adirondack Mountain towns, opening up the Adirondacks for commerce, tourists, and photographers. This early-1900s photograph shows a Delaware & Hudson coal-burning engine and train approaching West Rupert, Vermont.

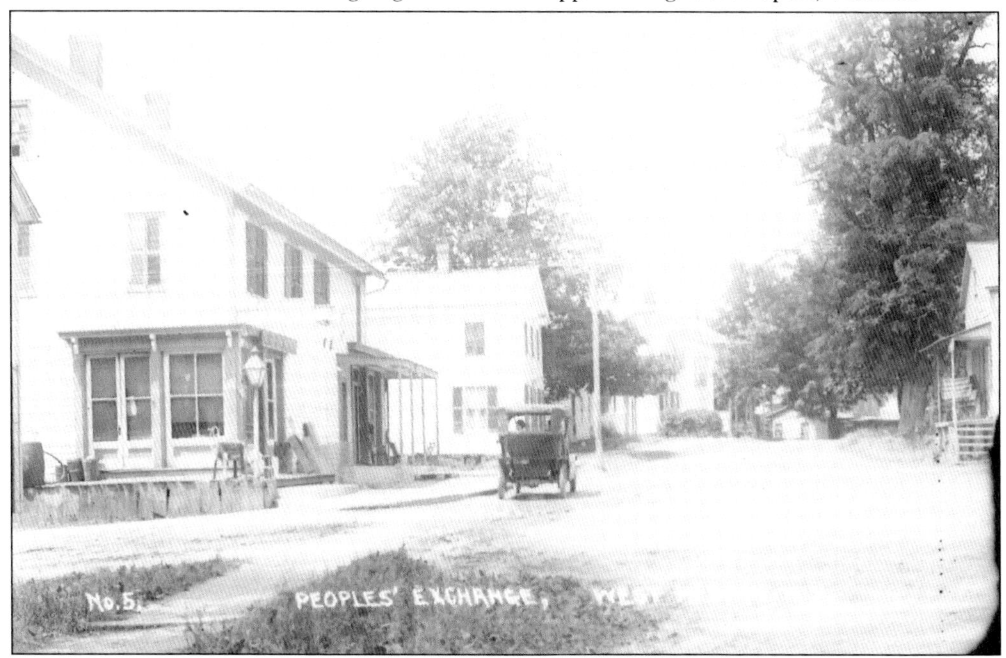

The Champlain Canal, the Delaware & Hudson Railway, and the Northern Turnpike all contributed to northern expansion. In the early 1900s, Robert A. Cruikshank, having taken over his father's photography business, traveled on State Route 22 and side roads in his automobile to capture the scenes north of Salem and in the eastern Adirondacks. The Peoples' Exchange, at Bedlam Corner on County Route 30, is seen here as one enters West Hebron.

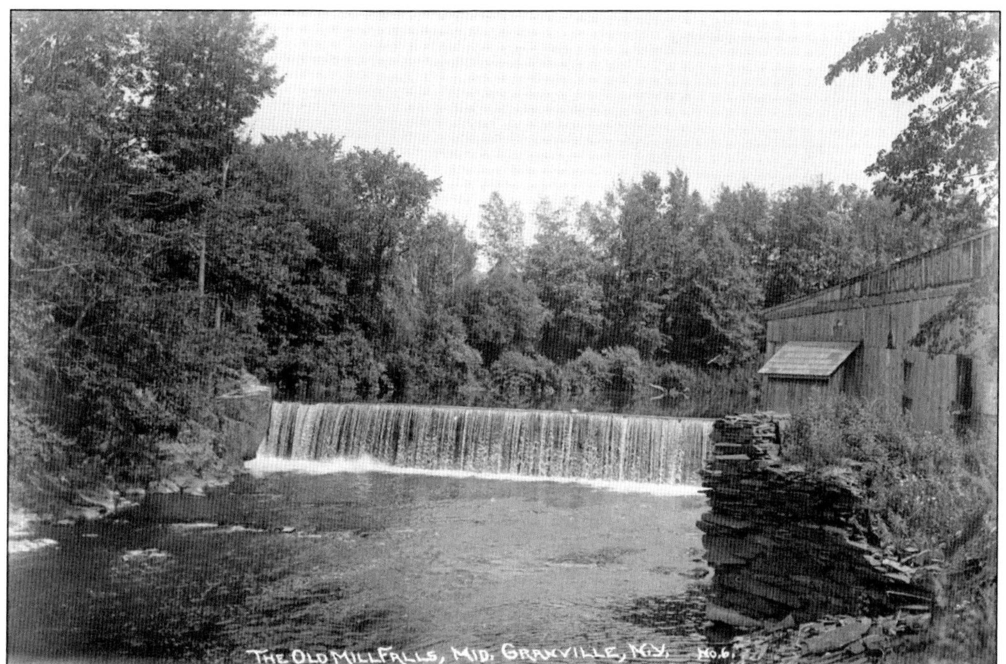

Wherever a suitable river ran, water powered the mills. This photograph shows the old mill on the Mettawee River in Middle Granville, New York. The river continues to be known for its native brook trout and rainbow trout fly-fishing. Unlike the westerly flow of the Battenkill to the Hudson River, the geography of Granville forces the Mettawee River north, where it empties into Lake Champlain.

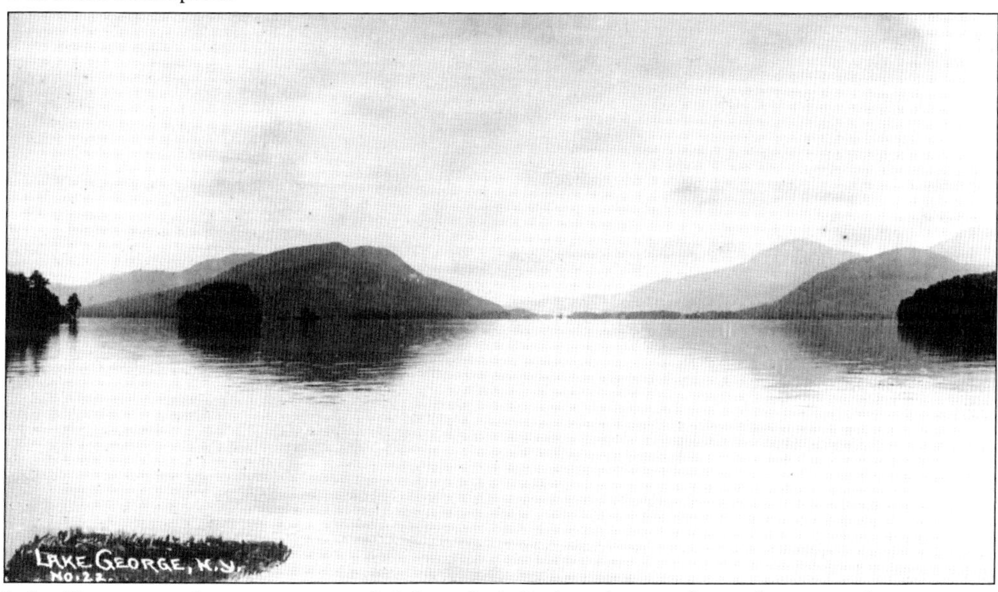

Lake George, in the now-protected Adirondack Park, is known for its beauty and pure water. This photograph shows the lake looking north toward the narrows. In 1646, Jesuit missionary Isaac Jogues traveled through the narrows, which was also used by the Iroquois Indians in their trade with French settlers on Lake Champlain. Missionary Jogues named the lake Lac du Saint Sacrement, or "Lake of the Blessed Sacrament."

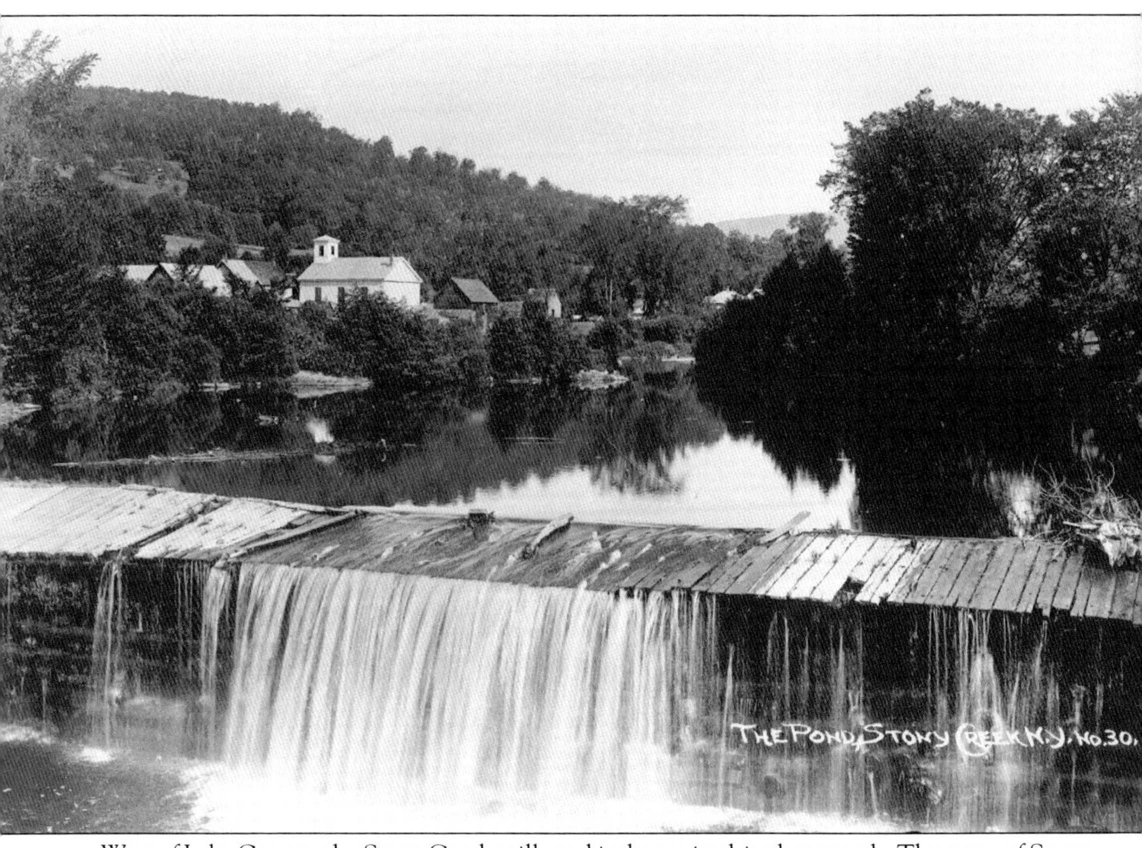

West of Lake George, the Stony Creek millpond is shown in this photograph. The town of Stony Creek, organized in 1852, contained a village called Creek Center. Surrounded by hemlock trees, the village was known for its tannery, which was one of its major businesses for many years, until the hemlock forest was depleted.

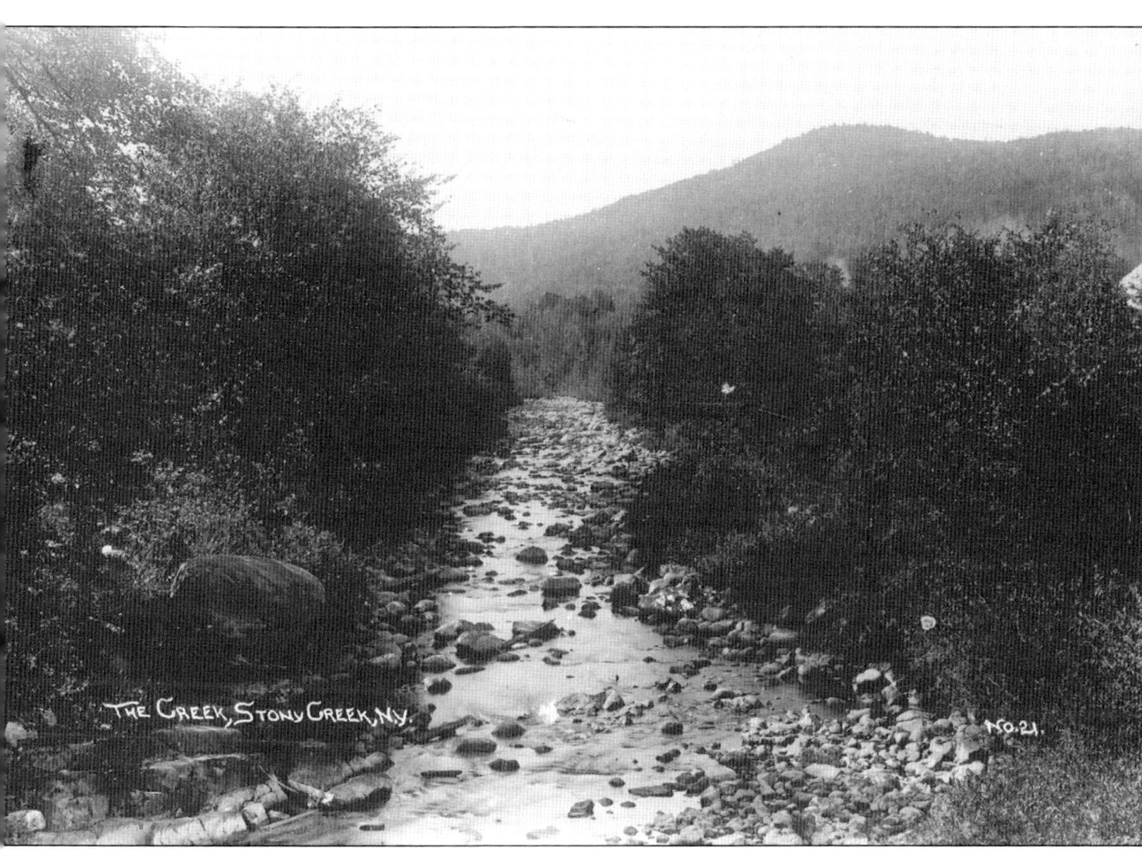

Stony Creek runs through the town for which it is named. This photograph shows the creek bed covered with granite stones. The availability of the stone and railroad transportation in 1852 encouraged granite businesses, such as Stony Creek Red Granite Company, Norcross Brothers, and Guildford's Beattie Quarry, to open. The granite was nationally known for its strength and was used in building Grant's Tomb and the West Point Monument.

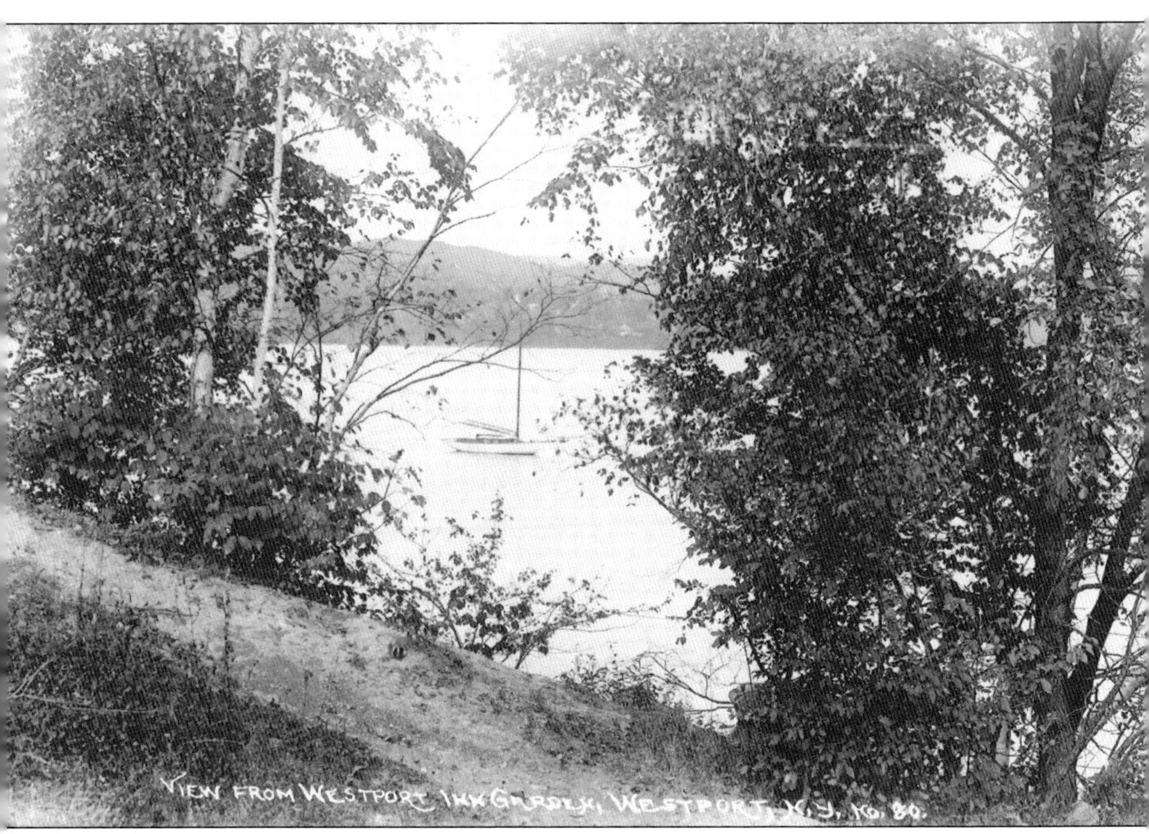

The Westport Inn, a fashionable stop for travelers, was on the banks of Lake Champlain. Here, a moored sailboat with gaff sail rests quietly in the bay. Westport was formed in 1815 and developed a logging and iron ore industry, both of which were important Adirondack industries. The railroads, built for shipping iron ore, garnet, and other natural products, also brought visitors to enjoy the wilderness.

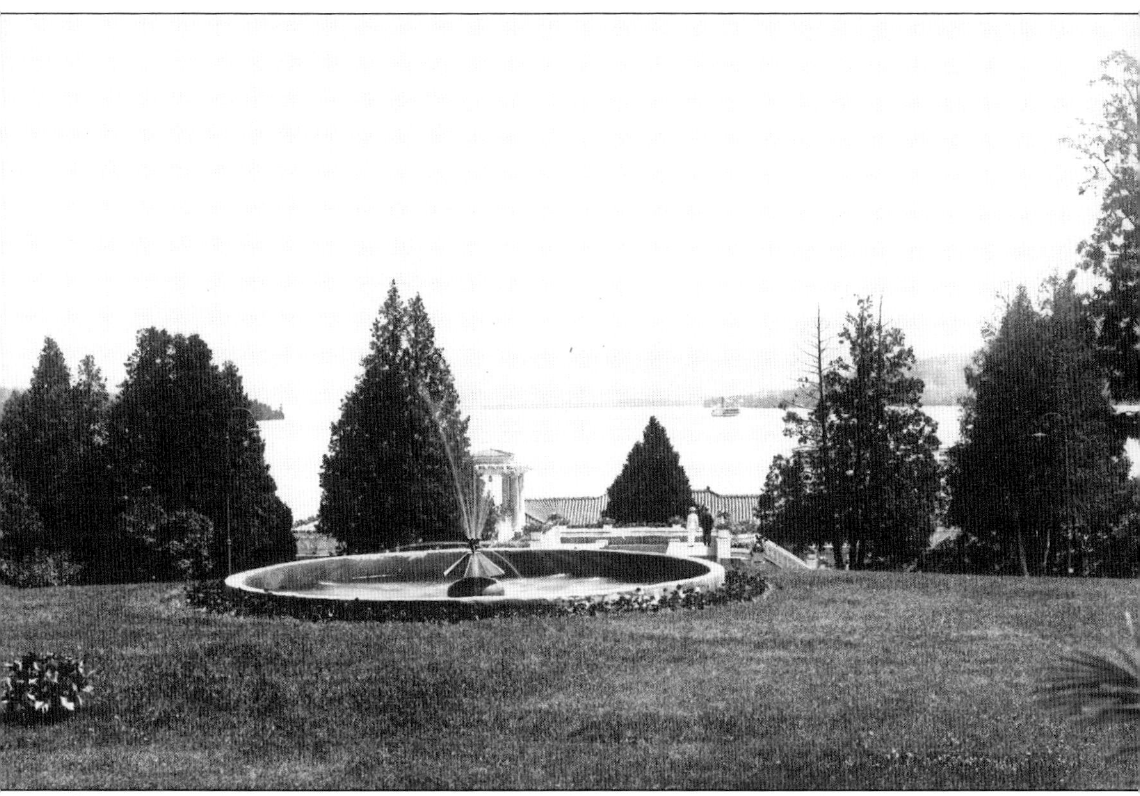

A fountain graced the garden of the Westport Inn, where guests could watch the passing steamboats carrying passengers and freight up and down the lake. The Champlain Transportation Company was the first, in 1826, eventually running two day boats and two night boats. By 1868, the Rutland & Burlington Railroad had taken ownership of the steamboat company to suit the Adirondack Railroad schedules.

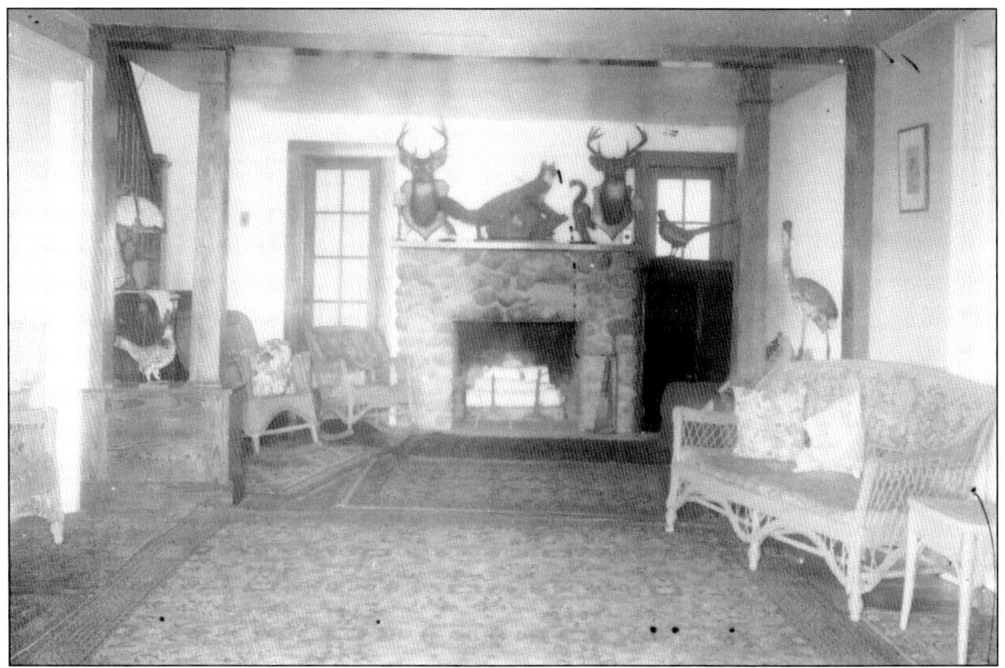

The lobby of the Westport Inn reflected the wild Adirondacks, giving the guests a taste of "roughing it." The wood-beamed lobby, featuring a cobblestone fireplace, stuffed wild animals and birds, and wicker furniture, made for a comfortable setting. The inn was demolished in 1967, and Ballard Park now occupies the lakeside site.

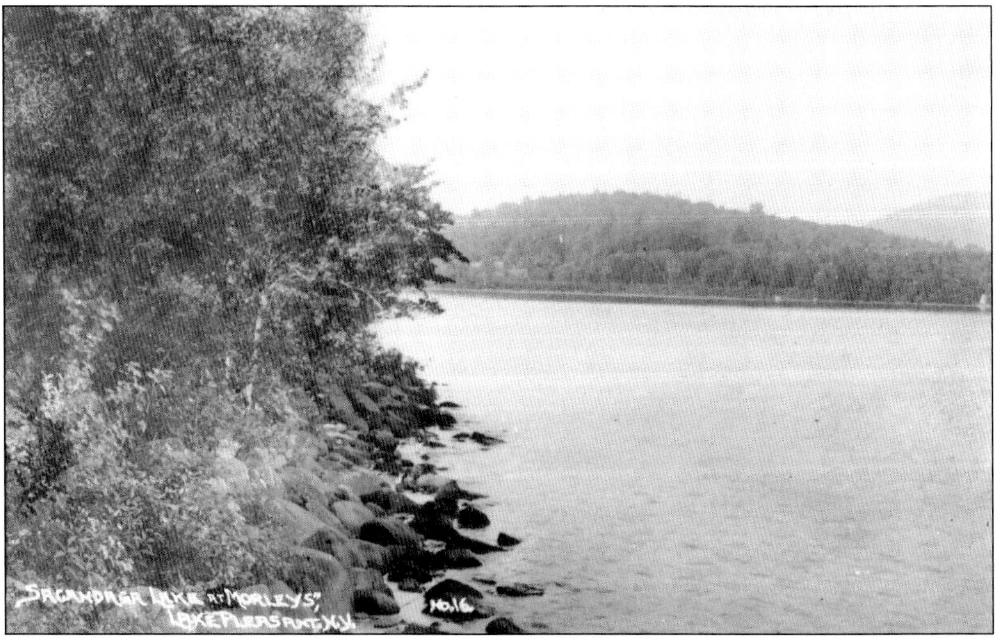

The 64-mile-long Sacandaga River flows south from Sacandaga Lake, in the town of Lake Pleasant, to create the 29-mile-long Great Sacandaga Lake and reservoir, completed in 1929. A total of 34 cemeteries and 3,872 graves had to be moved for the project. The Indian name for the river is Sachendaga, meaning "the drowned lands," which refers to the nearby swampland.

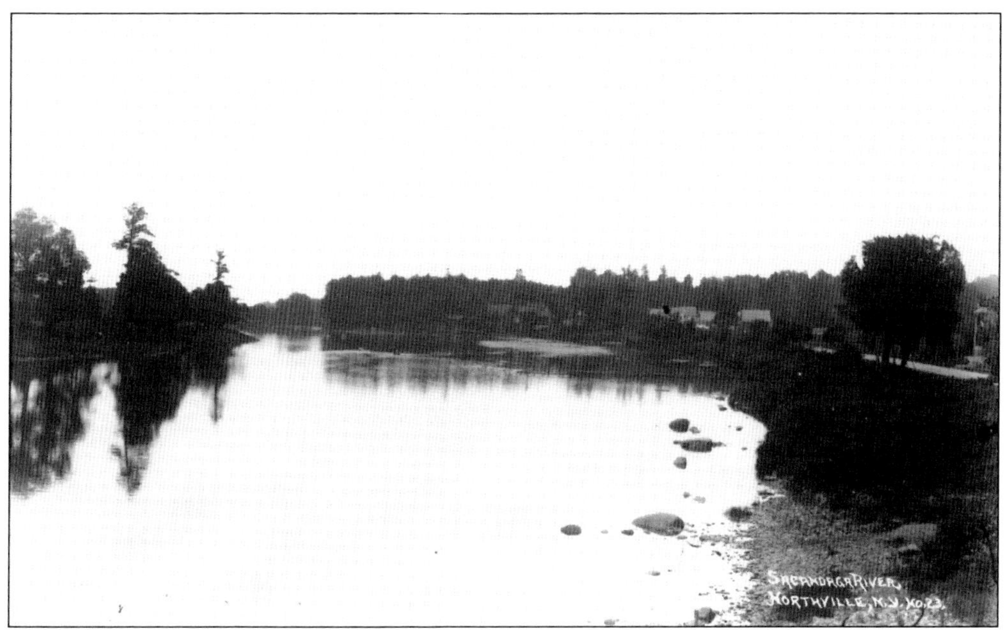

Northville, incorporated in 1873, is on the east side of the Sacandaga River as it enters the Great Sacandaga Lake. Northville was once situated on high ground above the Sacandaga Valley until the Conklingville Dam, built in 1929, flooded the valley. The Fonda, Johnstown & Gloversville Railroad track from Northville to Mayfield to Broadalbin, destroyed by the project, was paid $1.75 million.

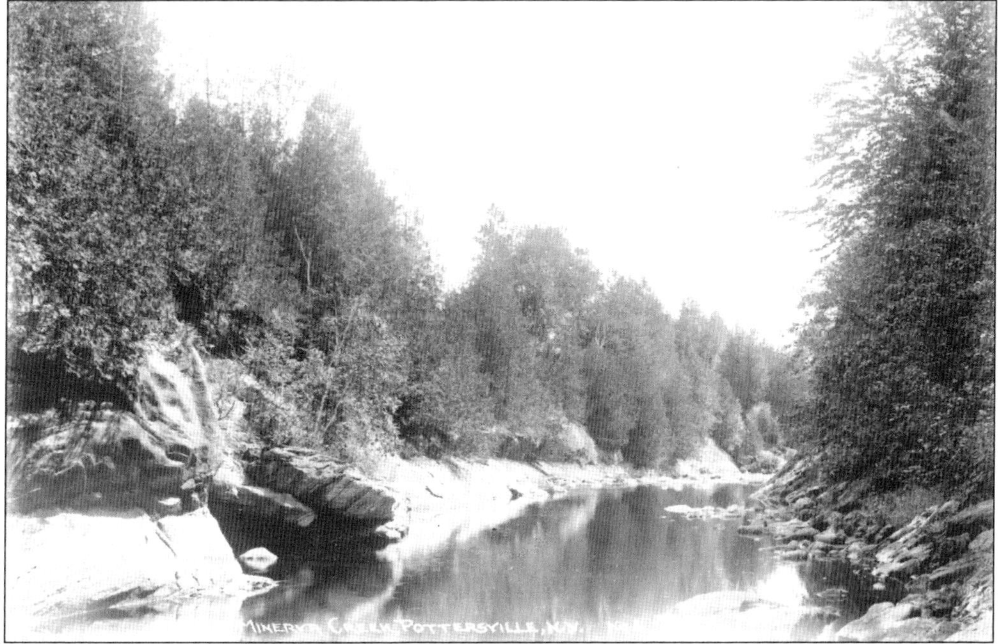

Minerva Creek is one of many Adirondack waterways, and the Minerva Creek bed in Pottersville is another good example of Adirondack geology. Granite and marble formations can be seen in the nearby Natural Stone Bridge & Caves Park, where the largest marble cave entrance in the east and the natural stone bridge are accessible to the public.

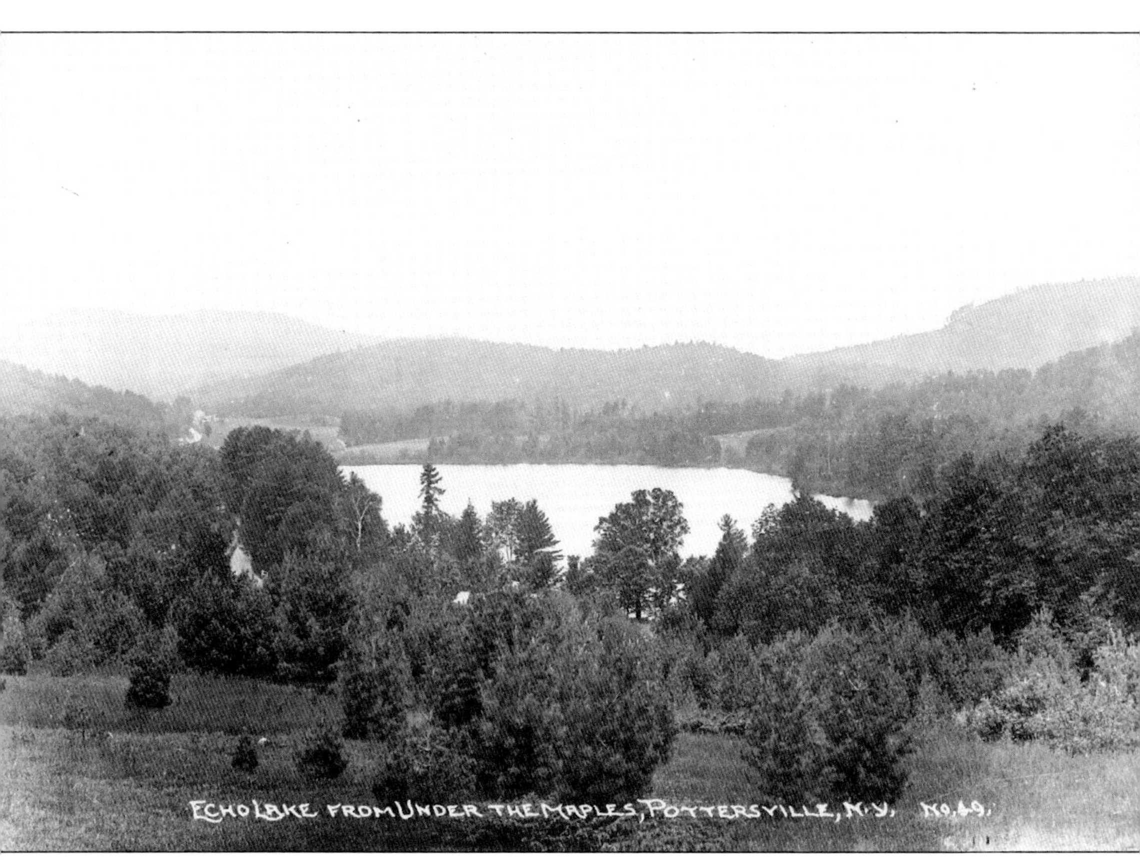

Like many of the Adirondack towns, Pottersville, organized in 1799, relied heavily on the lumber and tanning industries. When these early industries petered out, tourism became an important part of the economy. Today, the beauty and solitude of Echo Lake invites tourists and campers to vacation in Pottersville.

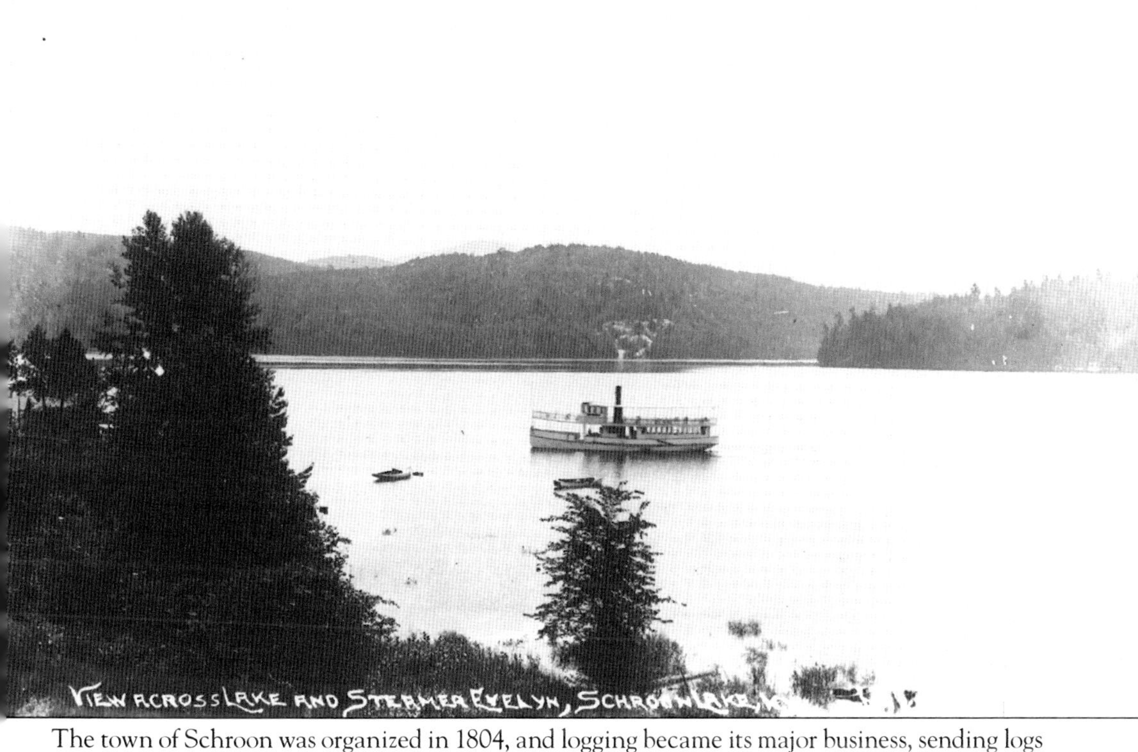

The town of Schroon was organized in 1804, and logging became its major business, sending logs down the Schroon River in the spring to sawmills at Warrensburg and Glens Falls. Vacationers took the Adirondack Railroad to Riparius and then took the stage to one of the steamboats on Schroon Lake. This early-1900s photograph shows the steamer *Evelyn* heading for the dock at the Leland House.

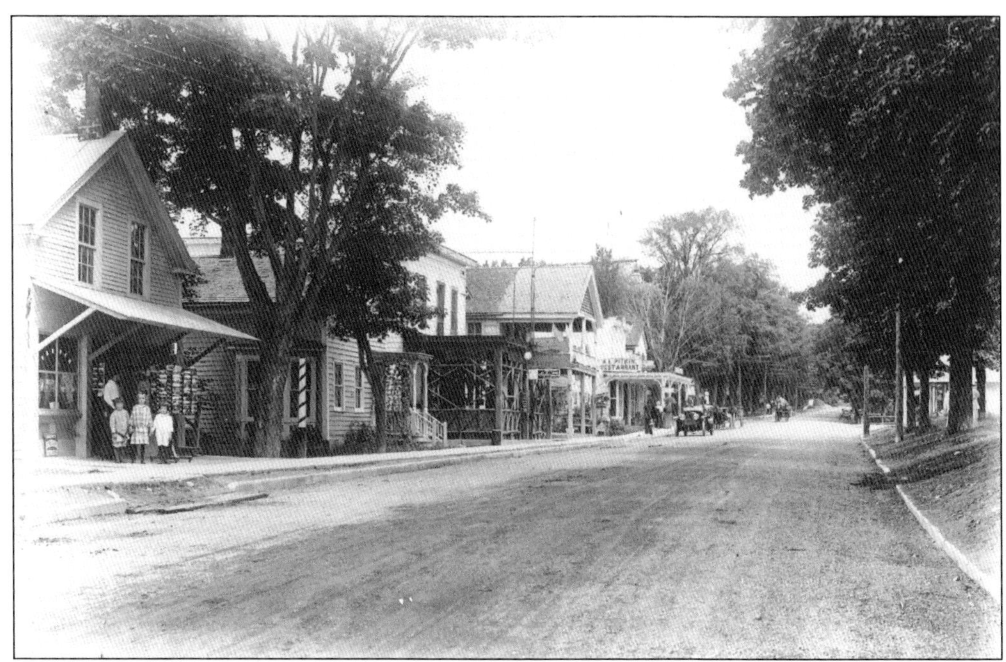

This late-1880s photograph shows Main Street in Schroon with a mother and her children standing in front of the barbershop and souvenir store. A rack of postcards, perhaps taken by Salem's Robert Cruikshank, can be seen behind them. The Pitkin Restaurant has customers, and motorcars share the road with horses and wagons.

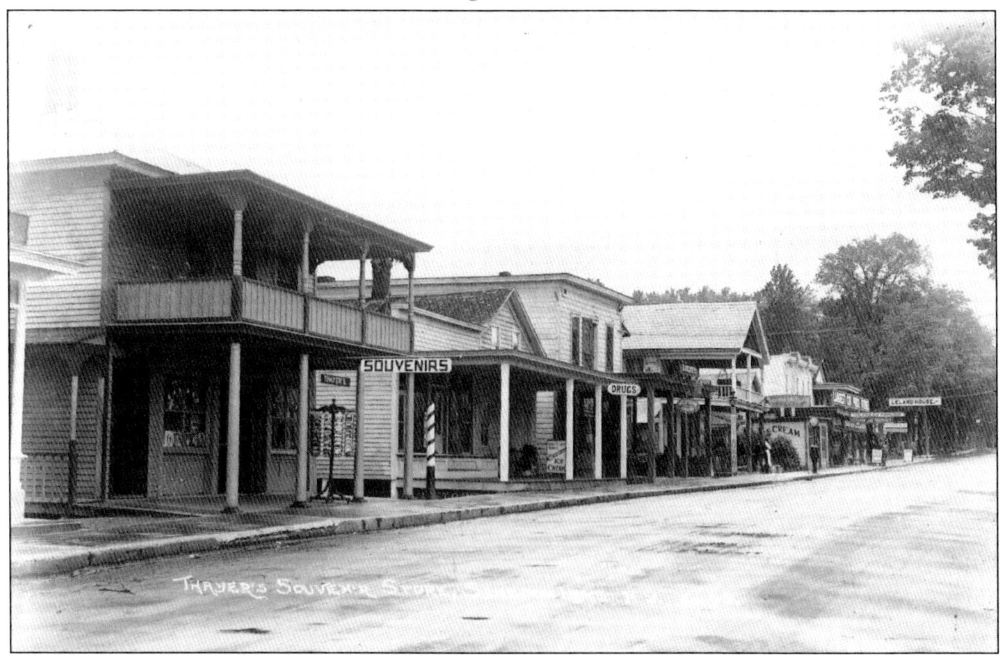

This photograph of Main Street in Schroon was taken later, around 1910, and shows improved building fronts. Thayer's Souvenir Store, drugstores, a restaurant, an ice cream parlor, and a sign pointing the way to the Leland House welcomed visitors. The Pitkin Restaurant sign had faded, as perhaps did its business.

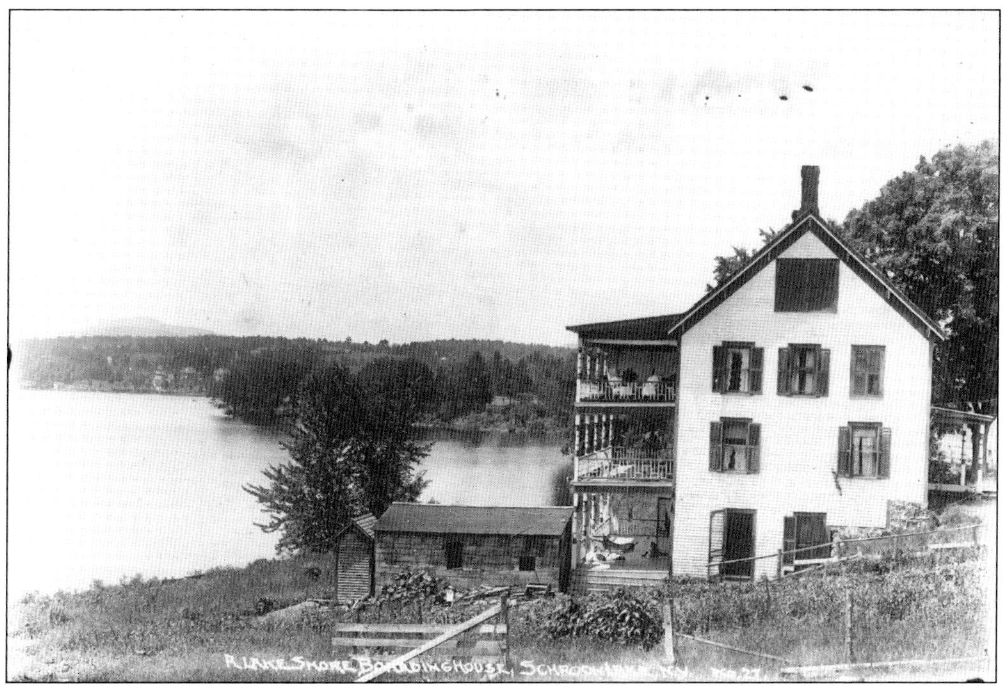

Not all visitors could afford to stay in the extravagant resort hotels like the Leland House. Numerous boardinghouses lined the Schroon Lake shores. This photograph shows one of the modest boardinghouses, a three-story house with three porches facing the lake. Stays in the Adirondacks were usually for two weeks or longer.

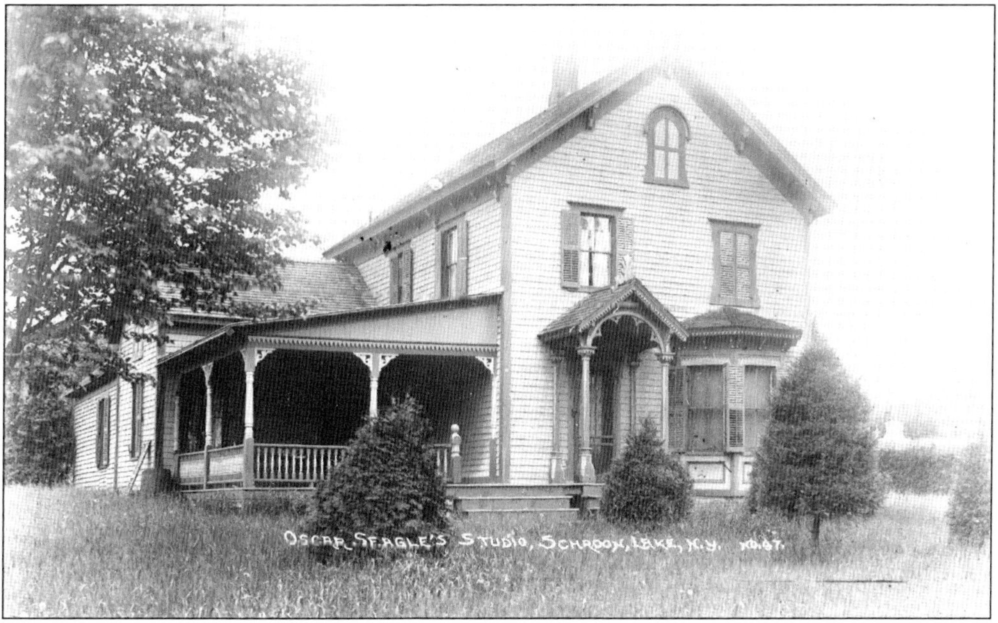

One of Schroon Lake's most famous personalities was Oscar Seagle, who founded the oldest singer-training program in the country. In 1915, he moved from Hague, on Lake George, to Schroon and opened the Seagle Music Colony, now known around the world. Pictured here is his first Schroon Lake studio.

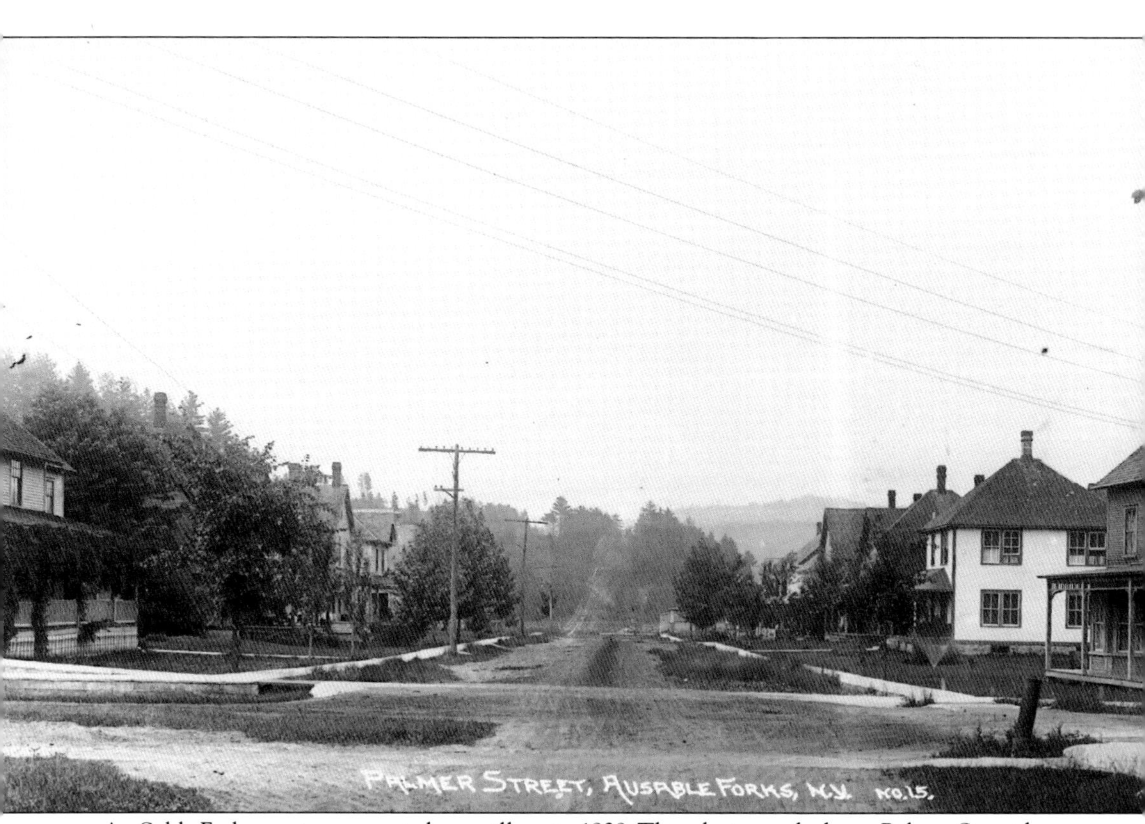

Au Sable Forks was incorporated as a village in 1839. This photograph shows Palmer Street homes and their fancy corbeled chimneys. Since wood was readily available, heating was most likely supplied by wood-burning fireplaces and furnaces. Nearby Palmer Hill was known for its iron ore deposits, which bolstered the economy for many years until the ore ran out.

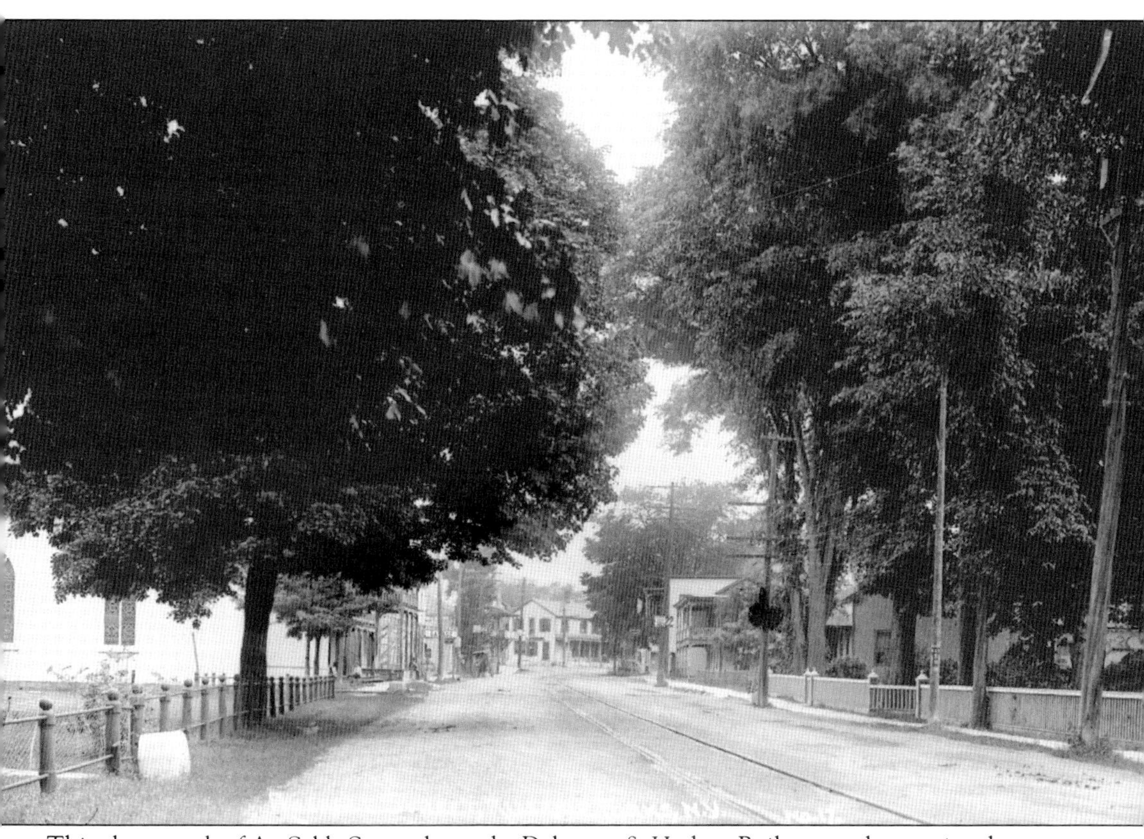

This photograph of Au Sable Street shows the Delaware & Hudson Railway tracks running down the middle of the tree-lined street. The Delaware & Hudson transported the iron ore from Palmer Hill mines to the iron ore furnaces. The name Au Sable is French, meaning "of the sand."

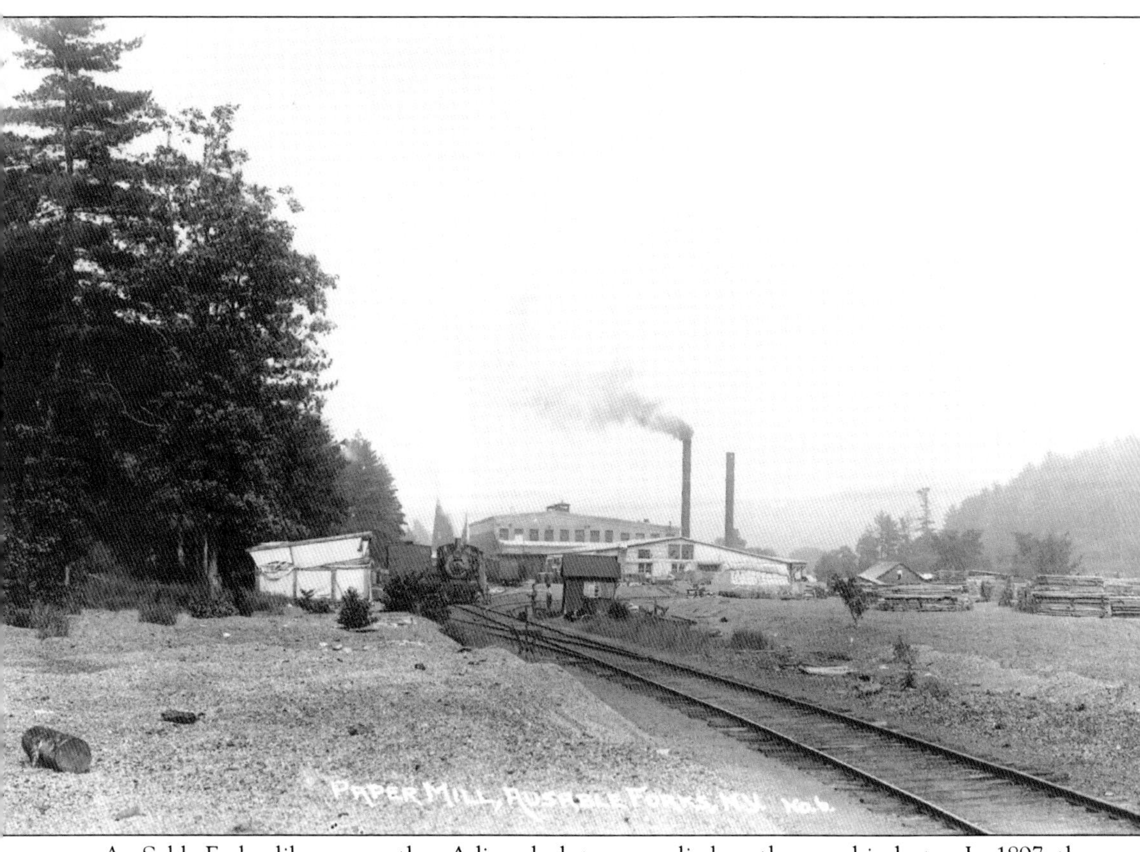

Au Sable Forks, like many other Adirondack towns, relied on the wood industry. In 1897, the largest manufacturer of pulpwood in town was the J.J. Rogers Pulp & Paper Mill. Pulpwood was delivered by train or floated down the Au Sable River to Lake Champlain. This photograph shows a train leaving a yard of sawn boards at one of the paper mills.

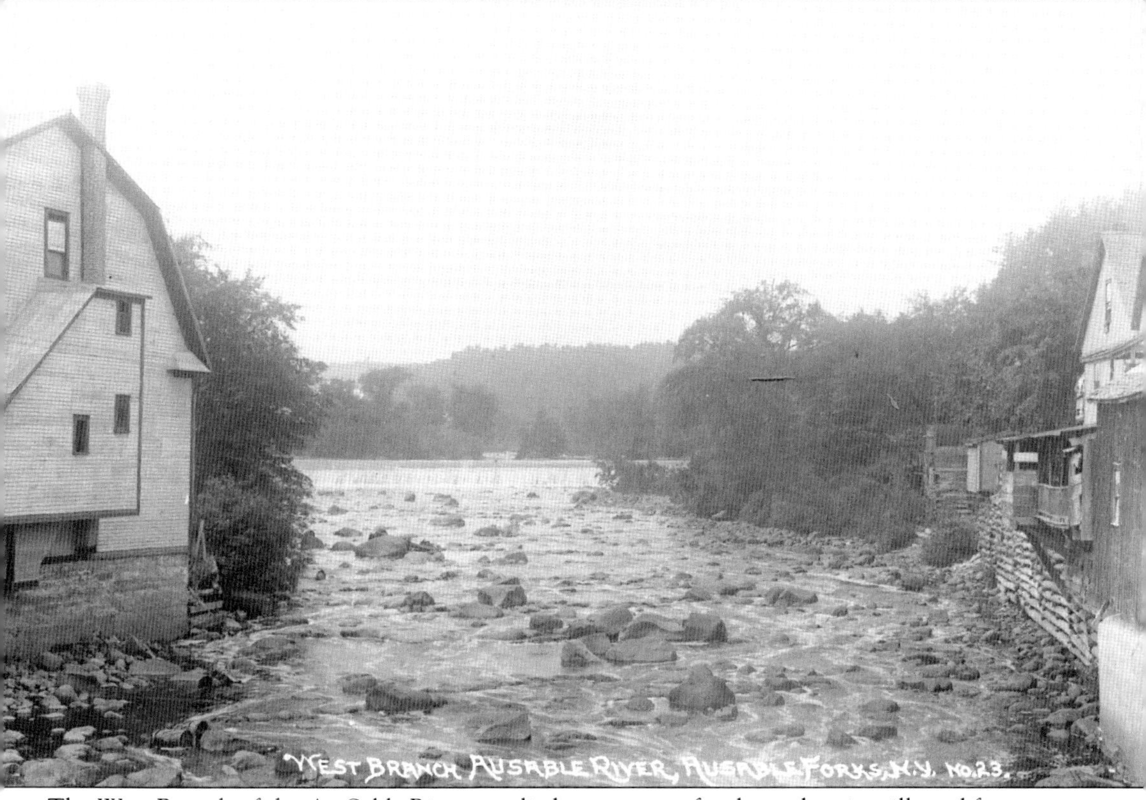

The West Branch of the Au Sable River supplied waterpower for the early gristmills and forges. The dam on the river can be seen in the background. The East and West Branches of the Au Sable River converge in Au Sable Forks, where it empties into Lake Champlain. Today, the West Branch is known for its fly-fishing.

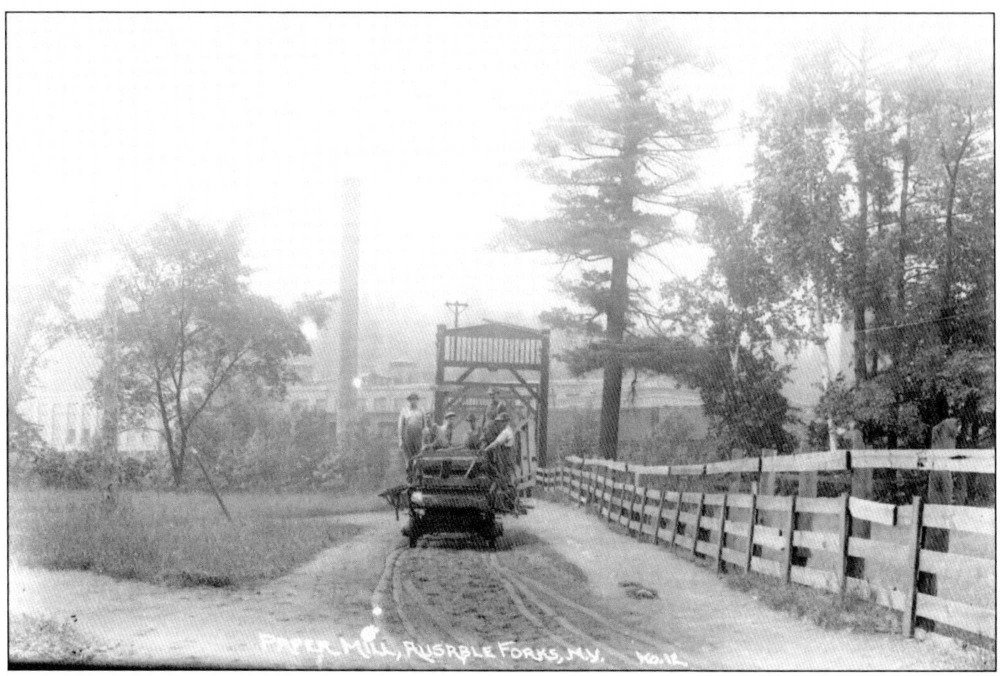

This photograph shows a group of pulp mill workers on a wagon about to cross the bridge to the J.J. Rogers Pulp & Paper Mill. When the iron ore business died, the paper industry took its place. Not seen in the photograph is the horse or oxen used to pull the wagon.

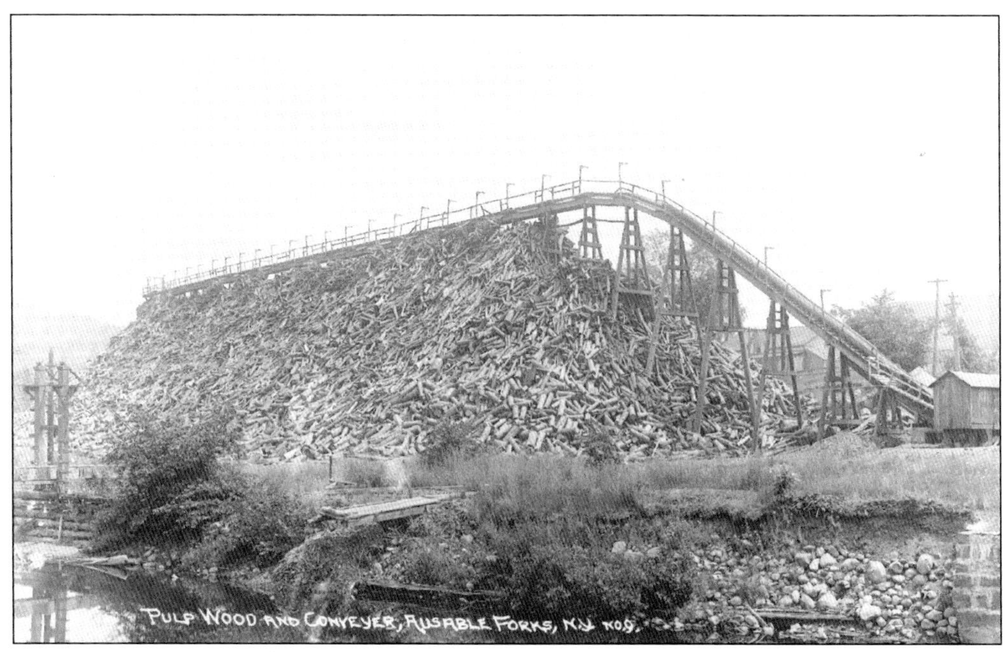

A pulpwood conveyer belt at the pulp mill is shown in this photograph. The pile of pulpwood that floated down the river to the mill site was now the basic ingredient, instead of rags, in making print paper. As demand grew for paper, the forests were overharvested until conservation measures came into being.

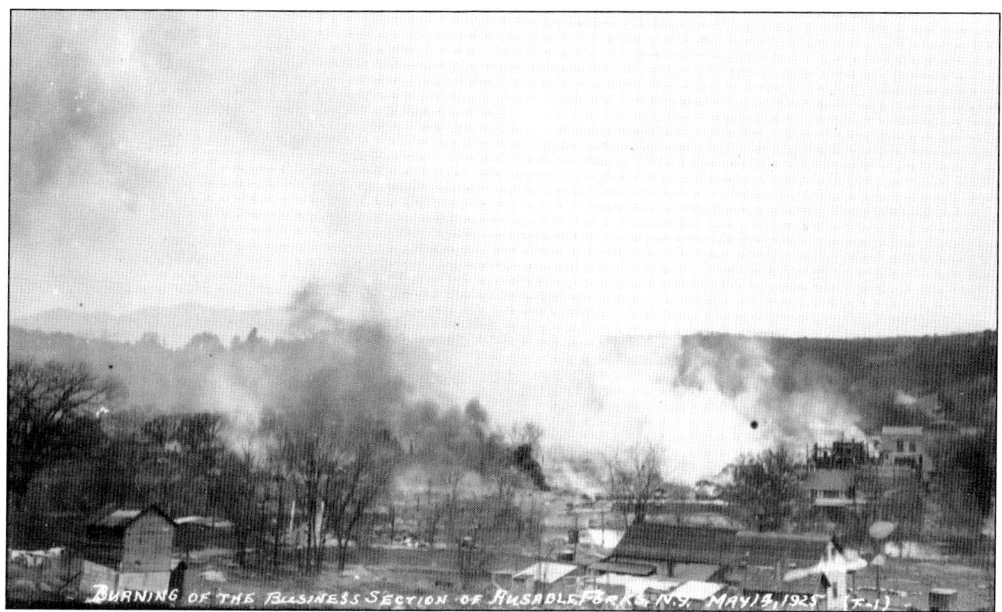

Fire was always a danger, as a lack of adequate fire equipment and trucks limited the capacity to put out a commercial Main Street fire once it got going. This photograph shows the business section of Au Sable Forks on fire on May 1, 1925. Following the fire, business owners rebuilt with brick, not wood.

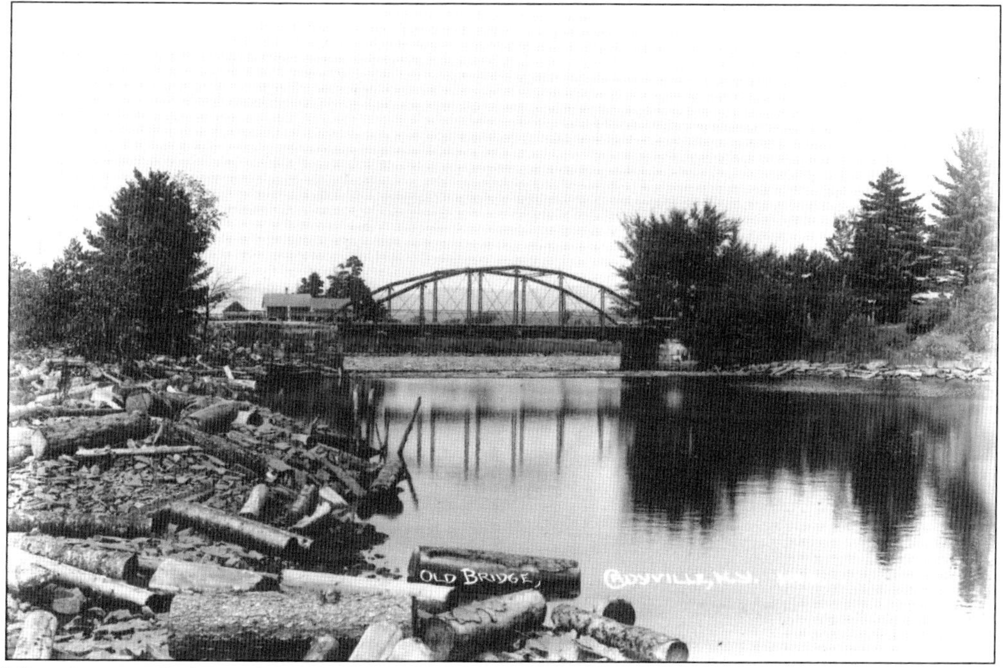

This photograph shows the Cadyville Bridge over the Sacandaga River, as well as pulp log leftovers along the riverbanks. In the spring floods, rafts of logs like those seen beyond the bridge were floated downriver to collection booms like those at the Rogers Pulp & Paper Mill, where conveyor belts made large piles of logs.

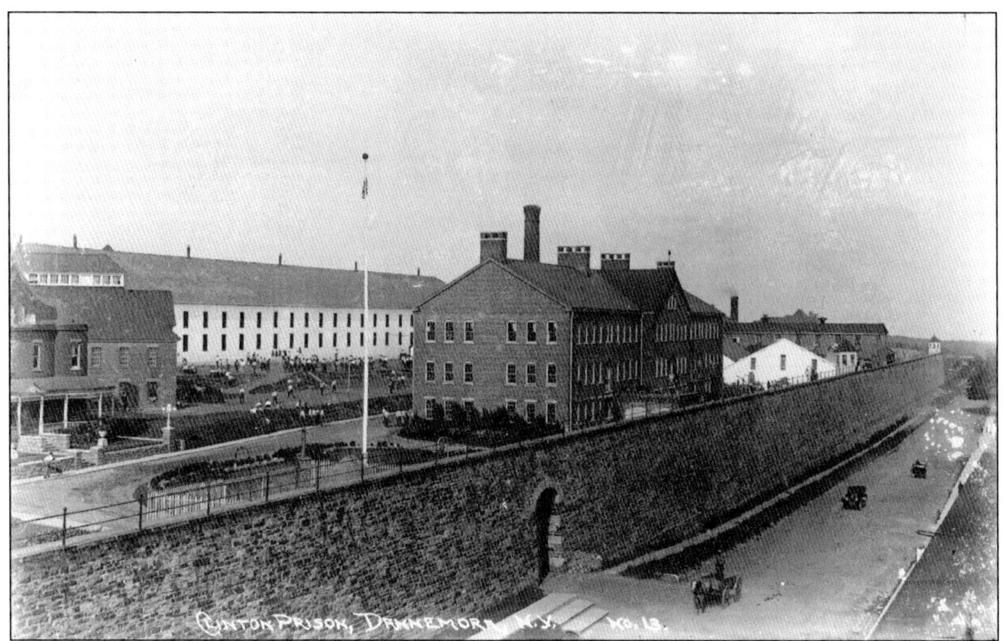

Clinton Prison, in Dannemora, 15 miles from Cadyville, was built in 1845. The Adirondack prison became known as the "hell hole," or "Siberia of North America." New York State "sent its most hardened and seasoned underworld characters" to this rural maximum security prison. On July 20, 1929, a group of 1,300 prisoners rioted, killing three guards. The New York State Police and the 20th Infantry were called in to put down the riot.

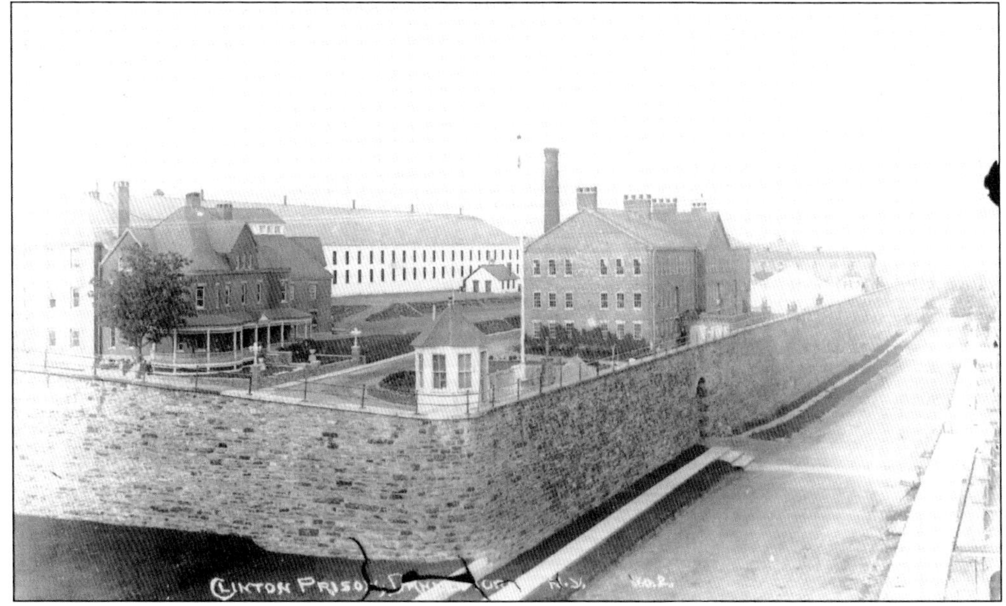

Over the years, Clinton Prison was expanded and high walls and guard towers were added, as seen in this 1925 photograph. Since many prisoners would arrive with tuberculosis, the Dannemora State Hospital was built in 1941 to take advantage of the clear mountain air. The hospital continues to operate today as a general hospital and dental facility. Today, the prison holds 2,700 prisoners and employs 1,400 guards.

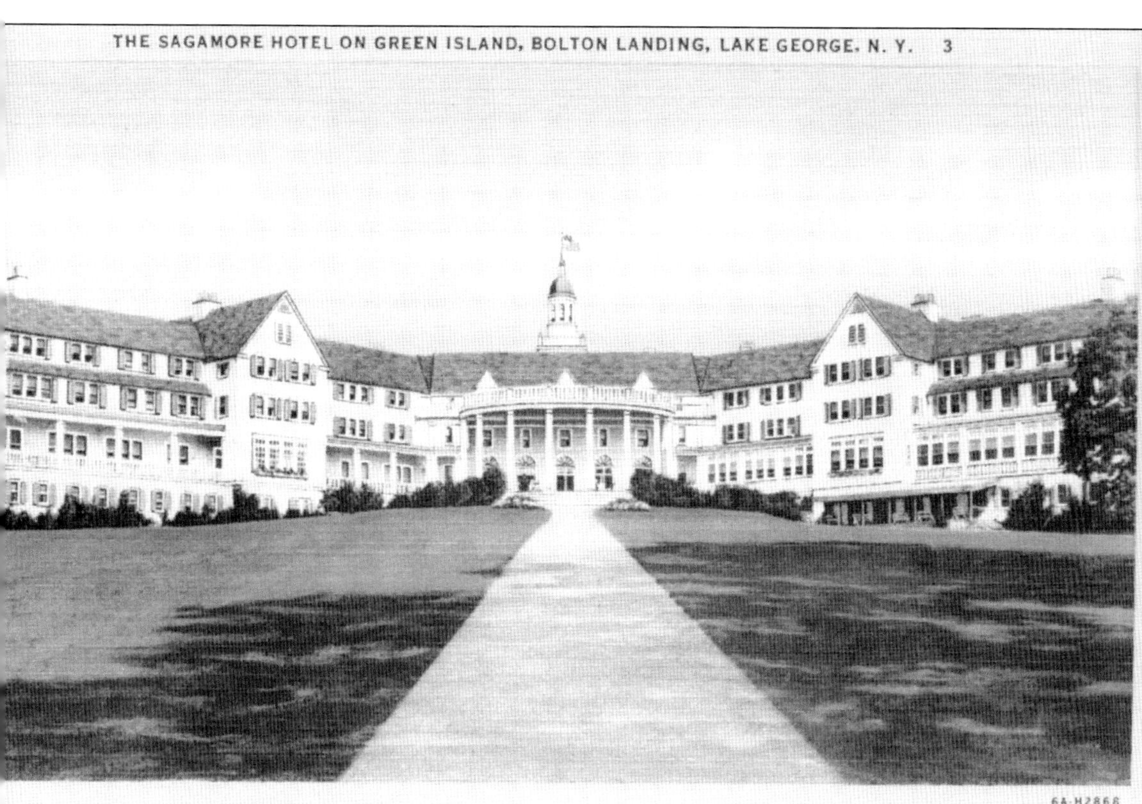

Unlike Clinton Prison, the Sagamore Hotel, in Bolton Landing on Lake George, seen in this c. 1950 postcard, shows more inviting accommodations. Originally built in 1883, the hotel was damaged by fires in 1893 and 1914 and rebuilt in 1930 in a grand style. After closing in 1981, the hotel was fully renovated and reopened in 1983. Today, it is a four-star resort with luxurious accommodations, attracting tourists to the lake and the Adirondack Park.

Consistent with our mission to preserve history on a local level, this book was printed in South Carolina on American-made paper and manufactured entirely in the United States. Products carrying the accredited Forest Stewardship Council (FSC) label are printed on 100 percent FSC-certified paper.

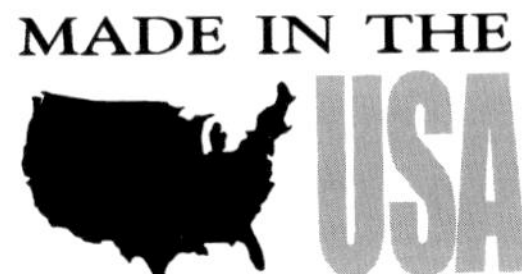